GREAT PREACHING ON
CHRISTMAS

GREAT PREACHING ON
CHRISTMAS

COMPILED BY
CURTIS HUTSON

SWORD of the LORD
PUBLISHERS
P.O. BOX 1099, MURFREESBORO, TN 37133

Copyright 1988 by

SWORD OF THE LORD PUBLISHERS

ISBN 0-87398-330-0

Printed and Bound in the United States of America

Table of Contents

I. HARRY IRONSIDE
    The Wondrous Birth of Our Wondrous Lord 11

II. T. DEWITT TALMAGE
    The Sky Anthem 23

III. J. C. RYLE
    Christ's Birth Announced 33

IV. CHARLES SPURGEON
    *The Song of the Angels; the Praise of
    the Shepherds* 49

V. CHARLES SPURGEON
    The Star and the Wise Men 71

VI. JOHN R. RICE
    How the Wise Men Found the Baby Jesus 91

VII. LEE ROBERSON
    Royalty in a Stable 103

VIII. KENNY MCCOMAS
    Don't Just Star-Gaze in Bethlehem This Christmas .. 113

IX. WILLIAM E. BIEDERWOLF
    If Christ Had Not Been Born, What Then? 121

X. D. L. MOODY
    Good News! 131

XI. T. T. SHIELDS
    A Christmas Message 143

XII. TOM MALONE
　　　The Infinite Christ 157

XIII. BILLY SUNDAY
　　　"Wonderful"! 167

XIV. LOUIS T. TALBOT
　　　The Names of Our Lord 177

XV. JOHN R. RICE
　　　Should a Christian Observe Christmas? 195

XVI. JOHN R. RICE
　　　*Decide This Christmas to Serve God Without
　　　Regard for Consequences* 205

XVII. JOE HENRY HANKINS
　　　"Good Tidings" 221

XVIII. R. G. LEE
　　　Consider Christmas 231

XIX. A Pastor's Wife
　　　A Thrilling Christmastime on the Frontier 247

Introduction

It was Christmastime. Two women, their arms filled with bundles and their coat collars raised against the wintry wind, walked past a large, downtown department store. In the window was a life-size scene of the Nativity: the Christ Child in the manger, Mary and Joseph, the kneeling shepherds, and the cattle standing nearby. "Can you beat that!" one of the women was overheard to say. "The churches are even barging in on Christmas!"

What irony—that some have drifted so far from the original significance of the Christmas season that the King of kings should be accused of "barging in" on His own birthday party!

Or what about this! Some 85 years ago George Bernard Shaw invented a society for the abolition of Christmas. For him Christmas was simply a "nuisance," supported by the "mob" as a "carnival of mendicity, gluttony and drunkenness." But after years of campaigning, Mr. Shaw had to admit his society was a failure. "So far," said he, "I am the only member."

Now contrast the above with this sweet story:

Wally was nine when asked to participate in the school's Christmas pageant. He was to be the innkeeper.

After many rehearsals, the long-awaited event occurred. Joseph and Mary came to the inn, and there was Wally, standing at the door with his lantern. "What do you want?" he asked.

"We seek lodging," replied Joseph.

"Go elsewhere; the inn is filled."

"But, Sir, we have asked everywhere in vain. We have traveled far and are very weary. Please, good innkeeper, this is my wife, heavy with child. You must have some small corner for her!"

Wally now looked down on Mary with pity. But the prompter called to Wally, "Go on with your lines."

So Wally continued: "There is no room here; begone—go on your way."

At this point, Joseph sadly placed his arms around Mary, Mary laid her head upon his shoulder, and the two started to move slowly away.

Wally stood there in the doorway, watching the forlorn couple with obvious concern and with a tear trickling down his cheek.

Suddenly the Christmas pageant became different from all others. "Don't go, Joseph!" Wally called out. "Bring Mary back!" And Wally's face lighted up with a bright smile. "You can have MY room!" His tender heart had made room for the Saviour.

Christmas lives on, its spirit having captured the hearts of both old and young. And the tender beauty of Christmas sentiment and Christmas singing and Christmas sermons affords an opportunity for the Gospel to enter many a life that is closed to God throughout most of the year.

Your heart will overflow with joy to read again of what happened in the little town of Bethlehem 2,000 years ago. Only one other event in history can compare with Christ's birth into the world and that is His death upon Calvary's cross.

The rapidly-expanding book publishing division of the Sword of the Lord Foundation is constantly adding new, refreshing volumes for the reading pleasure of God's people. These nineteen sermons by fifteen authors were chosen as the best on the subject of Christmas from the last fifty-three year's writing in THE SWORD OF THE LORD.

Some of these messages are addressed to the unsaved; others have a definite appeal to Christians to make first place in their hearts for Jesus.

Oh, the wondrous story, that in the town of Bethlehem was born the King of Glory!

Sword of the Lord Publishers

HARRY A. IRONSIDE
1876-1951

ABOUT THE MAN:

Few preachers had more varied ministries than this man. He was a captain in the Salvation Army, an itinerant preacher with the Plymouth Brethren, pastor of the renowned Moody Memorial Church in Chicago, and conducted Bible conferences throughout the world. Sandwiched between those major ministries, Ironside preached the Gospel on street corners, in missions, in taverns, on Indian reservations, etc.

Never formally ordained and with no experience whatever as a pastor, Ironside took over the 4,000-seat Moody Memorial Church in Chicago and often filled it to capacity for 18½ years. A seminary president once said of him, *"He has the most unique ministry of any man living."* Although he had little formal education, his tremendous mental capacity and photographic memory caused him to be called the "Archbishop of Fundamentalism."

Preaching—warm, soul-saving preaching—was his forte. Special speakers in his great church often meant nothing; the crowds came when he was there. He traveled constantly; at his prime, he averaged 40 weeks in the year on the road—always returning to Moody Memorial for Sunday services.

His pen moved, too; he contributed regularly to various religious periodicals and journals in addition to publishing 80 books and pamphlets. His writings included addresses or commentaries on the entire New Testament, all of the prophetic books of the Old Testament, and a great many volumes on specific Bible themes and subjects.

In 1951, Dr. Ironside died in Cambridge, New Zealand, and was buried there at his own request.

I.

The Wondrous Birth of Our Wondrous Lord

H. A. IRONSIDE

"And it came to pass in those days, that there went out a decree from Caesar Augustus, that all the world should be taxed. (And this taxing was first made when Cyrenius was governor of Syria.) And all went to be taxed, every one into his own city. And Joseph also went up from Galilee, out of the city of Nazareth, into Judaea, unto the city of David, which is called Bethlehem; (because he was of the house and lineage of David:) to be taxed with Mary his espoused wife, being great with child. And so it was, that, while they were there, the days were accomplished that she should be delivered. And she brought forth her firstborn son, and wrapped him in swaddling clothes, and laid him in a manger; because there was no room for them in the inn." —Luke 2:1-7.

The incarnation of our Lord is not merely a doctrinal tenet about which theologians of different schools may hold various views; it is a glorious reality, a wondrous fact, apart from which there could be no salvation for sinful men.

"When the fulness of the time was come, God sent forth his Son, made of a woman, made under the law, to redeem them that were under the law, that we might receive the adoption of sons." —Gal. 4:4,5.

The miraculous birth of our Saviour is one of the foundation stones of our Christian faith. It is the companion truth to that of His expiatory sacrifice on the cross. Because of this, it will generally be found that he who denies the one denies the other. Too much importance cannot therefore be attached to the historic fact that Jesus was born of a virgin mother and that the "child...born" was the "son...given" (Isa. 9:6).

He who deigned to enter human conditions by the birth in Bethlehem is the One "whose goings forth have been from of old, from everlasting" (Mic. 5:2). To deny this is to repudiate the truth of the Gospel, apart from which there is no hope for a lost world.

God Wonderfully Brought About That Jesus Was Born in Bethlehem, Fulfilling Prophecy

This passage connects very definitely with a prophecy which was given some 700 years before the events took place, which is found in chapter 5 of the book of Micah. Micah was contemporary with Isaiah, and both prophets predicted the coming of the days of the Messiah, our Lord Jesus Christ.

In verse 2 we read,

"But thou, Bethlehem Ephratah, though thou be little among the thousands of Judah, yet out of thee shall come forth unto me that is to be ruler in Israel; whose goings forth have been from of old, from everlasting."

It is rather interesting to note the next verse. You might expect the prophet to declare that immediately all Israel would recognize Him as their Messiah and find redemption through Him; but we read,

"Therefore will he give them up, until the time that she which travaileth hath brought forth: then the remnant of his brethren shall return unto the children of Israel."

How little chance there seemed, to almost the very last, of any possibility of the fulfillment of verse 2. It was given, as I have already said, 700 years before the Lord Jesus Christ was born. The Holy Spirit definitely indicated the place where He must be born—Bethlehem, a city of Judaea, David's city. It was not a very large city, but it is the most beautiful, to my mind, in all Palestine. For over a thousand years since the days of the first Crusade Bethlehem has been a Christian city, at least in name. It has not been given over to Mohammedanism, but has been a recognized Christian community. The prophet said that the Messiah must be born there, and he declared that this mysterious Child was to be One "whose goings forth have been from of old, from everlasting." The psalmist says, "From everlasting to everlasting, thou art God."

This Child, then, would be both God and Man—God and Man united in one Person, never again to be separated. This is the mystery of the incarnation.

Such was Micah's declaration, but it seemed until a very, very short time before the actual event took place that the prophecy could not be literally fulfilled. Almost up to the very last, Mary was dwelling in the city of Nazareth in the northern part of the land. In those days when one could only travel on foot or on the back of an ass or a camel, it took a long time to get from Nazareth to Jerusalem. It is very different today. One can make the journey in about three hours, with a stop or two, by automobile. It was not possible to travel that quickly in those days.

There was Mary at her home in Nazareth, expecting almost daily the birth of the wonderful Babe, the secret of whose conception she alone thoroughly understood, yet the prophecy said, "He must be born in Bethlehem." I wonder if Mary ever thought of the words of Micah. I wonder if Joseph was concerned. Did he know that the child must come into the world at Bethlehem? At any rate, they seemed to make no preparation for it.

Then we are told it came to pass in those days that there went out a decree from Caesar Augustus, that all the world should be taxed. He was the ruler of the ancient world. He had his throne in the city of Rome. And here was the prophecy which said that the Messiah must be born in Bethlehem, and there was Mary waiting in Nazareth. So God put it in the heart of the emperor that everyone must go to his own city, the city where he was born, in order to be enrolled for the taxing. This was God's way of bringing Mary and Joseph to Bethlehem on time, in order that His Word might not fail.

We are told this taxing was first made when Cyrenius was governor of Syria. The critics, those who try to find fault with the Bible and question its inspiration, used to point to verse 2 and say, "Now you have positive proof that the Gospel of Luke could not have been divinely inspired because you have an inaccuracy. Cyrenius ruled over Syria something like 6 A.D., really ten years after the actual birth of Christ, because He was born four years before the change of the calendar from B.C. to A.D." These objectors said Cyrenius was governor of Syria, which included Palestine, a number of years on from A.D. 6. This taxing could not have taken place in his time if it took place at the time when Christ was reputed to have been born.

God has been answering the critics in a very wonderful way in our day. The spade of the archaeologist has been turning up a great many remarkable things that have demonstrated the truth of the Bible. One of the leading archaeologists of the day wrote:

> I am acquainted with practically all the results of archaeological discovery for the last hundred years, and I have not discovered any that cast doubt on the Scripture, but hundreds of things have proved its statements to be absolutely accurate.

I have jotted down an item which I took from one of the records:

> It has been thought that Luke confused this census with that under Cyrenius, at 6 to 7 A.D., when he became governor the second time. Luke refers to that also in Acts 5:37 as "the days of the taxing."

But we know that Cyrenius had been governor of Syria before that, under the reign of Augustus, from B.C. 12 on to B.C. 3. It was during this period that the census was taken to which Luke refers here in his Gospel.

Men are too short-sighted and know too little, to find fault with the Bible. Just give us the opportunity to get more facts, and the Bible will always prove triumphant in every controversy. God had so ordered things that this enrollment had to take place, and that meant that Joseph and Mary must go to Bethlehem.

Jesus Born in a Stable

We read in verse 4:

"And Joseph also went up from Galilee, out of the city of Nazareth, into Judaea, unto the city of David, which is called Bethlehem; (because he was of the house and lineage of David)."

So it was that while there the days were accomplished that she should be delivered.

Thus we see God had set the whole world in motion—millions of people going to their own cities to be enrolled for the taxation, in order that one prophecy in the Old Testament might be fulfilled on time, and that Christ might be born in Bethlehem of Judaea.

They were not looking for Him down there. There was no welcome. Though Joseph was of the lineage of David and Mary a daughter of the house of David, there was no blare of trumpets when they arrived.

THE WONDROUS BIRTH OF OUR WONDROUS LORD

There was no reservation for them in the local inn. We read there was "no room for them in the inn." I suppose hundreds of people were crowding into Bethlehem. The wealthy would make reservations ahead and preempt the good places to stay. I can imagine Joseph and Mary coming, tired and worn after that long journey, and saying to the innkeeper, "Have you a comfortable place?" and the innkeeper saying, "You didn't make reservations. All the rooms have been taken." You can imagine there would not be much attention paid to this poor carpenter.

One cannot but wonder, however, whether the innkeeper himself ever realized what a wondrous Guest he had failed to find room for. One can well imagine what his feelings are today. He knows now that the child born that night was God's own Son, who had become Man, in grace, for our redemption. Surely, if he never learned on earth the identity of the family turned away from his door, he must regret now that he did not make it possible to entertain them, no matter how crowded the inn might have been.

Yet God had made provision. There was one place, if there was no room for His Son to be born in the inn, a place in a stable among the cattle. So we read, "She brought forth her firstborn son, and wrapped him in swaddling clothes, and laid him in a manger; because there was no room for them in the inn."

Do not think of the stable in which He was born as what we call a stable. It would not be a wooden barn but a cave cut in the limestone. When this place is shown to people in Bethlehem today, they say, "This is the cave in which Christ was born." One can see where the sheep, goats and oxen had been kept; and passing through a kind of a catacomb-like lane, you go into another cave where Jerome spent so many years while he translated the Bible into the Latin from the Greek. According to his own record, he said that his cave was right close by the one where Jesus Himself had been born.

It was in some such cave-stable that our blessed Lord was born. The little One was taken and wrapped in swaddling clothes, and for a cradle they put Him in a manger from which the cattle were accustomed to get their food.

The Wonderful Message of the Angels

"And there were in the same country shepherds abiding in the field,

keeping watch over their flock by night. And, lo, the angel of the Lord came upon them, and the glory of the Lord shone round about them: and they were sore afraid. And the angel said unto them, Fear not: for, behold, I bring you good tidings of great joy, which shall be to all people. For unto you is born this day in the city of David, a Saviour, which is Christ the Lord. And this shall be a sign unto you; Ye shall find the babe wrapped in swaddling clothes, lying in a manger. And suddenly there was with the angel a multitude of the heavenly host praising God, and saying, Glory to God in the highest, and on earth peace, good will toward men."— Luke 2:8-14.

Think of God's blessed Son becoming Man for our redemption! Born in a stable, cradled in a manger! We find all Heaven was stirred. In these early chapters of Luke, we get one song after another—the song of Elisabeth, the song of Zacharias, the song of Mary, and here we get the song of the angel. I know we do not actually get the word "song" here; it does not actually say the angel sang—but I am sure that the ordinary speech of the angels would be sweeter and more melodious than any song anybody could sing on earth.

All Heaven was moved. We are told:

"There were in the same country shepherds abiding in the field, keeping watch over their flocks by night, and lo, the angel of the Lord came upon them, and the glory of the Lord shone round about them, and they were sore afraid."

They had heard of angels appearing in time past. But 400 years had gone by since the last of the prophets, and there was no authentic record of angels being seen on earth until Gabriel appeared to Zacharias in the Temple. Now all Heaven was illuminated and a majestic being was actually visible to mortals.

They were sore afraid; but the angel said unto them, "Fear not; for, behold, I bring you good tidings of great joy which shall be to all people."

What a message—FEAR NOT! Gabriel twice before had used these same words, and this may have been Gabriel again. "Fear not; for behold, I bring you good tidings."

That is what the Gospel is. The word means "good tidings." Our English word *gospel* is just a slightly changed form of the old Anglo-Saxon *Gudspel*, which means "good tidings." So the angel came to preach the Gospel, and that word rings all through the Word of God.

The Gospel was preached to Abraham and to the people of Israel. The Gospel was preached all through the time or ministry of John the Baptist, and the Gospel is being proclaimed today in the power of the Holy Ghost, sent down from Heaven. It is God's message about His blessed Son.

There is only one Gospel. Paul says, "Though we or an angel from heaven preach any other gospel, let him be accursed." This was an angel from Heaven. If there be any who preach any other gospel than that which we have preached, let them be accursed. It is God's good news about His blessed Son. It takes on different forms at different times. It was the Gospel of the Kingdom, specifically, when our blessed Lord and the early apostles gave it forth.

Since Christ ascended to Heaven, the message has been sent down to earth, that a Saviour is seated at God's right hand. This tells of a finished work. It is called the "glorious gospel" because it leads to the glory, and the "everlasting gospel," for it is the Gospel for all ages. The Gospel will be the joy of our hearts for all eternity. It is all summed up in those wonderful words of John 3:16, "For God so loved the world, that he gave his only begotten Son, that whosoever believeth in him should not perish, but have everlasting life."

There are good tidings of great joy for *all* people, not just for the elect, not just for a limited number. All men everywhere are invited to put their trust in the Saviour whom God has sent into the world. We have the definite announcement of the Lord's birth as given by the Angel:

"Unto you is born this day in the city of David a Saviour, which is Christ the Lord.... And this shall be a sign unto you; Ye shall find the babe wrapped in swaddling clothes, lying in a manger."

Then we read that "suddenly there was with the angel, a multitude of the heavenly host, praising God and saying, Glory to God in the highest, and on earth *peace, good will* toward men." It seems strange to hear those words ringing down through the ages, when you think of the awful condition which prevails in the earth today.

Look where you will—there is no peace. Look at the lands abroad—there is war. Look out over our own land—it is strife between capital and labor, between different groups. There is misery and wretchedness everywhere—unrest on every hand; yet the angel said, "Peace, good will toward men."

Ah, but that peace was dependent upon receiving the Saviour whom

God had sent into the world. Alas, men rejected Him, refused Him; thus the world remains in its unhappy condition.

According to Micah, the Messiah is coming back again, when the rest of Israel shall return to their God.

How Simple Was the Faith of the Shepherds!

"And it came to pass as the angels were gone away from them into heaven, the shepherds said one to another, Let us now go even unto Bethlehem, and see this thing which is come to pass, which the Lord hath made known unto us. And they came with haste, and found Mary, and Joseph, and the babe lying in a manger. And when they had seen it, they made known abroad the saying which was told them concerning this child. And all they that heard it wondered at those things which were told them by the shepherds. But Mary kept all these things, and pondered them in her heart. And the shepherds returned, glorifying and praising God for all the things that they had heard and seen, as it was told unto them."—Luke 2:15-20.

The shepherds did not stop to question, but we read:

"It came to pass, as the angels were gone away from them into heaven, the shepherds said one to another, Let us now go even unto Bethlehem, and see this thing which is come to pass, which the Lord hath made known unto us."

I like the simplicity of their faith. They did not say, "Let us go and see *if* this thing has come to pass." They said, "Let us go and see this thing which *has* come to pass." They were persuaded even before they saw.

They hastened and came and found Mary and Joseph and the Babe lying in the manger; and when they had seen it they made known the saying which was told them concerning this Child.

The first evangelists of the new age were these simple shepherds who went out saying, "He has come," and, "We have seen Him. He was born in Bethlehem. We saw Him lying in a manger." They went forth proclaiming the advent of our blessed Lord Jesus Christ, and all who heard it wondered at those things which were told them by the shepherds.

Think of the virgin mother—what it must have meant to her! There she lay in the palace of straw! There—on the floor of the stable—there was the little Babe in the manger where she could reach Him with her delicately-shaped fingers, while all the time thinking what a wonderful message had come to her some months before, and now was the fulfillment. What does it all mean? Little could she see the wonderful results that would be manifested down through the ages, but she knew that God had come in in grace and visited His people.

We read that

"Mary kept all these things, and pondered them in her heart, and the shepherds returned, glorifying and praising God for all the things that they had heard and seen, as it was told unto them."

How our hearts rejoice in this story! We have read it over and over again, but it is always new; is it not? The sweetest story ever told—the coming to earth of our Lord Jesus Christ. No room for Him in the inn.

Is there room in your heart? Have you made room for Him? Have you received Him? Have you trusted Him? If you have never made room for Him before, won't you say now,

Come in, my Lord, come in,
And make my heart Thy home,
Come in and cleanse my soul from sin,
And dwell with me alone.

He wants to come in, and He will come in if you will open the door.

T. DEWITT TALMAGE
1832-1902

ABOUT THE MAN:

If Charles Spurgeon was the "Prince of Preachers," then T. DeWitt Talmage must be considered as one of the princes of the American pulpit. In fact, Spurgeon stated of Talmage's ministry: "His sermons take hold of my inmost soul. The Lord is with the mighty man. I am astonished when God blesses me but not surprised when He blesses him." He was probably the most spectacular pulpit orator of his time—and one of the most widely read.

Like Spurgeon, Talmage's ministry was multiplied not only from the pulpit to immense congregations, but in the printed pages of newspapers and in the making of many books. His sermons appeared in 3,000 newspapers and magazines a week, and he is said to have had 25 million readers.

And for 25 years, Talmage—a Presbyterian—filled the 4,000 to 5,000-seat auditorium of his Brooklyn church, as well as auditoriums across America and the British Isles. He counted converts to Christ in the thousands annually.

He was the founding editor of *Christian Herald,* and continued as editor of this widely circulated Protestant religious journal from 1877 until his death in 1902.

He had the face of a frontiersman and the voice of a golden bell; sonorous, dramatic, fluent, he was, first of all, an orator for God; few other evangelists had his speech. He poured forth torrents, deluges of words, flinging glory and singing phrases like a spendthrift; there was glow and warmth and color in every syllable. He played upon the heartstrings like an artist. One writer described him as the cultured Billy Sunday of his time. Many of his critics found fault with his methods; but they could not deny his mastery, nor could they successfully cloud his dynamic loyalty to his Saviour and Lord, Jesus Christ.

II.

The Sky Anthem

T. DEWITT TALMAGE

"Glory to God in the highest, and on earth peace, good will toward men." —Luke 2:14.

At last I have what I longed for—a Christmas Eve in the Holy Land. This is the time of year that Christ landed. This wintry month saw His arrival. This is the chill air through which He descended. I look up through these Christmas skies and I see no loosened star hastening southward to halt above Bethlehem, but all the stars suggest the Star of Bethlehem. No more need that any of them run along the sky to point downward. In quietude they kneel at the feet of Him who, though once an exile, is now enthroned forever.

Fresh from a visit to Bethlehem, I am full of the scenes suggested by a visit to that village. You know that whole region of Bethlehem is famous in Bible story. There were the waving harvests of Boaz, in which Ruth gleaned for herself and weeping Naomi. There David the warrior was thirsty, and three men of unheard-of self-sacrifice broke through the Philistine army to get him a drink. It was to that region that Joseph and Mary came to have their names enrolled in the census. That is what the Scripture means when it says they came "to be taxed," for people did not in those days rush after the assessors of tax any more than they now do.

The village inn was crowded with the strangers who had come up by the command of government to have their names in the census, so that Joseph and Mary were obliged to lodge in the stables. We have seen some of those large stone buildings, in the center of which the camels were kept, while running out from this center in all directions there were rooms, in one of which Jesus was born. Had His parents been more showily appareled, I have no doubt they would have found more comfortable entertainment.

That night in the field the shepherds, with crook and kindled fires, were watching their flocks, when, hark! to the sound of voices strangely sweet. Can it be that the maidens of Bethlehem have come out to serenade the weary shepherds? But now a light stoops upon them like the morning, so that the flocks arise, shaking their snowy fleece and bleating to their drowsy young. The heavens are filled with armies of light, and the earth quakes under the harmony as, echoed back from cloud to cloud, it rings over the midnight hills: "Glory to God in the highest, and on earth peace, good will toward men"! It seems as if the crown of royalty and dominion and power which Christ left behind Him was hung on the sky in sight of Bethlehem. Who knows but that that crown may have been mistaken by the Wise Men for the star running and pointing downward?

Indigence Not Always Significant of Degradation

My subject, in the first place, impresses me with the fact that indigence is not always significant of degradation. When princes are born, heralds announce it, and cannon thunder it, and flags wave it, and illuminations set cities on fire with the tidings. Some of us in England or America remember the time of rejoicing when the Prince of Wales was born. You can remember the gladness throughout Christendom at the nativity in the palace at Madrid.

But when our glorious Prince was born, there was no rejoicing on earth. Poor, and growing poorer, yet the heavenly recognition that Christmas night shows the truth of the proposition that indigence is not always significant of degradation. In all ages there have been great hearts throbbing under rags, tender sympathies under rough exterior, gold in the quartz, Parian marble in the quarry, and in every stable of privation wonders of excellence that have been the joy of the heavenly host.

All the great deliverers of literature and of nations were born in homes without affluence and from their own privation learned to speak and fight for the oppressed. Many a man has held up his pine-knot light from the wilderness until all nations and generations have seen it, and off his hard crust of penury has the bread of knowledge and religion been broken for the starving millions of the race. Poetry and science and literature and commerce and laws and constitutions and liberty, like Christ, were born in a manger.

All the great thoughts which have decided the destiny of nations started in obscure corners and had Herods who wanted to slay them and Iscariots who betrayed them and rabbles that crucified them and sepulchres that confined them until they burst forth in glorious resurrection.

Strong character, like the rhododendron, is an Alpine plant that grows faster in the storm. Men are like wheat, worth all the more for being flailed. Some of the most useful people would never have come to positions of usefulness had they not been grounded and pounded and hammered in the foundry of disaster.

When I see Moses coming up from the ark of bulrushes to be the greatest lawgiver of the ages, and Amos from tending the herds to make Israel tremble with his prophecies, and David from the sheepcote to sway the poet's pen and the king's sceptre, and Peter from the fishing-net to be the great preacher at the Pentecost, I find proof of the truth of my proposition that indigence is not always significant of degradation.

God Reveals Himself to Us While We Are at Our Post of Duty

My subject also impresses me with the thought that it is while at our useful occupations that we have the divine manifestations. Had those shepherds gone that night into Bethlehem and left their flocks at the mercy of the wolves, they would not have heard the song of the angels. In other words, that man sees most of God and Heaven who minds his own business. We all have our posts of duty, and, standing there, God appears to us. We are all shepherds or shepherdesses, and we have our flocks of cares and annoyances and anxieties, and we must tend them.

We sometimes hear very good people say, "If I had a month or a year or two to do nothing but attend to religious things, I would be a great deal better than I am now." You are mistaken. Generally the best people are the busy people.

Elisha was plowing in the field when the prophetic mantle fell on him.

Matthew was attending to his custom-house duties when Christ commanded him to follow.

James and John were mending their nets when Christ called them to be fishers of men. Had they been snoring in the sun, Christ would not have called their indolence into the apostleship.

Gideon was at work with the flail on the threshing-floor when he saw the angel.

Saul was with great fatigue hunting up the lost asses when he found the crown of Israel.

The prodigal son would never have reformed and wanted to have returned to his father's house if he had not first gone into business, though it was swine-feeding.

Not once out of a hundred times will a lazy man become a Christian. Those who have nothing to do are in very unfavorable circumstances for the receiving of divine manifestations. It is not when you are in idleness, but when you are, like the Bethlehem shepherds, watching your flocks, that the glory descends and there is joy among the angels of God over your soul, penitent and forgiven.

Christ Brings Joy, Not Sorrow

My subject also strikes at the delusion that the religion of Christ is dolorous and grief-infusing. The music that broke through the midnight heavens was not a dirge, but an anthem. It shook joy over the hills. It not only dropped upon the shepherds, but it sprang upward among the thrones.

The robe of a Saviour's righteousness is not black. The Christian life is not made up of weeping and cross-bearing and war-waging. Through the revelation of that Christmas night I find that religion is not a groan, but a song. In a world of sin and sickbeds and sepulchres, we must have trouble; but in the darkest night the heavens part with angelic song. You may, like Paul, be shipwrecked, but I exhort you to be of good cheer, for you who are trusting on Christ shall all escape safe to the land.

True religion does not show itself in the elongation of the face and the cut of the garb. The Pharisee who puts his religion into his phylactery has none left for his heart. Fretfulness and complaining do not belong to the family of Christian graces which move into the heart when the Devil moves out. Christianity does not frown upon amusements and recreations. It is not a cynic; it is not a shrew. It chokes not laughter, quenches no light, defaces no art. Among the happy, it is the happiest. It is just as much at home on the playground as it is in the church. It is just as graceful in the charade as it is in the psalm-book. It sings just as well in Surrey Gardens as it prays in St. Paul's. Christ died that we might live. Christ walked that we might ride. Christ wept that we might laugh.

Glorious Endings Sometimes Have Very Humble Beginnings

Again, my subject impresses me with the fact that glorious endings sometimes have very humble beginnings. The straw pallet was the starting point, but the shout in the midnight sky revealed what would be the glorious consummation. Christ on Mary's lap, Christ on the throne of universal dominion—what an humble starting! What a glorious ending!

Grace begins on a small scale in the heart. You see only men as trees walking. The grace of God in the heart is a feeble spark, and Christ has to keep both hands over it lest it be blown out.

What an humble beginning! But look at that same man when he has entered Heaven. No crown able to indicate His royalty. No palace able to signify His wealth. No sceptre able to symbolize His power and dominion. Drinking from the fountain that drips from the everlasting Rock. Among the harpers harping with their harps. On a sea of glass mingled with fire. Before the throne of God, to go no more out forever. The spark of grace that Christ had to keep both hands over lest it come to extinction, having flamed up into honor and glory and immortality. What humble starting! What glorious consummation!

The New Testament church was on a small scale. Fishermen watched it. Against the uprising walls crashed infernal enginery. The world said, **Anathema.** Ten thousand people rejoiced at every seeming defeat, and said, "Aha! aha! so we would have it." Martyrs on fire cried, "How long, O Lord, how long?"

Very humble starting, but see the difference at the consummation, when all the immortals of Heaven, rising on their thrones, beat time with their sceptres. Oh, what an humble beginning! What a glorious ending! Throne linked to a manger, heavenly mansions to a stable.

How Angels and Men Were Affected by the Birth of Christ

My subject also impresses me with the effect of Christ's mission upward and downward. Glory to God, peace to man! When God sent His Son into the world, angels discovered something new in God, something they had never seen before. Not power, not wisdom, not love. They knew all that before. But when God sent His Son into this world, then the angels saw the spirit of self-denial in God, the spirit of self-sacrifice in God.

It is easier to love an angel on his throne than a thief on the cross, a seraph in his worship than an adulteress in her crime. When the angels saw God—the God who would not allow the most insignificant angel in Heaven to be hurt—give up His Son, His only Son, they saw something that they had never thought of before. And I do not wonder that when Christ started out on the pilgrimage the angels in Heaven clapped their wings in triumph and called on all the hosts of Heaven to help them celebrate it and sang so loud that the Bethlehem shepherds heard it—"Glory to God in the highest."

But it was also to be a mission of peace to man. Infinite holiness, accumulated depravity—how could they ever come together? The Gospel bridges over the distance. It brings God to us. It takes us to God. God in us, and we in God. Atonement! Justice satisfied, sins forgiven, eternal life secured, Heaven built on a manger.

A Future Peace to a Warring World

But it was also to be the pacification of all individual and international animosities. What a sound this word of peace had in the Roman Empire, that boasted of the number of people it has massacred; that prided itself on the number of slain; that rejoiced at the trembling provinces. Gaul and Britain and Sicily and Corsica and Sardinia and Macedonia and Egypt had bowed to her sword and crouched at the cry of her war eagles. She gave her chief honor to Cipio and Fabius and Caesar—all men of blood. What contempt they must have had there for the penniless, unarmed Christ in the garb of a Nazarene, starting out to conquer all nations!

There never was a place on earth where that word of peace sounded so offensively to the ears of the multitude as in the Roman Empire. The greatest music they ever heard was the clanking chains of their captives. If all the blood that has been shed in battle could be gathered together it would upbear a navy. The club that struck Abel to the earth has its echo in the butcheries of all ages.

Oh, if we could now take our position on some high point and see the march of the world's armies, what a spectacle it would be!

There go the hosts of Israel through a score of Red Seas—one of water, the rest of blood.

There go Cyrus and his army, with infuriate yell, rejoicing over the fall of the gates of Babylon.

There goes Alexander, leading forth his hosts and conquering all the world but himself, the earth reeling with the battle-gash of Arbela and Persepolis.

There goes Ferdinand Cortes, leaving his butchered enemies on the tablelands once fragrant with vanilla and covered with groves of flowering cacao.

There goes the great Frenchman Napoleon, leading his army down through Egypt like one of its plagues and up through Russia like one of its own icy blasts. Yonder is the grave-trench under the shadow of Sebastopol. There are the ruins of Delhi and Allahabad, and yonder are the inhuman Sepoys committing their outrages and the brave regiments under Havelock avenging the insulted flag of Britain; while cut right through the heart of my native land is a trench in which there lie one million Northern and Southern dead. Oh, the tears! Oh, the blood! Oh, the long marches! Oh, the hospital wounds! Oh, the martyrdom! Oh, the death!

But brighter than the light which flashed on all these swords and shields and musketry is the light that fell on Bethlehem, and louder than the bray of the trumpets and the neighing of the chargers and the crash of walls and the groaning of the dying armies is the song that unrolls this moment from the sky, sweet as though all the bells of Heaven rung a jubilee, "Peace on earth, good will toward men."

Oh, when will the day come—God hasten it!—when the swords shall be turned into plowshares! There will be a song louder than the voice of the storm-lifted oceans, "Glory to God in the highest," and from all nations and kindred and people and tongues will come the response, "And on earth peace, good will toward men!"

On this Christmas Eve I bring you tidings of great joy. Pardon for all sin, comfort for all trouble and life for the dead. Shall we now take this Christ into our hearts? The time is passing. This is the closing of the year. How the time speeds by! Put your hand on your heart—one, two, three. Three times less it will beat. Life is passing like gazelles over the plain. Sorrows hover like petrels over the sea. Death swoops like a vulture from the mountains. Misery rolls up to our ears like waves. Heavenly songs fall to us like stars.

I wish you a merry Christmas, not with world dissipations, but merry with gospel gladness, merry with pardoned sin, merry with hope of reunion in the skies with all your beloved ones who have preceded you. In that grandest sense—a merry Christmas.

And God grant that in our final moment we may have as bright a vision as did the dying girl when she said, "Mother"—pointing with her thin white hand through the window—"Mother, what is that beautiful land out yonder beyond the mountains, the high mountains?"

"Oh," said the mother, "my darling, there are no mountains within sight of our home."

"Oh, yes," she said. "Don't you see them—that beautiful land beyond the mountains out there, just beyond the high mountains?"

The mother looked down into the face of her dying child and said, "My dear, I think that must be Heaven that you see."

"Well, then," she said, "Father, you come, and with your strong arms carry me over those mountains into that beautiful land beyond the high mountains."

"No," said the weeping father, "my darling, I cannot go with you."

"Well," she said, clapping her hands, "never mind, never mind. I see yonder a shining one coming. He is coming now, in His strong arms to carry me over the mountains to the beautiful land—over the mountains, over the high mountains!"

(From *500 Selected Sermons,* Baker Book House)

JOHN CHARLES RYLE
1816-1900

ABOUT THE MAN:

John Charles Ryle was born in Macclesfield, Cheshire (England) in 1816. At age 12, Ryle entered "prep school," leaving in 1827 to enter Eton, from which he graduated in 1834. He then enrolled at Oxford, and the year in which he graduated (1837) he was soundly converted.

In preparation for sharing his father's banking business, Ryle studied law in London. When in 1841 the bank failed and the family lost everything, each family member assisted his father in paying back every cent of indebtedness.

In that same year, young John was ordained and preached his first sermon December 19. He began his ministry at Exbury, and then went to Winchester. And from 1844 to 1861, he served at Helmingham. Here he went through the valley, burying his wife of less than two years in 1847 and his second wife in 1860. From 1861 to 1880 Ryle ministered at Stradbroke. Here he met and married his third wife.

At this church he had the workmen carve on the pulpit:
   WOE IS UNTO ME IF I PREACH NOT THE GOSPEL!

In 1880, John Charles Ryle was appointed the first Bishop of Liverpool. It was not easy to be a Bible believer in the Established Church, for you would not be recognized by those in authority and you would probably not be promoted or offered the "better churches."

He gathered around him like-minded Christians who wanted to share the Gospel and build churches. Instead of raising money to construct an ornate cathedral, Ryle used the funds available to extend the church, building 90 places of worship and staffing them with 136 ministers.

Always a man with a great heart, Ryle saw nothing wrong with cooperating with the non-conformists, including D. L. Moody and Ira Sankey when they came to Liverpool in 1883. His friendly attitude toward the Methodists rankled some of the most exclusive Anglican clergy, but their criticisms did not disturb him.

On February 1, 1900, Bishop Ryle resigned from his charge. He had lived to see nearly one-fourth of the parishes in his diocese staffed by Bible believers!

Not only was Bishop Ryle a faithful pastor, a noted preacher, an able administrator, but he was a prolific writer. He was the author of numerous expository works, chief among which is *Expository Thoughts on the Gospels*, a set that ought to be in every Bible student's library. *The Best of J. C. Ryle* is a good "sampler" for one not yet acquainted with this giant of the faith.

He went to be with the Lord on June 10, 1900, at the ripe old age of 84.

III.

Christ's Birth Announced

J. C. RYLE

"And in the sixth month the angel Gabriel was sent from God unto a city of Galilee, named Nazareth, To a virgin espoused to a man whose name was Joseph, of the house of David; and the virgin's name was Mary. And the angel came in unto her, and said, Hail, thou that art highly favoured, the Lord is with thee: blessed art thou among women. And when she saw him, she was troubled at his saying, and cast in her mind what manner of salutation this should be. And the angel said unto her, Fear not, Mary: for thou hast found favour with God. And, behold, thou shalt conceive in thy womb, and bring forth a son, and shalt call his name JESUS. He shall be great, and shall be called the Son of the Highest: and the Lord God shall give unto him the throne of his father David: And he shall reign over the house of Jacob for ever; and of his kingdom there shall be no end." —Luke 1:26-33.

We have in these verses the announcement of the most marvelous event that ever happened in this world—the incarnation and birth of our Lord Jesus Christ. It is a passage which we should always read with mingled wonder, love and praise.

1. Christ's Lowly Birth

We should notice, in the first place, the lowly and unassuming manner in which the Saviour of mankind came amongst us. The angel who announced His advent was sent to an obscure town of Galilee named Nazareth. The woman who was honored to be our Lord's mother was evidently in a humble position of life. Both in her station and dwellingplace, there was an utter absence of what the world calls greatness.

We need not hesitate to conclude that there was a wise providence in all this arrangement. The Almighty Counsel, which orders all things in Heaven and earth, could just as easily have appointed Jerusalem to be the place of Mary's residence as Nazareth, or could as easily have chosen the daughter of some rich scribe to be our Lord's mother as a poor woman. But it seemed good that it should not be so. The first advent of Messiah was to be an advent of humiliation. That humiliation was to begin even from the time of His conception and birth.

Let us beware of despising poverty in others and of being ashamed of it if God lays it upon ourselves. The condition of life which Jesus voluntarily chose ought always to be regarded with holy reverence. The common tendency of the day to bow down before rich men and make an idol of money ought to be carefully resisted and discouraged. The example of our Lord is a sufficient answer to a thousand groveling maxims about wealth, which pass current among men. "Though he was rich, yet for our sakes he became poor" (II Cor. 8:9).

Let us admire the amazing condescension of the Son of God. The Heir of all things not only took our nature upon Him, but took it in the most humbling form in which it could have been assumed. It would have been condescension to come on earth as a king and reign. It was a miracle of mercy passing our comprehension to come on earth as a poor man, to be despised, suffer and die. Let His love constrain us to live not to ourselves, but to Him. Let His example daily bring home to our conscience the precept of Scripture: "Mind not high things, but condescend to men of low estate" (Rom. 12:16).

2. The High Privilege of the Virgin Mary

We should notice, in the second place, the high privilege of the Virgin Mary. The language which the Angel Gabriel addresses to her is very remarkable. He calls her "highly favoured." He tells her that "the Lord is with her." He says to her, "Blessed art thou among women."

It is a well-known fact that the Roman Catholic Church pays an honor to the Virgin Mary hardly inferior to that which it pays to her blessed Son. She is formally declared by the Roman Catholic Church to have been "conceived without sin." She is held up to Roman Catholics as an object of worship, and prayed to as a mediator between God and man, no less powerful than Christ Himself.

For all this, there is not the slightest warrant in Scripture, and no warrant in the verses before us now nor in any other part of God's Word.

But while we say this, we must in fairness admit that no woman was ever so highly honored as the mother of our Lord. It is evident that one woman only out of the countless millions of the human race could be the means whereby God could be "manifest in the flesh," and the Virgin Mary had the mighty privilege of being that one.

By one woman, sin and death were brought into the world at the beginning. By the child-bearing of one woman, life and immortality were brought to light when Christ was born. No wonder this one woman was called "highly favoured" and "blessed."

One thing in connection with this subject should never be forgotten by Christians. There is a relationship to Christ within reach of us all, a relationship far nearer than that of flesh and blood, a relationship which belongs to all who repent and believe. "Whosoever shall do the will of God," says Jesus, "the same is my brother, and sister, and mother." "Blessed is the womb that bare thee" was the saying of a woman one day. But what was the reply? "Yea rather, blessed are they that hear the word of God, and keep it" (Mark 3:35; Luke 11:27).

3. Mary's Glorious Testimony to the Lord Jesus

We should notice, finally, in these verses the glorious account of our Lord Jesus Christ which the angel gives to Mary. Every part of the account is full of deep meaning and deserves close attention.

Jesus "shall be great," says Gabriel. Of His greatness we know something already. He has brought in a great salvation. He has shown Himself a Prophet greater than Moses. He is a great High Priest. And He shall be greater still when He shall be owned as a King.

Jesus "shall be called the Son of the Highest," says Gabriel. He was so before He came into the world. Equal to the Father in all things, He was from all eternity the Son of God. But He was to be known and acknowledged as such by the church. The Messiah was to be recognized and worshiped as nothing less than very God.

"The Lord God shall give unto him the throne of his father David," says Gabriel, "and he shall reign over the house of Jacob for ever." The literal fulfillment of this part of the promise is yet to come. Israel is yet to be gathered, the Jews yet to be restored to their own land and to look to Him whom they once pierced as their King and their God. Though the accomplishment of this prediction tarry, we may confidently wait for it. It shall surely come one day and not tarry (Hab. 2:3).

Finally, says Gabriel, 'Of the kingdom of Jesus there shall be no end.' Before His glorious kingdom the empires of this world shall one day go down and pass away. Like Nineveh, Babylon, Egypt, Tyre and Carthage, they shall all come to nothing one day, and the saints of the most High shall take the kingdom. Before Jesus every knee shall one day bow and every tongue confess that He is Lord. His kingdom alone shall prove an everlasting kingdom, and His dominion that which shall not pass away (Dan. 7:14,27).

The true Christian should often dwell on this glorious promise and take comfort in its contents. He has no cause to be ashamed of his Master. Poor and despised as he may often be for the Gospel's sake, he may feel assured that he is on the conquering side. The kingdoms of this world shall yet become the kingdoms of Christ. Yet a little time and He that shall come will come, and will not tarry (Heb. 10:37).

For that blessed day let us patiently wait and watch and pray. Now is the time for carrying the cross and for fellowship with Christ's sufferings. The day draws near when Christ shall take His great power and reign; and when all who have served Him faithfully shall exchange a cross for a crown.

Mary and Angel Gabriel

"Then said Mary unto the angel, How shall this be, seeing I know not a man? And the angel answered and said unto her, The Holy Ghost shall come upon thee, and the power of the Highest shall overshadow thee: therefore also that holy thing which shall be born of thee shall be called the Son of God. And, behold, thy cousin Elisabeth, she hath also conceived a son in her old age: and this is the sixth month with her, who was called barren. For with God nothing shall be impossible. And Mary said, Behold the handmaid of the Lord; be it unto me according to thy word. And the angel departed from her." —Luke 1:34-38.

The Incarnation Reverently Told

Let us mark in these verses the reverent and discreet manner in which the Angel Gabriel speaks of the great mystery of Christ's incarnation. In reply to the question of the virgin, "How shall this be?" he uses these remarkable words: "The Holy Ghost shall come upon thee, and the power of the Highest shall overshadow thee."

We shall do well to follow the example of the angel in all our reflections on this deep subject. Let us ever regard it with holy reverence and abstain from those unseemly and unprofitable speculations upon it, in which some have unhappily indulged. Enough for us to know that "the Word was made flesh," and that when the Son of God came into the world, a real "body was prepared for him," so that He "took part of our flesh and blood," and was "made of a woman" (John 1:14; Heb. 10:5; Heb. 2:14; Gal. 4:4).

Here we must stop. The manner in which all this was effected is wisely hidden from us. If we attempt to pry beyond this point, we shall but darken counsel by words without knowledge and rush in where angels fear to tread. In a religion which really comes down from Heaven, there must needs be mysteries. Of such mysteries in Christianity, the incarnation is one.

Jesus Conceived of the Holy Ghost

Let us mark, in the second place, the prominent place assigned to the Holy Ghost in the great mystery of the incarnation. We find it written, "The Holy Ghost shall come upon thee."

An intelligent reader of the Bible will probably not fail to remember that the honor here given to the Spirit is in precise harmony with the teaching of Scripture in other places. In every step of the great work of man's redemption we shall find special mention of the work of the Holy Ghost.

Did Jesus die to make atonement for our sins? It is written that "through the eternal Spirit he offered himself without spot to God" (Heb. 9:14).

Did He rise again for our justification? It is written that He "was quickened by the Spirit" (I Pet. 3:18).

Does He supply His disciples with comfort between the time of His first and second advent? It is written that the Comforter whom He promised to send is "the Spirit of truth" (John 14:17).

Let us take heed that we give the Holy Ghost the same place in our personal religion which we find Him occupying in God's Word. Let us remember that all that believers have and are and enjoy under the Gospel, they owe to the inward teaching of the Holy Spirit. The work of each of the three Persons of the Trinity is equally and entirely needful to the salvation of every saved soul. The election of God the Father, the blood of God the Son and the sanctification of God the Spirit ought never be separated in our Christianity.

Nothing Impossible With God

Let us mark, in the third place, the mighty principle which the Angel Gabriel lays down to silence all objections about the incarnation. "With God nothing shall be impossible."

A hearty reception of this great principle is of immense importance to our own inward peace. Questions and doubts will often arise in men's minds about many subjects in religion. They are the natural result of our fallen estate of soul. Our faith at the best is very feeble. Our knowledge at its highest is clouded with much infirmity. And among many antidotes to a doubting, anxious, questioning state of mind, few will be found more useful than that before us now—a thorough conviction of the almighty power of God. With Him who called the world into being and formed it out of nothing, everything is possible. Nothing is too hard for the Lord.

There is no sin too black and bad to be pardoned. The blood of Christ cleanseth from all sin. There is no heart too hard and wicked to be changed. The heart of stone can be made a heart of flesh. There is no work too hard for a believer to do. We may do all things through Christ strengthening us. There is no trial too hard to be borne. The grace of God is sufficient for us. There is no promise too great to be fulfilled. Christ's words never pass away, and what He has promised He is able to perform. There is no difficulty too great for a believer to overcome. When God is for us, who shall be against us? The mountain shall become a plain.

Let principles like these be continually before our minds. The angel's receipt is an invaluable remedy. Faith never rests so calmly and peacefully as when it lays its head on the pillow of God's omnipotence.

Mary Accepted God's Will

Let us mark, in the last place, the meek and ready acquiescence of the Virgin Mary in God's revealed will concerning her. She says to the angel, "Behold the handmaid of the Lord; be it unto me according to thy word."

There is far more of admirable grace in this answer than at first sight appears. A moment's reflection will show us that it was no light matter to become the mother of our Lord in this unheard of and mysterious way. It brought with it, no doubt, at a distant period great honor; but it brought with it for the present no small danger to Mary's reputation, and no small trial to Mary's faith. All this danger and trial the holy virgin was willing and ready to risk. She asks no further questions. She raises no further objections. She accepts the honor laid upon her with all its attendant perils and inconveniences. "Behold," she says, "the handmaid of the Lord."

Let us seek in our daily practical Christianity to exercise the same blessed spirit of faith which we see here in the Virgin Mary. Let us be willing to go anywhere and do anything and be anything, whatever be the present and immediate inconvenience, so long as God's will is clear and the path of duty is plain. The words of good Bishop Hall on this passage are worth remembering. "All disputations with God after His will is known, arise from infidelity. There is not a more noble proof of faith than to captivate all the powers of our understanding and will to our Creator, and without all questionings to go blindfold whither He will lead us."

Mary and Elizabeth

"And Mary arose in those days, and went into the hill country with haste, into a city of Juda; And entered into the house of Zacharias, and saluted Elisabeth. And it came to pass, that, when Elisabeth heard the salutation of Mary, the babe leaped in her womb; and Elisabeth was filled with the Holy Ghost: And she spake out with a loud voice, and said, Blessed art thou among women, and blessed is the fruit of thy womb. And whence is this to me, that the mother of my Lord should come to me? For, lo, as soon as the voice of thy salutation sounded in mine ears, the babe leaped in my womb for joy. And blessed is she that believed: for there shall be a performance of those things which were told her from the Lord."—Luke 1:39-45.

Sweet Christian Fellowship

We should observe in this passage the benefit of fellowship and communion between believers. We read of a visit paid by the Virgin Mary to her cousin Elizabeth. We are told in a striking manner how the hearts of both these holy women were cheered and their minds lifted up by this interview. Without this visit Elizabeth might never have been so filled with the Holy Ghost as we are here told she was; Mary might never have uttered that song of praise which is now known all over the church of Christ. The words of an old divine are deep and true: "Happiness communicated doubles itself. Grief grows greater by concealing; joy, by expression."

We should always regard communion with other believers as an eminent means of grace. It is a refreshing break in our journey along the narrow way to exchange experience with our fellow-travelers. It helps us insensibly and it helps them, and so is a mutual gain. It is the nearest approach that we can make on earth to the joy of Heaven. "As iron sharpeneth iron, so doth the countenance of a man his friend." We need reminding of this. The subject does not receive sufficient attention, and the souls of believers suffer in consequence. There are many who fear the Lord and think upon His name, and yet forget to speak often one to another (Mal. 3:16).

First, let us seek the face of God; then let us seek the face of God's friends. If we did this more and were more careful about the company we keep, we should oftener know what it is to be "filled with the Holy Ghost."

Elizabeth's Spiritual Knowledge

We should observe in this passage the clear spiritual knowledge which appears in the language of Elizabeth. She uses an expression about the Virgin Mary which shows that she herself was deeply taught of God. She calls her "the mother of my Lord."

Those words, "my Lord," are so familiar to our ears that we miss the fullness of their meaning. At the time they were spoken they implied far more than we are apt to suppose. They were nothing less than a distinct declaration that the child who was to be born of the Virgin Mary was the long-promised Messiah, the "Lord" of whom David in spirit had prophesied, the Christ of God. Viewed in this light, the expression is a wonderful example of faith, a confession worthy to be placed alongside that of Peter when he said to Jesus, "Thou art the Christ."

Let us remember the deep meaning of the words, "The Lord," and beware of using them lightly and carelessly. Let us consider that they rightly apply to none but Him who was crucified for our sins on Calvary. Let the recollection of this fact invest the words with a holy reverence and make us careful how we let them fall from our lips.

There are two texts connected with the expression which should often come to our minds. In one it is written, "No man can say that Jesus is the Lord but by the Holy Ghost." In the other it is written, "Every tongue shall confess that Jesus Christ is Lord, to the glory of God the Father" (I Cor. 12:3; Phil. 2:11).

Mary's Remarkable Faith

Finally, we should observe in these verses the high praise which Elizabeth bestows upon the grace of faith. "Blessed," she says, "is she that believed."

We need not wonder that this holy woman should thus commend faith. No doubt she was well acquainted with the Old Testament Scriptures. She knew the great things that faith had done. What is the whole history of God's saints in every age but a record of men and women who obtained a good report by faith? What is the simple story of all, from Abel downwards, but a narrative of redeemed sinners who believed and so were blessed?

By faith they embraced promises. By faith they lived. By faith they walked. By faith they endured hardships. By faith they looked to an unseen Saviour and good things yet to come. By faith they battled with the world, the flesh and the Devil. By faith they overcame and got safe home. Of this goodly company the Virgin Mary was proving herself one. No wonder Elizabeth said, "Blessed is she that believed."

Do we know anything of this precious faith? This, after all, is the question that concerns us. Do we know anything of the faith of God's elect, the faith which is of the operation of God (Titus 1:2; Col. 2:12)? Let us never rest till we know it by experience. Once knowing it, let us never cease to pray that our faith may grow exceedingly. Better a thousand times be rich in faith than rich in gold. Gold will be worthless in the unseen world to which we are all traveling. Faith will be owned in that world before God the Father and the holy angels. When the great white throne is set and the books are opened, when the dead are called from their graves and, receiving their final sentence, the value of faith will at length be fully known—men will learn then, if they never learned before, how true are the words, "Blessed are they that believed."

Mary's Hymn of Praise

"And Mary said, My soul doth magnify the Lord, And my spirit hath rejoiced in God my Saviour. For he hath regarded the low estate of his handmaiden: for, behold, from henceforth all generations shall call me blessed. For he that is mighty hath done to me great things; and

holy is his name. And his mercy is on them that fear him from generation to generation. He hath shewed strength with his arm; he hath scattered the proud in the imagination of their hearts. He hath put down the mighty from their seats, and exalted them of low degree. He hath filled the hungry with good things; and the rich he hath sent empty away. He hath holpen his servant Israel, in remembrance of his mercy; As he spake to our fathers, to Abraham, and to his seed for ever. And Mary abode with her about three months, and returned to her own house."—Luke 1:46-56.

These verses contain the Virgin Mary's famous hymn of praise, in the prospect of becoming the "mother of our Lord." Next to the Lord's Prayer, perhaps, few passages of Scripture are better known than this. Wherever the Church of England Prayer-book is used, this hymn forms part of the evening service. And we need not wonder that the compilers of that Prayer-book gave it so prominent a place. No words can express more aptly the praise for redeeming mercy which ought to form part of the public worship of every branch of Christ's church.

Mary Knew the Scripture

Let us mark, first, the full acquaintance with Scripture which this hymn exhibits. We are reminded as we read it of many expressions in the book of Psalms. Above all, we are reminded of the song of Hannah, in the book of Samuel (I Sam. 2:2-10). It is evident that the memory of the blessed virgin was stored with Scripture. She was familiar—whether by hearing or by reading—with the Old Testament. And so, when out of the abundance of her heart her mouth spoke, she gave vent to her feelings in scriptural language. Moved by the Holy Ghost to break forth into praise, she chooses language which the Holy Ghost had already consecrated and used.

Every year we live, let us strive to become more deeply acquainted with Scripture. Let us study it, search into it, dig into it, meditate on it, until it dwells in us richly (Col. 2:16). In particular, let us labor to make ourselves familiar with those parts of the Bible which, like the book of Psalms, describe the experience of the saints of old. We shall find it most helpful to us in all our approaches to God. It will supply us with the best and most suitable language both for the expression of our wants and thanksgivings. Such knowledge of the Bible can doubtless never be attained without regular, daily study. But the time spent on such study is never misspent. It will bear fruit after many days.

Mary's Humility as a Sinner Needing a Saviour

Let us mark, second, in this hymn of praise, the Virgin Mary's deep humility. She who was chosen of God to the high honor of being Messiah's mother, speaks of her own "low estate" and acknowledges her need of a "Saviour." She does not let fall a word to show that she regarded herself as a sinless, "immaculate" person. On the contrary, she uses the language of one who has been taught by the grace of God to feel her own sins, and so far from being able to save others, requires a Saviour for her own soul. We may safely affirm that none would be more forward to reprove the honor paid by the Romish church to the Virgin Mary than the Virgin Mary herself.

Let us copy this holy humility of our Lord's mother while we stedfastly refuse to regard her as a mediator, or to pray to her. Like her, let us be lowly in our own eyes and think little of ourselves. Humility is the highest grace that can adorn the Christian character. It is a true saying of an old divine, that "a man has just so much Christianity as he has humility." It is the grace which, of all, is most becoming to human nature. Above all, it is the grace which is within the reach of every converted person.

All are not rich. All are not learned. All are not highly gifted. All are not preachers. But all children of God may be clothed with humility.

Mary's Thankfulness

Let us mark, third, the lively thankfulness of the Virgin Mary. It stands out prominently in all the early part of her hymn. Her 'soul magnifies the Lord.' Her 'spirit rejoices in God.' 'All generations shall call her blessed.' 'Great things have been done for her.' We can scarcely enter into the full extent of feelings which a holy Jewess would experience on finding herself in Mary's position. But we should try to recollect them as we read her repeated expressions of praise.

We too shall do well to walk in Mary's steps in this matter and cultivate a thankful spirit. It has ever been a mark of God's most distinguished saints in every age. David in the Old Testament and St. Paul in the New are remarkable for their thankfulness. We seldom read much of their writings without finding them blessing and praising God.

Let us rise from our beds every morning with a deep conviction that we are debtors and that every day we have more mercies than we deserve. Let us look around us every week, as we travel through the world, and see whether we have not much to thank God for. If our hearts are in the right place, we shall never find any difficulty in building an Ebenezer. Well would it be if our prayers and supplications were more mingled with thanksgiving (I Sam. 7:12; Phil. 4:6).

Mary Knew How God Had Dealt With Other Christians

Let us mark, fourth, the experimental acquaintance with God's former dealings with His people, which the Virgin Mary possessed. She speaks of God as One whose "mercy is on them that fear him"; as One who 'scatters the proud, and puts down the mighty...and sends the rich empty away'; as One who 'exalteth them of low degree, and filleth the hungry with good things.' She spoke, no doubt, in recollection of Old Testament history. She remembered how Israel's God had put down Pharaoh and the Canaanites and the Philistines and Sennacherib and Haman and Belshazzar. She remembered how He had exalted Joseph and Moses and Samuel and David and Esther and Daniel; and never allowed His chosen people to be completely destroyed. And in all God's dealings with herself—in placing honor upon a poor woman of Nazareth—in raising up Messiah in such a dry ground as the Jewish nation seemed to have become—she traced the handiwork of Israel's covenant God.

The true Christian should always give close attention to Bible history and the lives of individual saints. Let us often examine the "footsteps of the flock" (Song of Sol. 1:8). Such study throws light on God's mode of dealing with His people. He is of one mind. What He does for and to them in time past, He is likely to do in time to come. Such study will teach us what to expect, check unwarrantable expectations and encourage us when cast down. Happy is that man whose mind is well stored with such knowledge. It will make him patient and hopeful.

Mary Knew and Laid Hold of Bible Promises

Let us mark, last, the firm grasp which the Virgin Mary had of Bible promises. She ends her hymn of praise by declaring that God has 'blessed Israel in remembrance of his mercy,' and that He has done "as he spake to our fathers, to Abraham and to his seed for ever." These words show clearly that she remembered the old promise made to Abraham, "In thee shall all nations of the earth be blessed." And it is evident that in the approaching birth of her Son, she regarded this promise as about to be fulfilled.

Let us learn from this holy woman's example to lay firm hold on Bible promises. It is of the deepest importance to our peace to do so. Promises are, in fact, the manna that we should daily eat and the water that we should daily drink as we travel through the wilderness of this world. We see not yet all things put under us. We see not Christ and Heaven and the Book of Life and the mansions prepared for us. We walk by faith, and this faith leans on promises. But on those promises we may lean confidently. They will bear all the weight we can lay on them. We shall find one day, like the Virgin Mary, that God keeps His word and that what He has spoken, so He will always in due time perform.

(From Ryle's *Expository Thoughts on the Gospels*.)

CHARLES HADDON SPURGEON
1835 - 1892

ABOUT THE MAN:

Many times it has been said that this was the greatest preacher this side of the Apostle Paul. He began preaching at the age of 16. At 25 he built London's famous Metropolitan Tabernacle, seating around 5,000. It was never large enough. Even when traveling he preached to 10,000 eager listeners a week. Crowds thronged to hear him as they came to hear John the Baptist by the River Jordan. The fire of God was on him as on the Prophet Elijah facing assembled Israel at Mount Carmel.

Royalty sat in his Tabernacle, as did washerwomen. Mr. Gladstone had him to dinner; and cabbies refused his fare, considering it an honor to drive for this "Prince of Preachers." To a housewife kneading bread, he would say, "Have you ever tried the Bread of life?" Many a carpenter was asked, "Have you ever tried to build a house on sand?"

He preached in all the principal cities of England, Scotland and Ireland. And although invited to the United States on several occasions, he was never able to visit this country.

HOW GREAT WAS HIS HEART: for preachers, so the Pastors' College was founded; for orphans, so the orphans' houses came to be; for people around the world, so his literature poured forth in an almost unmeasurable volume. He was a national voice; so every national issue affecting morals, religion or the poor had his interpretation, his counsel.

Oh, but his passion for souls! You can see it in every sermon.

Spurgeon published thousands of poems, tracts, sermons and songs.

HIS MESSAGE TO LOST SINNERS WILL LIVE AS LONG AS THE GOSPEL IS PREACHED.

IV.

The Song of the Angels; the Praise of the Shepherds

CHARLES H. SPURGEON

Part I

The Song of the Angels

"And suddenly there was with the angel a multitude of the heavenly host praising God, and saying, Glory to God in the highest, and on earth peace, good will toward men."—Luke 2:13,14.

Angels had been present on many august occasions; they had joined in many a solemn chorus to the praise of their Almighty Creator.

They were present at the creation: "The morning stars sang together, and all the sons of God shouted for joy." They had seen many a planet fashioned between the palms of Jehovah and wheeled by His eternal hands through the infinitude of space. They had sung solemn songs over many a world which the Great One had created. We doubt not they had often chanted, "Blessing and honour, and glory, and majesty, and power, and dominion, and might, be unto him that sitteth on the throne," manifesting Himself in the work of creation. I doubt not, too, that their songs had gathered force through ages. As when first created, their first breath was song, so when they saw God create new worlds, then their song received another note; they rose a little higher in the gamut of adoration.

But this time, when they saw God stoop from His throne and become a Babe, hanging upon a woman's breast, they lifted their notes higher still; and reaching to the uttermost stretch of angelic music, they gained the highest notes of the living scale of praise and sang, "Glory to God in the highest," for higher in goodness they felt God could not go. Thus their highest praise they gave to Him in the highest act of His Godhead.

If it be true that there is a hierarchy of angels, rising tier upon tier in magnificence and dignity—if the apostle teaches us that there be "angels, and principalities, and powers, and thrones, and dominions," amongst these blest inhabitants of the upper world—I can suppose that when the intelligence was first communicated to those angels that are to be found upon the outskirts of the heavenly world, when they looked down from Heaven and saw the newborn Babe, they sent the news backward to the place whence the miracle first proceeded, singing:

> **Angels, from the realms of glory,**
>   **Wing your downward flight to earth:**
> **Ye who sang creation's story,**
>   **Now proclaim Messiah's birth:**
> **Come and worship,**
> **Worship Christ, the newborn King.**

And as the message ran from rank to rank, at last the presence-angels who perpetually watch around the throne of God, took up the strain and, gathering up the song of all the inferior grades of angels, surmounted the divine pinnacle of harmony with their own solemn chant of adoration, upon which the entire host shouted, "The highest angels praise Thee... Glory to God in the highest." Aye, no mortal can ever dream how magnificent was that song!

Then, note: if angels shouted before and when the world was made, their hallelujahs were more full, more strong, more magnificent, if not more hearty, when they saw Jesus Christ born of the Virgin Mary to be man's Redeemer—"Glory to God in the highest."

Salvation Is God's Highest Glory

What is the instructive lesson to be learned from this first syllable of the angel's song? Why this: that salvation is God's highest glory. He is glorified in every dew drop that twinkles to the morning sun. He is magnified in every wood flower that blossoms in the copse, although it live to blush unseen and waste its sweetness on the forest air. God is glorified in every bird that warbles on the spray, in every lamb that skips the mead.

From the tiny minnow to the huge leviathan, do not all creatures that swim the water bless and praise His name? Do not all created things extol Him? Is there aught beneath the sky, *save man*, that doth not glorify God? Do not the stars exalt Him when they write His name upon

THE SONG OF THE ANGELS; THE PRAISE OF THE SHEPHERDS

the azure of Heaven in their golden letters? The psalmist says: "The heavens declare the glory of God; and the firmament sheweth his handiwork. Day unto day uttereth speech, and night unto night sheweth knowledge."

Does not lightning adore Him when it flashes its brightness in arrows of light piercing the midnight darkness? Do not thunders extol Him when they roll like drums in the march of the God of armies? Do not all things exalt Him—from the least even to the greatest?

But sing, sing, oh, universe, till thou hast exhausted thyself; thou canst not afford a song so sweet as the song of Incarnation! Though creation may be a majestic organ of praise, it cannot reach the compass of the golden canticle—Incarnation! There is more in that than in creation, more melody in Jesus in the manger than in worlds on worlds rolling their grandeur round the throne of the Most High.

Pause, Christian, and consider. See how every attribute is here magnified. Lo! what *wisdom* is here. God becomes man that He may be just and the Justifier of the ungodly. Lo! what *power*, for where is power so great as when it concealeth power? What power, that Godhead should unrobe itself and become Man! Behold, what *love* is thus revealed to us when Jesus becomes a Man! Behold, what *faithfulness!* How many promises are this day kept? How many solemn obligations are this hour discharged? What *grace*, and yet what *justice!* For it was in the person of that newborn Child that the law must be fulfilled, and in His precious body must vengeance find recompense for injuries done to divine righteousness.

All the attributes of God were in that little Child most marvelously displayed and veiled. Tell me one attribute of God that is not manifest in Jesus, and your ignorance shall be the reason why you have not seen it so. The whole of God is glorified in Christ; and though some part of the name of God is written in the universe, it is here best read—in Him who was the Son of Man, yet the Son of God.

Conceive the whole sun to be focused to a single point, yet so softly revealed as to be endurable by the tenderest eye. Even thus the glorious God is brought down for man to see Him born of a woman. Think of it. The express image of God in mortal flesh! The Heir of all things cradled in a manger! Marvelous is this! Glory to God in the Highest! He has never revealed Himself before as He now manifests Himself in Jesus.

But let me say one word more. We must learn from this, that if salvation glorifies God, glorifies Him in the highest degree and makes the highest creatures praise Him, this one reflection may be added—then that doctrine which glorifies man in salvation cannot be the Gospel. For salvation glorifies God.

The angels sang, "Glory to *God* in the highest." They believe in no doctrine which uncrowns Christ and puts the crown upon the head of mortals. They believe in no system of faith which makes salvation dependent upon the creature and which really gives the creature the praise.

No, my brethren; there may be some preachers who delight to preach a doctrine that magnifies man; but in their gospel angels have no delight. The only glad tidings that made the angels sing are those that put God first, God last, God midst and God without end, in the salvation of His creatures, and put the crown wholly and alone upon the head of Him who saves without a helper. "Glory to God in the highest" is the angels' song.

Peace on Earth

When they had sung this, they sang what they had never sung before. "Glory to God in the highest" was an old, old song. They had sung that from before the foundations of the world. But, now, they sang as it were a new song before the throne of God: for they added this stanza—*"on earth, peace."*

They did not sing that in the Garden of Eden—there was peace there—but it seemed a thing of course, and scarce worth singing of. There was more than peace there; for there was glory to God there.

But, now, man had fallen, and since the day when cherubim with fiery swords drove out the man, there had been no peace on earth, save in the breasts of some believers who had obtained peace from the living fountain of this incarnation of Christ. Wars had raged from the ends of the world. Men had slaughtered one another, heaps on heaps. There had been wars within as well as wars without. Conscience had fought with man; Satan had tormented man with thoughts of sin. There had been no peace on earth since Adam fell.

But, now, when the newborn King made His appearance, the swaddling band with which He was wrapped up was the white flag of peace. That manger was the place where the treaty was signed, whereby warfare should be stopped between man's conscience and himself, man's conscience and his God. It was then, that day, the trumpet blew—

THE SONG OF THE ANGELS; THE PRAISE OF THE SHEPHERDS   53

"Sheathe the sword, O man, sheathe the sword, O conscience, for God is now at peace with man, and man at peace with God."

Do you not feel, my brethren, that the Gospel of God is peace to man? Where else can peace be found but in the message of Jesus? Go, legalist, work for peace with toil and pain, and thou shalt never find it. Go, thou who trustest in the law: go thou to Sinai; look to the flames that Moses saw, and shrink and tremble and despair; for peace is nowhere to be found but in Him of whom it is said: "This man shall be peace."

And what a peace it is, beloved! It is peace like a river, and righteousness like the waves of the sea. It is the peace of God that passeth all understanding, which keeps our hearts and minds through Jesus Christ our Lord. This sacred peace between the pardoned soul and God the Pardoner; this marvelous at-one-ment between the sinner and his Judge, this was it that the angels sang when they said, "Peace on earth."

It is through our Lord Jesus being born that there is already a measure of peace on earth and boundless peace yet to come. The day cometh when nations shall learn war no more. The Prince of Peace shall snap the spear of war across His knee. He, the Lord of all, shall break the arrows of the bow, the sword and the shield and the battle, and He shall do it in His own dwellingplace, even in Zion, which is more glorious and excellent than all the mountains of prey.

As surely as Christ was born in Bethlehem He will yet establish a universal monarchy of peace, of which there shall be no end. So let us sing if we value the glory of God, for the newborn Child reveals it; let us sing if we value peace on earth, for He is come to bring it.

Let us labor if we can to make peace. Now, old gentleman, you won't take your son in, for he has offended you. Fetch him in. "Peace on earth," you know. Make peace in your family.

Now, brother, you have made a vow that you will never speak to your brother again. Go after him and say, "Oh, my dear fellow, let not this day's sun go down upon our wrath." Fetch him in and give him your hand.

Now, Mr. Tradesman, you have an opponent in the trade about whom you have said some very hard words lately. Make the matter up today or tomorrow or as soon as you can.

Oh, if thou hast anything on thy conscience, anything that prevents thy having peace of mind, pray to God to give thee peace; for it is peace on earth, mind, peace in thyself, peace with thyself, peace with thy fellowmen, peace with thy God. And do not rest till thou canst say,

> **With the world, myself, and Thee**
> **I, ere I sleep, at peace will be.**

Good Will Toward Men

Then, the angels wisely ended their song with a third note: "Good will toward men."

Philosophers have said that God has a good will toward man, but I never knew any man who derived much comfort from their philosophical assertions. Wise men have thought from what we have seen in creation that God had much good will toward man or else His works would never have been so constructed for their comfort. But I never heard of any man who could risk his soul's peace upon such a faint hope as that.

But I have not only heard of thousands, but I know them, who are quite sure that God has a good will toward men; and if you ask their reason, they will give a full and perfect answer. "He has good will toward man, for He gave His Son." No greater proof of kindness between the Creator and His subjects can possibly be afforded than when the Creator gives His only begotten and well-beloved Son to die.

Though the first note is Godlike, though the second note is peaceful, this third note melts my heart the most. Some think of God as if He were a morose being who hated all mankind. Some picture Him as if He were some abstract subsistence taking no interest in our affairs. Hark ye! God has "good will toward men."

Well, all that good will means, and more, God has to you, ye sons and daughters of Adam. Swearer, though you have cursed God, He has not fulfilled His curse on you. He has good will toward you, though you have no good will toward Him. Infidel, though you have sinned high and hard against the Most High, He has said no hard things against you, for He has good will toward men.

Poor sinner, thou hast broken His laws. Thou art half afraid to come to the throne of His mercy lest He should spurn thee. Hear thou this, and be comforted: God has good will toward men, so good a will that He has said, and said it with an oath, too, "As I live, saith the Lord, I have no pleasure in the death of him that dieth, but had rather that he should turn unto me and live"; so good a will moreover that He has even condescended to say, "Come now, and let us reason together . . . : though your sins be as scarlet, they shall be as white as snow; though they be red like crimson, they shall be as wool."

And if you ask, "Lord, how shall I know that Thou hast this good will toward me?" He points to yonder manger and says, "Sinner, if I had not a good will toward thee, would I have parted with My Son? If I had not good will toward the human race, would I have given up My Son to become one of that race that He might by so doing redeem them from death?"

Ye who doubt the Master's love, look ye to that circle of angels; see their blaze of glory; hear their song; then let your doubts die away in that sweet music and be buried in a shroud of harmony. He has good will to men. He is willing to pardon. He passes by iniquity, transgression and sin. And, mark thee: if Satan shall then add, "But though God hath good will, yet He cannot violate His justice. Therefore His mercy may be ineffective, and you may die," then listen to that first note of the song, "Glory to God in the highest," and reply to Satan and all his temptations that when God shows good will to a penitent sinner, there is not only peace in the sinner's heart, but it brings glory to every attribute of God; and so He can be just and yet justify the sinner and glorify Himself.

Prophetic

There are some prophetic utterances contained in these words.

The angels sang, "Glory to God in the highest, and on earth peace, good will toward men." But when I look around, what see I in the wide, wide world? Not God honored but the heathen bowing down before their idols. When I look about me, I see tyranny lording it over the bodies and souls of men. I see God forgotten; I see a worldly race pursuing mammon; I see a bloody race pursuing Moloch; I see ambition riding like Nimrod over the land, God forgotten, His name dishonored.

And was this all the angels sang about? Is this all that made them sing, "Glory to God in the highest"? Ah! no. There are brighter days approaching.

They sang, "Peace on earth." But I hear still the clarion of war and the cannon's horrid roar. Not yet have they turned the sword into plowshare and the spear into pruning-hook! War still reigns.

Is this all that the angels sang about? And whilst I see wars to the ends of the earth, am I to believe that this was all the angels expected? No, brethren. The angels' song is big with prophecy; it travaileth in birth with glories.

A few more years and he who lives them out shall see why angels sang. A few more years and He who will come shall come and will not tarry. Christ the Lord will come again, and when He cometh He shall cast the idols from their thrones. He shall dash down every fashion of heresy and every shape of idolatry. He shall reign from pole to pole with illimitable sway, reign, when, like a scroll, yon blue heavens have passed away.

No strife shall vex Messiah's reign, no blood shall then be shed. They'll hang the useless helmet high, and study war no more. The hour is approaching when the temple of Janus shall be shut forever, and when cruel Mars shall be hooted from the earth. The day is coming when the lion shall eat straw like the ox, when the leopard shall lie down with the kid, when the weaned child shall put his hand upon the cockatrice' den and play with the asp.

The hour approacheth. The first streaks of the sunlight have made glad the age in which we live. Lo, He comes with trumpets and with clouds of glory! He shall come for whom we look with joyous expectation, whose coming shall be glory to His redeemed and confusion to His enemies.

Brethren, when the angels sang this, there was an echo through the long aisles of a glorious future. The echo was—

**Hallelujah! Christ the Lord
God Omnipotent shall reign.**

PART II

The Praise of the Shepherds

"And when they had seen it, they made known abroad the saying which was told them concerning this child. And all they that heard it wondered at those things which were told them by the shepherds. But Mary kept all these things, and pondered them in her heart. And the shepherds returned, glorifying and praising God for all the things that they had heard and seen, as it was told unto them."—Luke 2:17-20.

I. THE SHEPHERDS HONORED JESUS BY PUBLISHING ABROAD HIS BIRTH

In the first place, we find that some celebrated the Saviour's birth by

THE SONG OF THE ANGELS; THE PRAISE OF THE SHEPHERDS

PUBLISHING ABROAD what they had heard and seen. Truly we may say of them that *they had something* to rehearse in men's ears well worth the telling.

1. What a Message They Had!

That for which prophets and kings had waited long, had at last arrived—and arrived to them. They had found out the answer to the perpetual riddle. They might have run through the streets with the ancient philosopher, crying, "Eureka! Eureka!" for their discovery was far superior to his. They had found out no solution to a mechanical problem or metaphysical dilemma, but their discovery was second to none ever made by men in real value, since it has been like the leaves of the tree of life to heal the nations and a river of water of life to make glad the city of God.

They had seen angels; they had heard them sing a song all strange and new. They had seen more than angels—they had beheld the angel's King, the Angel of the Covenant whom we delight in. They had heard the music of Heaven, and when near that manger the ear of their faith had heard the music of earth's hope, a mystic harmony which should ring all down the ages—the grave, sweet melody of hearts attuned to praise the Lord and the glorious swell of the holy joy of God and man rejoicing in glad accord.

They had seen God incarnate—such a sight that he who gazeth on it must feel his tongue unloosed, unless indeed an unspeakable astonishment should make him dumb. Be silent when their eyes had seen such a vision? Impossible! To the first person they met outside that lowly stable door they began to tell their matchless tale, and they wearied not till nightfall, crying, "Come and worship! Come and worship Christ, the newborn King!"

As for us, beloved, have we also not something to relate which demands utterance? If we talk of Jesus, who can blame us? This, indeed, might make the tongue of him who sleeps to move—the mystery of God incarnate for our sake, bleeding and dying that we might neither bleed nor die, descending that we might ascend and wrapped in swaddling bands that we might be unwrapped of the graveclothes of corruption.

Here is such a story, so profitable to all hearers that he who repeats it the most often does best, and he who speaks the least hath most reason to accuse himself for sinful silence.

2. Angels Singing to Shepherds: Simple, Sublime

They had something to tell, and *that something had in it the inimitable blending which is the secret sign and royal mark of Divine authorship; a peerless marrying of sublimity and simplicity;* angels singing! to shepherds! Heaven bright with glory—bright at midnight! God! A Babe! The Infinite! An Infant of a span long! The Ancient of Days! Born of a woman!

What more simple than the inn, the manger, a carpenter, his wife, a child? What more sublime than a "multitude of the heavenly host" waking the midnight with their joyous chorales and God Himself in human flesh made manifest?

A child is but an ordinary sight; but what a marvel to see that Word which was "in the beginning with God, tabernacling among us that we might behold his glory—the glory as of the only begotten of the Father, full of grace and truth."

Brethren, we have a tale to tell as simple, as sublime. What simpler?— "Believe and live." What more sublime?—"God was in Christ reconciling the world unto himself!" A system of salvation so wonderful that angelic minds cannot but adore as they meditate upon it, yet so simple that the children in the Temple may fitly hymn its virtues as they sing, "Hosanna! Blessed is he that cometh in the name of the Lord."

What a splendid combining of the sublime and the simple have we in the great atonement offered by the incarnate Saviour! Oh, make known to all men this saving truth!

3. They Receive the Message From Heaven

The shepherds need no excuse for making everywhere the announcement of the Saviour's birth, *for what they told they first received from Heaven.* Their news was not muttered in their ears by Sybilline oracles, not brought to light by philosophic search, not conceived in poetry nor found as treasure trove among the volumes of the ancient, but revealed to them by that notable gospel preacher who led the angelic host and testified, "Unto you is born this day, in the city of David, a Saviour, which is Christ the Lord."

When Heaven entrusts a man with a merciful revelation, he is bound to deliver the good tidings to others.

What, keep that a secret whose utterance eternal mercy makes to charm the midnight air? To what purpose were angels sent, if the message were not to be spread abroad? According to the teaching of our own beloved Lord, we must not be silent, for He bids us, "What ye hear in secret that reveal ye in public; and what I tell you in the ear in closets, that proclaim ye upon the housetops."

Beloved, you have heard a voice from Heaven. You twice-born men, begotten again unto a lively hope, have heard the Spirit of God bearing witness of God's truth with you and teaching you of heavenly things. You then must keep this Christmas by telling to your fellowmen what God's own Holy Spirit has seen fit to reveal to you.

4. They Had Seen Jesus for Themselves

But though the shepherds told what they heard from Heaven, remember that *they spoke of what they had seen below.* They had, by observation, made those truths most surely their own which had first been spoken to them by revelation.

No man can speak of the things of God with any success until the doctrine which he finds in the book, he finds also in his heart. We must bring down the mystery and make plain by knowing, by the teaching of the Holy Ghost, its practical power on the heart and conscience.

My brethren, the Gospel which we preach is most surely revealed to us by the Lord; but, moreover, our hearts have tried and proved, have grasped, have felt, have realized its truth and power. If we have not been able to understand its heights and depths, yet we have felt its mystic power upon our heart and spirit. It has revealed sin to us better; it has revealed to us our pardon. It has killed the reigning power of sin; it has given us Christ to reign over us, the Holy Spirit to dwell within our bodies as in a temple. Now *we must* speak.

I do not urge any of you to speak of Jesus who merely know the Word as you find it in the Bible—your teaching can have but little power—but I do speak earnestly to you who know its mighty influence upon the heart, who have not only heard of the Babe but have seen Him in the manger, taken Him up in your own arms and received Him as being born to you, a Saviour to you, *Christos,* the anointed for you, Jesus, the Saviour from sin for you.

Beloved, can you do otherwise than speak of the things which you have seen and heard? God has made you to taste and to handle of this good Word of life, and you must not, you dare not hold your peace; but you *must* tell to friends and neighbors what you have felt within.

5. The Shepherds Were Poor, Ignorant Men, but They Published It

These were shepherds, *unlettered men.* I will warrant you they could not read in a book. There is no probability that they even knew a single letter. They were shepherds, but they preached right well. And whatever some may think, preaching is not to be confined to those learned gentlemen who have taken their degrees at Oxford or at Cambridge or at any college or university.

It is true that learning need not be an impediment to grace and may be a fitting weapon in a gracious hand, but often the grace of God has glorified itself by the plain, clear way in which unlettered men have understood the Gospel and proclaimed it.

I would not mind asking the whole world to find a Master of Arts now living who has brought more souls to Christ Jesus than Richard Weaver. If the whole bench of bishops have done a tenth as much in the way of soul winning as that one man, it is more than most of us give them credit for. Let us give to our God all the glory, but still let us not deny the fact that this sinner saved, with the brogue of the collier still about him, fresh from the coal pit, tells the story of the cross by God's grace in such a way that Right Reverend Fathers in God might humbly sit at his feet to learn the way to reach the heart and melt the stubborn soul.

It is true that an uneducated brother is not fitted for all work—he has his own sphere—but he is quite able to tell of what he has seen and heard; and so it strikes me is every man in a measure. If you have seen Jesus and heard His saving voice; if you have received truth as from the Lord, felt its tremendous power as coming from God to you; if you have experienced its might upon your own spirit, you can surely tell out what God has written within.

If you cannot get beyond that into the deeper mysteries, into the more knotty points, well, there are some who can, and so you need not be uneasy; but you can at least reveal the first and foundation truths, and they are by far the most important.

If you cannot speak in the pulpit, if as yet your cheek would mantle with a blush and your tongue would refuse to do her office in the presence of many, there are your children—you are not ashamed to speak before them. There is the little cluster round the hearth on Christmas night; there is the little congregation in the workshop; there is a little audience somewhere to whom you might tell out of Jesus' love.

Do not get beyond what you know; do not plunge into what you have not experienced, for if you do, you will be out of your depth, and then very soon you will be floundering and making confusion worse confounded. Go as far as you know. Since you do know yourself a sinner and Jesus a great Saviour, talk about those two matters, and good will come of it. Beloved, each one in his own position, telling what he has heard and seen—publish that abroad among the sons of men.

6. They Had Authority From God: So Do You

But *were they authorized?* It is a great thing to be authorized! Unauthorized ministers are most shameful intruders! Unordained men entering the pulpit who are not in the apostolical succession—very horrible indeed! The Puseyite mind utterly fails to fathom the depth of horror which is contained in the idea of an unauthorized man preaching and a man out of the apostolical succession daring to teach the way of salvation.

To me this horror seems very like a schoolboy's fright at a hobgoblin which his fears had conjured up. I think if I saw a man slip through the ice into a cold grave and I could rescue him from drowning, it would not be so very horrible to be the means of saving him, though I may not be employed by the Royal Humane Society.

I imagine if I saw a fire and heard a poor woman screaming at an upper window, who was likely to be burned alive, it would not be so very dreadful a matter, if I should wheel the fire escape up to the window and preserve her life, though I might not belong to the regular Fire Brigade.

If a company of brave volunteers should chase an enemy out of their own county, I do not know that it would be anything so shocking, although a whole army of mercenaries might be neglecting their work in obedience to some venerable military rubric which rendered them incapable of effective service.

But mark you! The shepherds and others like them are in the apostolic succession, and they are authorized by divine ordinance, for every man who hears the Gospel is authorized to tell it to others.

Do you want authority? Here it is in confirmation strong from Holy Writ: "Let him that heareth say, Come"—that is, let every man who truly hears the Gospel bid others come to drink of the water of life. This is all the warrant you require for preaching the Gospel according to your ability.

It is not every man who has ability to preach the Word. It is not every man that we should like to hear preach it in the great congregation. For if all were mouth, what a great vacuum the church would be. Yet every Christian in some method should deliver the glad tidings. Our wise God takes care that liberty of prophesying shall not run to riot, for He does not give efficient pastoral and ministerial gifts to very many; yet every man according to his gifts, let him minister. Every one of you, though not in the pulpit, yet in the pew, in the workshop, somewhere, anywhere, everywhere, do make known the savour of the Lord Jesus. Be this your authority: "Let him that heareth say, Come."

I never thought of asking any authority for crying "Fire" when I saw a house burning; I never dreamed of seeking any authority for doing my best to rescue a poor perishing fellowman, nor do I mean to seek it now! All the authority we want is not the authority which can stream from prelates decorated with lawn sleeves, but that which comes direct from the great Head of the church. He gives it to everyone who hears the Gospel and teaches his fellowman to "know the Lord."

Here is one way for you to keep a right holy and, in some sense, a right merry Christmas. Imitate these humble men, of whom it is said, "When they had seen it, they made known abroad the saying which was told them concerning this child."

II. THEY HAD HOLY WONDER, ADMIRATION AND ADORATION!

We set before you now another mode of keeping Christmas—that is, by HOLY WONDER, ADMIRATION AND ADORATION. "And all they that heard it wondered at those things which were told them by the shepherds." We shall have little to say of those persons who merely wondered and did nothing more.

1. A Temporary Admiration Without Holy Commitment?

Many are set a-wondering by the Gospel. They are content, pleased to hear it; if not in itself something new, yet there are new ways of putting it, and they are glad to be refreshed with the variety. The preacher's voice is unto them as the sound of one who giveth a goodly tune upon an instrument. They are glad to listen. They are not sceptics, they do not cavil, they raise no difficulties; they just say to themselves, *It is an excellent Gospel, it is a wonderful plan of salvation. Here is most astonishing love, most extraordinary condescension.*

Sometimes they marvel that these things should be told them by shepherds. They can hardly understand how unlearned and ignorant men should speak of these things or how such things should ever get into these shepherds' heads, where they can have learned them. How is it that they seem so earnest about them? What kind of operation must they have passed through to be able to speak as they do? But after holding up their hands and opening their mouths for about nine days, the wonder subsides, and they go their way and think no more about it.

There are many of you who are set a-wondering whenever you see a work of God in your district. You hear of somebody converted who was a very extraordinary sinner, and you say, *It is very wonderful!* There is a revival. You happen to be present at one of the meetings when the Spirit of God is working gloriously. You say, *Well, this is a singular thing! very astonishing!* Even the newspapers can afford a corner at times for very great and extraordinary works of God the Holy Spirit. But there all emotion ends; it is all wondering and nothing more.

I trust it will not be so with any of us that we shall not think of the Saviour and of the doctrines of the Gospel which He came to preach simply with amazement and astonishment, for this will work us but little good.

On the other hand, there is another mode of wondering which is akin to adoration, if it be not adoration. I think it would be very difficult to draw a line between holy wonder and real worship, for when the soul is overwhelmed with the majesty of God's glory, though it may not express itself in song or even utter its voice with bowed head in humble prayer, yet it silently adores.

I am inclined to think that the astonishment which sometimes seizes upon the human intellect at the remembrance of God's greatness and goodness is, perhaps, the purest form of adoration which ever rises from mortal men to the throne of the Most High. I recommend this kind of wonder to those of you who from the quietness and solitariness of your lives are scarcely able to imitate the shepherds in telling out the tale to others: you can at least fill up the circle of the worshipers before the throne by wondering at what God has done.

2. We Should Marvel and Praise Such Amazing Grace

Let me suggest to you that holy wonder at what God has done should be very natural to you. That God should consider His fallen creature, man, and instead of sweeping him away with the besom of destruction should devise a wonderful scheme for his redemption, and that He should Himself undertake to be man's Redeemer and to pay his ransom price, is, indeed, marvelous!

Probably it is most marvelous to you in its relation to yourself, that *you* should be redeemed by blood; that God should forsake the thrones and royalties above to suffer ignominiously below for you. If you know yourself, you can never see any adequate motive or reason in your own flesh for such a deed as this. "Why such love to me?" you will say.

If David sitting in his house could only say, "Who am I, O Lord God, and what is mine house, that thou hast brought me hitherto?" what should you and I say? Had we been the most meritorious of individuals and had unceasingly kept the Lord's commands, we could not have deserved such a priceless boon as incarnation: but sinners, offenders who revolted and went from God further and further, what shall we say of this incarnate God dying for us but, "Herein is love, not that we loved God but that he loved us."

Let your soul lose itself in wonder, for wonder is in this way a very practical emotion. Holy wonder will lead you to grateful worship. Being astonished at what God has done, you will pour out your soul with astonishment at the foot of the golden throne with the song, "Blessing, and honour, and glory, and majesty, and power, and dominion, and might be unto Him who sitteth on the throne and doeth these great things to me."

Being filled with this wonder will cause you a godly watchfulness. You will be afraid to sin against such love as this. Feeling the presence of the mighty God in the gift of His dear Son, you will put off your shoes from off your feet, because the place whereon you stand is holy ground. You will be moved at the same time to a glorious hope. If Jesus has given Himself to you, if He has done this marvelous thing on your behalf, you will feel that Heaven itself is not too great for your expectation and that the rivers of pleasure at God's right hand are not too sweet or too deep for you to drink thereof.

Who can be astonished at anything when he has once been astonished at the manger and the cross? What is there left after one has seen the wonderful Saviour?

The nine wonders of the world! Why, you may put them all into a nutshell—machinery and modern art can excel them all; but this one wonder is not the wonder of earth only but of Heaven and earth, and even Hell itself. It is not the wonder of the olden time but the wonder of all time and eternity. They who see human wonders a few times, at last cease to be astonished. The noblest pile that architect ever raised, at last fails to impress the onlooker.

But not so this marvelous temple of incarnate Deity. The more we look, the more we are astonished. The more we become accustomed to it, the more have we a sense of its surpassing splendor of love and grace.

There is more of God, let us say, to be seen in the manger and the cross than in the sparkling stars above, the rolling deep below, the towering mountain, the teeming valleys, the abodes of life or the abyss of death. Let us then spend some choice hours of this festive season in holy wonder such as will produce gratitude, worship, love and confidence.

III. THE SHEPHERDS RETURNED TO BUSINESS

The last piece of holy Christmas work is to come. "The shepherds returned," we read in verse 20, "GLORIFYING AND PRAISING GOD for all the things that they had heard and seen, as it was told unto them." Returned to what? *Returned to business* to look after the lambs and sheep again. Then if we desire to glorify God, we need not give up our business.

1. You Can Glorify God in the Shepherds' Field or Your Store or Job

Some people get the notion that the only way in which they can live for God is by becoming ministers, missionaries or Bible women. Alas! how many of us would be shut out from any opportunity of magnifying the Most High if this were the case! The shepherds went back to the sheep pens glorifying and praising God.

Beloved, it is not office, it is earnestness; it is not position, it is grace which will enable us to glorify God.

God is most surely glorified in that cobbler's stall where the godly worker as he plies the awl sings of the Saviour's love, ay, glorified far more than in many a prebendal stall where official *religiousness* performs its scanty duties. The name of Jesus is glorified by yonder carter as he drives his horse and blesses his God or speaks to his fellow laborer by the roadside as much as by yonder divine who, throughout the country like Boanerges, is thundering out the Gospel. God is glorified by our abiding in our vocation.

Take care you do not fall out of the path of duty by leaving your calling. Take care you do not dishonor your profession while in it. Think not much of yourselves, but do not think too little of your callings.

There is no trade which is not sanctified by the Gospel. If you turn to the Bible, you will find the most menial forms of labor have been in some way or other connected either with the most daring deeds of faith or else with persons whose lives have been otherwise illustrious.

Keep to your calling, brother! Keep to your calling! Whatever God has made thee, when He calls thee, abide in that, unless thou art quite sure that He calls thee to something else. The shepherds glorified God though they went back to their trade.

They glorified God *though they were shepherds*. As we remarked, they were not men of learning. So far from having an extensive library full of books, it is probable they could not read a word; yet they glorified God.

This takes away all excuse for you good people who say, "I am no scholar. I never had any education. I never went even to a Sunday school." Ah, but if your heart is right, you can glorify God.

Never mind, Sarah; do not be cast down because you know so little. Learn more if you can, but make good use of what you do know.

Never mind, John; it is indeed a pity that you should have had to toil so early as not to have acquired even the rudiments of knowledge; but do not think that you cannot glorify God. If you would praise God, live a holy life; you can do that by His grace, at any rate, without scholarship.

If thou wouldst do good to others, be good thyself; and that is a way which is as open to the most illiterate as it is to the best taught. Be of good courage! Shepherds glorified God, and so may you.

Remember—there is one thing in which they had a preference over the Wise Men. They wanted a star to lead them; the shepherds did not. They went wrong even with a star, stumbled into Jerusalem; the shepherds went straight away to Bethlehem.

Simple minds sometimes find a glorified Christ where learned heads, much puzzled with their lore, miss Him. A good doctor used to say,

"Lo, these simpletons have entered into the kingdom, while we learned men have been fumbling for the latch." It is often so. So, ye simple minds, be ye comforted and glad.

2. It Glorifies God to Praise Him as They Did

The way in which these shepherds honored God is worth noticing. They did it by praising Him. Let us think more of sacred song than we sometimes do. When the song is bursting in full chorus from the thousands in this house, it is but a noise in the ear of some men. But inasmuch as many true hearts, touched with the love of Jesus, are keeping pace with their tongues, it is not a mere noise in God's esteem; there is a sweet music in it that makes glad His ear. What is the great ultimatum of all Christian effort?

When I stood here the other morning preaching the Gospel, my mind was fully exercised with the winning of souls, but I seemed while preaching to get beyond that. I thought, *Well, that is not the chief end after all — the chief end is to glorify God; and even the saving of sinners is sought by the right-minded as the means to that end.* Then it struck me all of a sudden — *If in Psalm-singing and hymn-singing we do really glorify God, we are doing more than in the preaching; because we are not then in the means — we are close upon the great end itself.*

If we praise God with heart and tongue, we glorify Him in the surest possible manner. We are really glorifying Him then. "Whoso offereth praise glorifieth me," saith the Lord.

Sing then, my brethren! Sing not only when you are together, but sing alone. Cheer your labor with Psalms and hymns and spiritual songs. Make glad the family with sacred music.

We sing too little, I am sure, yet the revival of religion has always been attended with the revival of Christian psalmody. Luther's translations of the Psalms were of as much service as Luther's discussions and controversies. And the hymns of Charles Wesley and Cennick and Toplady and Newton and Cowper aided as much in the quickening of spiritual life in England as the preaching of John Wesley and George Whitefield.

We want more singing. Sing more and murmur less. Sing more and slander less. Sing more and cavil less. Sing more and mourn less.

God grant us to glorify God by praising Him, as these shepherds did.

3. They Praised God for the Good News of the Gospel

I have not quite done with them. What was the subject of their praise? It appears that they *praised God for what they had heard.* If we think of it—there is good reason for blessing God every time we hear a gospel sermon. What would souls in Hell give if they could hear the Gospel once more and be on terms in which salvation grace might come to them! What would dying men give whose time is all but over, if they could once more come to the house of God and have another warning, another invitation!

My brethren, what would you give sometimes when you are shut up by sickness and cannot meet with the great congregation, when your heart and your flesh cry out for the living God! Well, praise God for what you have heard.

You have heard the faults of the preacher; let him mourn them. You have heard his Master's message; do you bless God for that? Scarcely will you ever hear a sermon which may not make you sing if you are in a right mind.

George Herbert says, "Praying is the end of preaching." So it is. But praising is its end, too.

Praise God that you hear there is a Saviour! Praise God that you hear that the plan of salvation is very simple! Praise God that you have a Saviour for your own soul! Praise God that you are pardoned, that you are saved!

4. They Praised for What They Had Personally Seen

Praise Him for what you have heard, but observe, *they also praised God for what they had seen.* Look at verse 20—"heard and seen." There is the sweetest music—what we have experienced, what we have felt within, what we have made our own—the things that we have made touching the King. Mere hearing may make some music, but the soul of song must come from seeing with the eye of faith.

And, dear friends, you who have seen with that God-given eyesight, I pray you, let not your tongues be steeped in sinful silence but loud to the praise of sovereign grace. Wake up your glory and awake psaltery and harp.

THE SONG OF THE ANGELS; THE PRAISE OF THE SHEPHERDS   69

One point for which they praised God was *the agreement between what they had heard and what they had seen.* Observe the last sentence—"As it was told them."

Have you not found the Gospel to be in yourselves just what the Bible said it would be? Jesus said He would give you grace—have you not had it? He promised you rest—have you not received it? He said that you should have joy and comfort and life through believing in Him—have you not had all these? Are not His ways ways of pleasantness and His paths paths of peace?

Surely you can say with the queen of Sheba, "The half has not been told me." I have found Christ more sweet than His servants could set Him forth as being. I looked upon the likeness as they painted it, but it was a mere daub as compared with Himself—the King in His beauty.

I have heard of the goodly land, but it floweth with milk and honey more richly and sweetly than men were ever able to tell me when in their best trim for speech! Surely, what we have seen keeps pace with what we have heard. Let us then glorify and praise God for what He has done.

This word to those who are not yet converted, and I have done. I do not think you can begin at verse 17, but I wish you would begin at verse 18. You cannot begin at the 17th—you cannot tell to others what you have not felt; so do not try it. Neither teach in the Sunday school, nor attempt to preach if you are not converted.

Unto the wicked God saith, "What hast thou to do to declare my statutes?" But I would to God you would begin with the 18th verse—wondering! Wondering that you are spared—wondering that you are out of Hell—wondering that still doth His good Spirit strive with the chief of sinners. Wonder that this morning the Gospel should have a word for you after all your rejections of it and sins against God.

I should like you to begin there, because then I should have good hope that you would go on to the next verse and change the first letter, and so go from wondering to pondering.

O sinner, I wish you would ponder the doctrines of the cross. Think of thy sin, God's wrath, judgment, Hell, thy Saviour's blood, God's love, forgiveness, acceptance, Heaven—think on these things. Go from wondering to pondering.

And then I would to God thou couldst go on to the next verse—from pondering to glorifying. Take Christ, look to Him, trust Him. Then sing, "I am forgiven," and go thy way a believing sinner, and therefore a sinner saved, washed in the blood, and clean. Then go back after that to verse 17 and begin to tell to others.

But as for you Christians who are saved, I want you to begin this very afternoon at the 17th.

> **Then will I tell to sinners round**
> **What a dear Saviour I have found:**
> **I'll point to Thy redeeming blood,**
> **And say—"Behold the way to God!"**

Then when the day is over, get up to your chambers and wonder, admire and adore; spend half an hour in pondering and treasuring up the day's work and the day's hearing in your hearts, and then close all with that which never must close—go on tonight, tomorrow and all the days of your life, glorifying and praising God for all the things that you have seen and heard.

May the Master bless you for Jesus Christ's sake. Amen.

V.

The Star and the Wise Men

CHARLES H. SPURGEON

"Now when Jesus was born in Bethlehem of Judaea in the days of Herod the king, behold, there came wise men from the east to Jerusalem, Saying, Where is he that is born King of the Jews? for we have seen his star in the east, and are come to worship him. When they had heard the king, they departed; and, lo, the star, which they saw in the east, went before them, till it came and stood over where the young child was. When they saw the star, they rejoiced with exceeding great joy."—Matt. 2:1,2,9,10.

See the glory of our Lord Jesus Christ, even in His state of humiliation! He is born of lowly parents, laid in a manger and wrapped in swaddling bands, but oh, the principalities and powers in the heavenly places are in commotion!

First, one angel descends to proclaim the advent of the newborn King, and suddenly there is with him a multitude of the heavenly host singing glory unto God. Nor was the commotion confined to the spirits above; for in the heavens which overhang this earth there is a stir. A star is deputed on behalf of all the stars, as if he were the envoy and plenipotentiary of all worlds to represent them before their King. This star is put in commission to wait upon the Lord, to be His herald to men afar off, His usher to conduct them to His Presence, and His bodyguard to sentinel His cradle.

Earth, too, is stirred. Shepherds have come to pay the homage of simple-minded ones; with all love and joy they bow before the mysterious Child. And after them from afar come the choice and flower of their generation, the most studious minds of the age. Making a long and difficult journey, they too at last arrive, the representatives of the Gentiles.

Lo! the kings of Seba and Sheba offer gifts—gold, frankincense and myrrh. Wise Men, the leaders of their peoples, bow down before Him and pay homage to the Son of God. Wherever Christ is, He is honorable. 'Unto you that believe He is honorable.' In the day of small things, when the cause of God is denied entertainment and is hidden away with things which are despised, it is still most glorious. Christ, though a Child, is still King of kings; though among the oxen, He is still distinguished by His star.

If Wise Men of old came to Jesus and worshiped, should not we come also? My intense desire is that we all may pay homage to Him of whom we sing, "Unto us a child is born; unto us a son is given." Let those of us who have long worshiped worship anew with yet lowlier reverence and intenser love.

And God grant—oh, that He would grant it!—that some who are far off from Him spiritually, as the Magi were far off locally, may come today and ask, "Where is He that is born King of the Jews? for we have come to worship Him." May feet that have been accustomed to broad roads, but unaccustomed to the narrow path, this day pursue that way till they see Jesus and bow before Him with all their hearts, finding salvation in Him.

These Wise Men came naturally, traversing the desert; let us come spiritually, leaving our sins. These were guided by the sight of a star; let us be guided by faith in the divine Spirit, by the teaching of His Word and all those blessed lights which the Lord uses to conduct men to Himself. Only let us come to Jesus.

It was well to come unto the Babe Jesus, led by the feeble beams of a star; you shall find it still more blessed to come to Him now that He is exalted in the highest heavens, and by His own light reveals His own perfect glory. Delay not, for this day He cries, "Come unto me, all ye that labour and are heavy laden, and I will give you rest" (Matt. 11:28).

Let us try to do three things. First, let us *gather light from this star;* second, let us *gather wisdom from these Wise Men;* and third, let us *act as wise men helped by our own particular star.*

I. LET US GATHER FROM THIS STAR

May the Spirit of the Lord enable us so to do.

I suppose you have each one his own imagination as to what this star was. It would seem to have been altogether supernatural and not a star or a comet of the ordinary kind. It was not a constellation nor a singular conjunction of planets; there is nothing in the Scriptures to support such a conjecture. In all probability it was not a star in the sense in which we now speak of stars; for we find that it moved before the Wise Men, then suddenly disappeared, and again shone forth to move before them. It could not have been a star in the upper spheres like others, for such movements would not have been possible.

Some have supposed that the Wise Men went in the direction in which the star shone forth in the heavens and followed the changes of its position, but it could not in that case have been said that it stood over the place where the young Child was. If the star was at its zenith over Bethlehem, it would have been in its zenith over Jerusalem too; for the distance is so small that it would not have been possible to observe any difference in the position of the star in the two places.

It must have been a star occupying quite another sphere from that in which the planets revolve. We believe it to have been a luminous appearance in midair probably akin to that which led the children of Israel through the wilderness, which was a cloud by day and a pillar of fire by night. Whether it was seen in the daylight or not we cannot tell.

Chrysostom and the early fathers are wonderfully positive about many things which Scripture leaves in doubt, but as these eminent divines drew upon their imagination for their facts, we are not under bonds to follow them. They aver that this star was so bright as to be visible all day long.

If so, we can imagine the Wise Men traveling day and night; but if it could be seen only by night, the picture before us grows far more singular and weird-like as we see these Easterners quietly pursuing their starlit way, resting *perforce* when the sun was up, but noiselessly hurrying at night through slumbering lands. These questions are not of much importance to us; therefore, we will not dwell long upon them.

Only here is a first lesson:

1. If It Should Ever Be That Men Should Fail to Preach the Gospel, God Can Conduct Souls to His Son by a Star

Ah! say not only by a star, but by a stone, a bird, a blade of grass, a drop of dew.

**Remember that Omnipotence
Has servants everywhere.**

Therefore, despond not when you hear that one minister has ceased to preach the Gospel or that another is fighting against the vital truth of God. Their apostasy shall be to their own loss rather than to the hurt of Jesus and His church. And sad though it be to see the lamps of the sanctuary put out, yet God is not dependent upon human lights. He is the Shekinah light of His own holy place. Mortal tongues, if they refuse to preach His Word, shall have their places supplied by books in the running brooks and sermons in stones. "The stone shall cry out of the wall, and the beam out of the timber shall answer it."

When chief priests and scribes have all gone out of the way, the Lord puts stars into commission. And once more in very deed the heavens are telling the glory of God and the firmament is showing His handiwork. Sooner than lack speakers for the incarnate God, mountains and hills shall learn eloquence and break forth into testimony. Jehovah's message shall be made known to the utmost ends of the earth. Hallelujah!

Now, when the Lord does use a star to be His minister, what is the order of His ministry? We may learn by this enquiry what kind of ministry God would have ours to be if we are stars in His right hand. We also shine as lights in the world; let us see how to do it.

We notice that:

2. Star-Preaching Is All About Christ

We do not know what the color of the star was nor its shape nor to what magnitude it had attained. These items are not recorded. But what is recorded is of much more importance. The Wise Men said, "We have seen *his* star."

Then the star which the Lord will use to lead men to Jesus must be Christ's own star. The faithful minister, like this star, belongs to Christ; he is Christ's own man in the most emphatic sense.

Before we can expect to be made a blessing, we must ourselves be blessed of the Lord. If we would cause others to belong to Jesus, we must belong wholly to Jesus ourselves. Every beam in that star shone forth for Jesus.

It was *His* star, always, and only, and altogether. It shone not for itself, but only as *His* star: as such it was known and spoken of—"we have seen his star."

As I have already said, there is no note taken of any peculiarity that it had except this one—that it was the star of the King.

I wish that you and I, whatever our eccentricities or personalities may be, may never make so much of them as to attract men's attention to them. May we never dwell upon our attainments or our deficiencies, but may we always observe this: we are men of God, we are ambassadors of Christ, we are Christ's servants and do not attempt to shine for ourselves or to make ourselves conspicuous. We labor to shine for Him, that His way may be known upon earth, His saving health among all people.

It is well for us to forget ourselves in our message, to sink ourselves in our Master. We know the names of several of the stars, yet they may each one envy that star which remains anonymous but can never be forgotten because men who sought the King of Israel knew it as *"his star."*

Though you be but a very little star, twinkling for Jesus; however feeble your light may be, be it plain that you are *His* star, so that if men wonder *what* you are, they may never wonder *whose* you are, for on your very forefront it may be written, "Whose I am and whom I serve." God will not lead men to Christ by us unless we are Christ's heartily, wholly, unreservedly.

In His temple our Lord uses no borrowed vessels; every bowl before the altar must be His own. It is not consistent with the glory of God for Him to use borrowed vessels. He is not so poor as to come to that. This lesson is worthy of all acceptation.

Are you in a hurry to preach, young man? Are you sure you are Christ's? Do you think it must be a fine thing to hold a company of people listening to your words? Have you looked at it in another light? Have you weighed the responsibility of having to speak as Christ would have you speak and of yielding yourself in your entire personality to the utterance of the mind of God? You must be consecrated and concentrated if you hope to be used of the Lord. If you have one ray or ten thousand rays, all must shine with the one design of guiding men to Jesus. You have nothing now to do with any object, subject, design or endeavor, but Jesus only. In Him and for Him and to Him must you live henceforth, or you will never be used of the Lord to conduct either wise men or babes to Jesus. See ye well to it that perfect consecration be yours.

Note, next, that:

3. True Star-Preaching Leads to Christ

The star was Christ's star itself, but it also led others to Christ. It did this very much because it moved in that direction. It is a sad thing when a preacher is like a signpost pointing the way but never following it on his own account. Such were those chief priests at Jerusalem. They could tell where Christ was born, but they never went to worship Him; they were indifferent altogether to Him and to His birth. The star that leads to Christ must always be going to Christ.

Men are far better drawn by example than driven by exhortation. Personal piety alone can be owned of God to the production of piety in others. "Go," say you, but they will not go. Say, "Come," and lead the way, then they will come. Do not the sheep follow the shepherd? He who would lead others to Christ should go before them himself, having his face towards his Master, his eyes towards his Master, his steps towards his Master, his heart towards his Master. We are so to live that we may be an example.

Oh, that all who think themselves to be stars would themselves diligently move towards the Lord Jesus. The star in the East led Wise Men to Christ because it went that way itself. There is a wisdom in example which truly Wise Men are quick to perceive. This star had such an influence upon those men that they could not but follow it; it charmed them across the desert. Such a charm may reside in you and in me, and we may exercise a powerful ministry over many hearts, being to them as loadstones, drawing them to the Lord Jesus.

Happy privilege! We would not merely show the road, but induce our neighbors to enter upon it. We read of one of old, not that they told him of Jesus but that "they brought him to Jesus." We are not only to tell the story of the cross, but we are to persuade men to fly to the Crucified One for salvation.

Did not the king in the parable say to his servants, "Compel them to come in"? Assuredly He girds His own messengers with such compelling power that men cannot hold out any longer but must follow their lead and bow at the King's feet.

The star did not draw, "as it were with a cart rope," nor by any force, material and physical; yet it drew these Wise Men from the remote East right to the manger of the newborn Child. And so, though we have no arm of the law to help us, nor patronage nor pomp of eloquence, nor parade of learning, yet we have a spiritual power by which we draw to Jesus thousands who are our joy and crown.

The man sent of God comes forth from the divine presence permeated with a power which makes men turn to the Saviour and live. Oh that such power might go forth from all God's ministers, yea, from all God's servants engaged in street-preaching, in Sunday schools, in tract-visitation, and in every form of holy service!

God uses those whose aim and intent it is to draw men to Christ. He puts His Spirit into them, by which Spirit they are helped to set forth the Lord Jesus as so lovely and desirable that men run to Him and accept His glorious salvation. It is a small thing to shine, but it is a great thing to draw. Any castaway may be brilliant; but only the real saint will be attractive for Jesus.

I would not pray to be an orator, but I do pray to be a soul winner. Do not aim at anything short of leading men to Jesus. Do not be satisfied to lead them to orthodox doctrine or merely to bring them to a belief in those views which you hold to be scriptural, valuable as that may be. It is to the Person of the incarnate God that we must bring them; to His feet we must conduct them that they may worship Him. Our mission is not accomplished; it is a total failure unless we conduct our hearers to the house where Jesus dwells and then stand over them, keeping watch over their souls for Jesus' sake.

Once more:

4. The Star Which God Used in This Case Was a Star That Stopped at Jesus

It went before the Wise Men till it brought them to Jesus, and then it stood still over the place where the young Child was.

I admire the manner of this star. There are remarkable stars in the theological sky at the present time. They have led men to Jesus, so they say, and now they lead them into regions beyond, of yet undeveloped thought. The Gospel of the Puritans is "old-fashioned"; these men have discovered that it is unsuitable for the enlarged intellects of the times; and so these stars would guide us further still. To this order of wandering stars I do not belong myself, and I trust I never shall. Progress beyond the Gospel I have no desire for. "God forbid that I should glory save in the cross of our Lord Jesus Christ" (Gal. 6:14).

When the star had come to the place where the young Child was, it stood still. So should the gracious mind become settled, fixed, immovable. The Wise Men knew where to find that star and where to find the young Child by it: so be it with us.

Oh, you who have hitherto been diligent in leading souls to Christ, never indulge for a single moment the notion that you need a broader philosophy or a deeper spirituality than is to be found in Jesus. Abide in Him. Cry, "O God, my heart is fixed; my heart is fixed."

There is nothing beyond Christ which is worth a moment's thought. Do not lose your paradise in Christ for another taste of that tree of knowledge-of-good-and-evil which ruined our first parents. Stick you to the old points: your one subject—Christ; your one object—to bring men to Christ; your one glory—the glory of Christ. Standing by your Lord, and there alone, from this day to the last day, you will secure a happy, honored and holy life.

They said of Greece after her fall that it had become so ruined that you might search for Greece in Greece and fail to find it.

I fear I must say that some professed preachers of the Gospel have roamed so far away from it that you cannot find the Gospel in their gospel nor Christ Himself in the Christ they preach. So far have some diverged from the grand essential soul-saving truth beyond which no man ought to dare to think of going, that they retain nothing of Christianity but the name.

All that is beyond truth is a lie; anything beyond revelation is at best a minor matter, and most probably is an old wives' fable, even though he may be of the masculine gender who invented it.

Stand you to your colors, you who hope to be used of the Lord. Abide so that men shall find you in twenty years' time shining for Jesus and pointing to the place where the Saviour is to be found, even as you are doing now. Let Jesus Christ be your ultimatum. Your work is done when you bring souls to Jesus and help to keep them there by being yourself "steadfast, unmovable." Be not carried away from the hope of your calling, but hold fast even the form of sound words, for it may be that in letting go the form, you may lose the substance also.

Now that we have somewhat rejoiced in the light of the star, let us:

II. GATHER WISDOM FROM THE WISE MEN

Perhaps you have heard the "much speaking" of tradition as to who they were, whence they came and how they traveled. In the Greek church, I believe, they know their number, their names, the character of their retinue and what kind of ornaments were on their dromedaries' necks.

Details which are not found in the Word of God you may believe or not, at your pleasure, and you will be wise if your pleasure is not to believe too much. We only know that they were Magi, Wise Men from the East, possibly of the old Parsee religion, watchers if not worshipers of the stars. We will not speculate about them but learn from them.

They did not content themselves with admiring the star and comparing it with other stars and taking notes as to the exact date of its appearance and how many times it twinkled and when it moved and all that, but:

1. They Practically Used the Teaching of the Star

Many are hearers and admirers of God's servants, but they are not wise enough to make fit and proper use of the preaching. They notice the peculiarity of the preacher's language, how much he is like one divine, how much he is unlike another, whether he coughs too often or speaks too much in his throat, whether he is too loud or too low, whether he has not a provincial tone, whether there may not be about him a commonness of speech approaching to vulgarity; or, on the other hand, whether he may not be too florid in his diction. Such fooleries as these are the constant observations of men for whose souls we labor. They are perishing and yet toying with such small matters.

With many it is all they go to the house of God for—to criticize in this paltry fashion. I have seen them come to this place with opera glasses, as if they came hither to inspect an actor who lived and labored to amuse their leisure hours. Such is the sport of fools.

But these were Wise Men, and therefore practical men. They did not become stargazers and stop at the point of admiring the remarkable star; but they said, "Where is he that is born King of the Jews? for we have seen his star in the east, and are come to worship him." They set out at once to find the newborn King, of whose coming the star was the signal.

Oh, how I wish that you were all wise in this same manner! I would sooner preach the dullest sermon that was ever preached than preach the most brilliant that was ever spoken if I could by that poor sermon lead you quite away from myself to seek the Lord Jesus Christ. That is the one thing I care about. Will you never gratify me by enquiring after my Lord and Master?

I long to hear you say, "What is the man talking about? He speaks about a Saviour. We will have that Saviour for ourselves. He talks about pardon through the blood of Christ. He speaks about God coming down among men to save them. We will find out if there is any reality in this pardon, any truth in this salvation. We will seek Jesus and find for ourselves the blessings which are reported to be laid up in Him." If I heard you all saying this, I should be ready to die of joy.

Is not this a good day on which to set out to find your Saviour? Some of you who have postponed it long; would it not be well to set out at once ere this expiring year has seen its last day?

These men appear to have set out as soon as they discovered the star. They were not among those who have time to waste in needless delays. "There is the star," said they. "Away we go beneath its guidance. We are not satisfied with a star. We go to find the King whose star it is!" And so they set out to find Christ immediately and resolutely.

2. Being Wise Men, They Persevered in Their Search After Him

We cannot tell how far they journeyed. Traveling was extremely difficult in those times. There were hostile tribes to avoid, the broad rivers of the Tigris and the Euphrates to cross, trackless deserts to penetrate; but they made nothing of difficulty or danger. They set out for Jerusalem, and to Jerusalem they came, seeking the King of the Jews.

If it be true that God has taken upon Himself our nature, we ought to resolve to find a Saviour. The distance and the expense ought to be nothing so long as we may but reach Him. Were the Christ in the bowels of the earth or in the heights of Heaven, we ought not rest till we come at Him.

Everything that was necessary for their expedition the Wise Men soon gathered together, regardless of expense, and off they went following the star that they might discover the Prince of the kings of the earth.

At length they came to Jerusalem. Here new trials awaited them. It must have been a great trouble to them when they asked, "Where is he that is born King of the Jews?" and the people shook their heads as if they thought the question an idle one. Neither rich nor poor in the metropolitan city knew anything of Israel's King. The ribald multitude replied, "Herod is king of the Jews. Mind how you speak of another king, or your head may have to answer for it. The tyrant brooks no rival."

The Wise Men must have been more astonished still when they found that Herod was troubled. They were glad to think that He was born who was to usher in the age of gold; but Herod's face grew blacker than ever at the bare mention of a king of the Jews. His eyes flashed, and a thundercloud was upon his brow. A dark deed of murder will come of it, though for the moment he conceals his malice. There is tumult all through the streets of Jerusalem, for no man knows what grim Herod may do now that he has been roused by the question, "Where is he that is born King of the Jews?"

Thus there was a ferment in Jerusalem, beginning at the palace, but this did not deter the Wise Men from their search for the promised Prince. They did not pack up their bales and go back and say, "It is useless to try to discover this questionable personage who is unknown even in the country of which He is King and who appears to be terribly unwelcome to those who are to be His subjects. We must leave to another day the solution of the question: 'Where is he that is born King of the Jews?'"

These earnest-minded seekers were not dispirited by the clergy and the learned men when they came together. To the chief priests and scribes the question was put, and they answered the inquiry as to where Christ would be born, but not a mother's son among them would go with the Wise Men to find this newborn King.

Strange apathy! Alas, how common! Those who should have been leaders were no leaders; they would not even be followers of that which is good, for they had no heart toward Christ. The Wise Men rose superior to this serious discouragement. If the clergy would not help them, they would go to Jesus by themselves.

Oh, if you are wise you will say, *I will find Christ alone if none will join me. If I dig to the center, I will find Him. If I fly to the sun, I will find Him. If all men put me off, I will find Him. If the ministers of the Gospel appear indifferent to me, I will find Him. The kingdom of Heaven of old suffered violence, and the violent took it by force, and so will I.*

The first Christians had to leave behind all the authorized teachers of the day and come out by themselves. It will be no strange thing if you should have to do the same. Happy will it be if you are determined to go through floods and flames to find Christ; for He will be found of you. Thus these men were wise because, having started on the search, they persevered in it till they found the Lord and worshiped Him.

3. They Were Wise Because, When They Again Saw the Star, "They Rejoiced With Exceeding Great Joy"

While inquiring among the priests at Jerusalem, they were perplexed; but when the star shone out again, they were at ease and full of joy. This joy they expressed, so that God had it recorded.

In these days very wise people think it necessary to repress all emotion and appear like men of stone or ice. No matter what happens, they are stoical and raised far above the enthusiasm of the vulgar. It is wonderful how fashions change and folly stands for philosophy. But these Wise Men were children enough to be glad when their perplexity was over and the clear light shone forth.

It is a good thing when a man is not ashamed to be happy because he hears a plain, unmistakable testimony for the Lord Jesus. It is good to see the great man come down from his pedestal and, like a little child, rejoice to hear the simple story of the cross. Give me the hearer who looks not for the fineries but cries out, "Lead me to Jesus! I want a guide to Jesus, and nothing else will suit me."

Why, truly, if men did but know the value of things they would rejoice more to see a preacher of the Gospel than a king. If the feet of the heralds of salvation be blessed, how much more their tongues when they tell out the tidings of a Saviour.

These Wise Men, with all their mystic learning, were not ashamed to rejoice because a little star lent them its beams to conduct them to Jesus. We unite with them in rejoicing over a clear gospel ministry. For us all else is darkness, sorrow and vexation of spirit; but that which leads us to our own glorious Lord is spirit and light and life. Better the sun should not shine than that a clear Gospel should not be preached. We reckon that a country flourishes or decays according as gospel light is revealed or withdrawn.

4. These Wise Men Enter In

Now follow these men a little further. They have come to the house where the young Child is. What will they do? Will they stand looking at the star? No.

The star stands still, but they are not afraid to lose its radiance and behold the Sun of righteousness. They did not cry, "We see the star, and that is enough for us. We have followed the star, and it is all we need to do." Not at all. They lift the latch and enter the lowly residence of the Babe. They see the star no longer, and they have no need to see it; for there is He that is born King of the Jews. Now the true Light has shone upon them from the face of the Child; they behold the incarnate God.

Oh, how wise you will be if, when you have been led to Christ by any man, you do not rest in the man but must see Christ for yourselves. How much I long that you may enter into the fellowship of the mystery, pass through the door and come and behold the young Child and bow before Him.

Our woe is that so many are so unwise. We are only their guides, but they are apt to make us their end. We point the way, but they do not follow the road; they stand gazing upon us. The star is gone; it did its work and passed away. Jesus remains, and the wise men live in Him.

Will any of you be so foolish as to think only of the dying preacher and forget the ever-living Saviour? Come, be wise, and hasten to your Lord at once.

5. These Men Were Wise Because When They Saw the Child They Worshiped

Theirs was not curiosity gratified but devotion exercised. We, too, must worship the Saviour. He has not come to put away our sins and yet to leave us ungodly and self-willed.

Oh, you who have never worshiped the Christ of God, may you be led to do so at once! He is God over all, blessed forever; adore Him! Was God ever seen in such a worshipful form before? Will you not worship God when He thus comes down to you and becomes your brother, born for your salvation? Here nature itself suggests worship. Oh, may grace produce it! Let us hasten to worship where shepherds and Wise Men and angels have led the way.

Here let my sermon come to a pause even as the star did. Enter the house and worship! Forget the preacher. Let the starlight shine for other eyes. Jesus was born that you might be born again. He lived that you might live. He died that you might die to sin. He is risen, and today He maketh intercession for transgressors that they may be reconciled to God through Him.

Come, then; believe, trust, rejoice, adore! If you have neither gold, frankincense, nor myrrh, bring your faith, your love, your repentance, and falling down before the Son of God pay Him the reverence of your hearts.

And now I turn to my third and last point, which is this:

III. LET US ACT AS WISE MEN UNDER THE LIGHT OF OUR STAR

We too have received light to lead us to the Saviour. I might say that for us many stars have shone to that blessed end. I will, however, on this point content myself with asking questions.

1. Do You Think That There Is Some Light for You in Your Particular Vocation, Some Call From God in Your Calling?

Listen to me, and then listen to God. These men were watchers of the stars; therefore a star was used to call them. Certain other men soon after were fishermen, and by means of an amazing take of fish the Lord Jesus made them aware of His superior power, and then He called them to become fishers of men. For a stargazer—a star; for a fisherman—a fish. The Master-Fisher hath a bait for each one of us, and oftentimes He selects a point in our own calling to be the barb of the hook.

Were you busy yesterday at your counter? Did you hear no voice saying, "Buy the truth and sell it not"? When you closed the shop last night, did you not bethink yourself that soon you must close it for the last time? Do you make bread? and do you never ask yourself, "Has my soul eaten the Bread of Heaven?"

Are you a farmer? Do you till the soil? Has God never spoken to you by those furrowed fields and these changing seasons and made you wish that your heart might be tilled and sown? Listen! God is speaking! How I wish that your common vocation would be viewed by you as concealing within itself the door to your high vocation. Oh, that the Holy Spirit would turn your favorite pursuits into opportunities for His gracious work upon you.

I wish that those of you who conclude that your calling could never draw you to Christ would make a point of seeing whether it might not be so. We are to learn from ants and swallows and cranes and conies; surely we need never be short of tutors.

It did seem that a star was an unlikely thing to head a procession of Eastern sages, yet it was the best guide that could be found. And so it may seem that your trade is an unlikely thing to bring you to Jesus, yet the Lord may so use it.

There may be a message from the Lord to thee in many a left-handed providence. A voice for wisdom may come to thee from the mouth of an ass, a call to a holy life may startle thee from a bush, a warning may flash upon thee from a wall; or a vision may impress thee in the silence of night when deep sleep falleth upon men. Only be thou ready to hear and God will find a way of speaking to thee. Answer the question as the wise men would have answered it, and say, "Yes, in our calling there is a call to Christ."

Then, again:

2. What Should You and I Do Better in This Life Than Seek After Christ?

The Wise Men thought all other pursuits of small account compared with this.

"Who is going to attend to that observatory and watch the rest of the stars?" They shake their heads and say they do not know. These things must wait. They have seen *His* star, and they are going to worship Him.

But who will attend to their wives and families, and all besides, while they make this long journey? They reply that every lesser thing must subordinate to the highest thing. Matters must be taken in proportion, and search after the King of the Jews, who is the Desire of all nations, is so out of all proportion great that all the rest must go.

Are not you, also, wise enough to judge in this sensible fashion? If you were to take a week and give it wholly to your own soul and to seeking Christ, would it not be well spent? How can you live with your soul in jeopardy?

Oh, that you would say, "I must get this matter right; it is an all-important business, and I must see it secure." This would be no more than common sense. If you are driving and a trace is broken, do you not stop the horse and set the harness right? How, then, can you go on with the chariot of life when all its harness is out of order and a fall means eternal ruin? If you will stop driving to arrange a buckle for fear of accident, I would beg of you to stop anything and everything to see to the safety of your soul.

See how the engineer looks to the safety valve. Are you content to run more desperate risks? If your house were not insured and you carried on a hazardous trade, the probability is you would feel extremely anxious until you had arranged that matter. But your soul is uninsured, and it may burn forever. Will you not give heed to it? I beseech you, be just to yourself. Be kind to yourself. Oh! see to your eternal well-being.

When we do come near to Jesus, let us ask ourselves this question:

3. Do We See More in Jesus Than Other People Do?

We read in the Scriptures that when these Wise Men saw the young Child they fell down and worshiped Him. Other people might have come in and seen the Child and said, "Many children are as interesting as this poor woman's Babe." Ay, but as these men looked, they saw.

All eyes are not so blessed. Carnal eyes are blind; but these men saw the Infinite in the Infant; the Godhead gleaming through the Manhood; the glory hiding beneath the swaddling bands. Undoubtedly there was a spiritual splendor about this matchless Child!

We read that Moses' father and mother saw that he was a "goodly child." They saw he was "fair unto God," says the original. But when these men saw that holy thing which is called the Son of the Highest, they discovered in Him a glory all unknown before. Then was His star in the ascendant to them: He became their all in all, and they worshiped with all their hearts.

Have you discovered such glory in Christ? "Oh!" says one, "you are always harping upon Christ and His glory. You are a man of one idea!" Precisely so. My one idea is that He is "altogether lovely," and that there is nothing out of Heaven nor in Heaven that can be compared with Him even in His lowest and weakest estate.

Have you ever seen as much as that in Jesus? If so, go you, and rejoice in Him. If not, pray God to open your eyes until, like the Wise Men, you see and worship.

Last, learn from these Wise Men that when they worshiped they did not permit it to be a mere empty-handed adoration. Ask yourself:

4. What Shall I Render Unto the Lord?

Bowing before the young Child, they offered "gold, frankincense and myrrh," the best of metals and the best of spices; an offering to the King of gold; an offering to the Priest of frankincense; an offering to the Child of myrrh.

Wise Men are generous men. Consecration is the best education. Today it is thought to be wise to be always receiving; but the Saviour said,

"It is more blessed to give than to receive." God judges our hearts by that which spontaneously comes from them; hence the sweet cane bought with money is acceptable to Him when given freely. He doth not tax His saints or weary them with incense; but He delights to see in them that true love which cannot express itself in mere words but must use gold and myrrh, works of love and deeds of self-denial, to be the emblems of its gratitude.

You will never get into the heart of happiness till you become unselfish and generous. You have but chewed the husks of religion which are often bitter; you have never eaten of the sweet kernel until you have felt the love of God constraining you to make sacrifice.

JOHN R. RICE
1895-1980

ABOUT THE MAN:

Preacher...evangelist...revivalist...editor...counselor to thousands...friend to millions—that was Dr. John R. Rice, whose accomplishments were nothing short of miraculous. Known as "America's Dean of Evangelists," Dr. Rice made a mighty impact upon the nation's religious life for some sixty years, in great citywide campaigns and in Sword of the Lord Conferences.

At age nine, after hearing a sermon on "The Prodigal Son," John went forward to claim Christ as Saviour. In 1916, with only $9.35 in his pocket, he rode off on his cowpony toward Decatur Baptist College. He was now on the road to becoming a world-renowned evangelist, although he was then totally unaware of God's will for his life.

There was many a twist and turn before Rice rode through the open door into full-time preaching—the army, marriage, graduate work, more seminary, assistant pastor, pastor—then FINALLY, where God planned to use him most—in full-time evangelism.

Dr. Rice and his ministry were always colorful (born in Cooke County, in Texas, December 11, 1895, and often called "Will Rogers of the Pulpit" because of their likeness and mannerisms)—and controversial. CONTROVERSIAL—and correctly so—because of his intense stand against modernism and infidelity and his fight for the Fundamentals.

Dr. Rice lived and died a man of convictions—intense convictions. But, like many other strong fighters for the Faith, Rice was also marked with a sincere spirit of compassion. Those who knew him best knew a man who loved them. In preaching, in prayer, and in personal life, Rice wept over sinners and with saints. But there is more....

Less than seventy-one hours before the dawning of 1981, one of the most prolific pens in all Christendom was stilled. Dr. John R. Rice left behind a legacy in writing of more than 200 titles, with a combined circulation of over 61 million copies. And through October of 1981, a total of 24,058 precious souls reported trusting Christ through his ministries, not counting those saved in his crusades nor in foreign countries where his literature has been translated.

And who but God knows the influence of THE SWORD OF THE LORD magazine which he started and edited for forty-six years!

And while "Twentieth Century's Mightiest Pen"—and man—has been stilled, thank God, the fruit remains! Though dead, he continues to speak.

VI.

How the Wise Men Found the Baby Jesus

JOHN R. RICE

"Now when Jesus was born in Bethlehem of Judaea in the days of Herod the king, behold, there came wise men from the east to Jerusalem, Saying, Where is he that is born King of the Jews? for we have seen his star in the east, and are come to worship him. When Herod the king had heard these things, he was troubled, and all Jerusalem with him. And when he had gathered all the chief priests and scribes of the people together, he demanded of them where Christ should be born. And they said unto him, In Bethlehem of Judaea: for thus it is written by the prophet, And thou Bethlehem, in the land of Juda, art not the least among the princes of Juda: for out of thee shall come a Governor, that shall rule my people Israel. Then Herod, when he had privily called the wise men, enquired of them diligently what time the star appeared. And he sent them to Bethlehem, and said, Go and search diligently for the young child; and when ye have found him, bring me word again, that I may come and worship him also. When they had heard the king, they departed; and, lo, the star, which they saw in the east, went before them, till it came and stood over where the young child was. When they saw the star, they rejoiced with exceeding great joy. And when they were come into the house, they saw the young child with Mary his mother, and fell down, and worshipped him: and when they had opened their treasures, they presented unto him gifts; gold, and frankincense, and myrrh. And being warned of God in a dream that they should not return to Herod, they departed into their own country another way."—Matt. 2:1-12.

The coming of Jesus showed the world in a sad light. We would never know how wicked is the human heart but for what men did to Jesus

Christ. The crucifixion showed that God loved the world, but it also showed that the world hated God!

So the birth of Christ revealed men. "There was no room for them in the inn" when Jesus was born. Herod planned to murder the Baby Jesus, and all Jerusalem was troubled when they heard that the long-looked-for King of the Jews was born.

Most of the world knew little and cared less when a virgin gave birth to the Son of God. A few shepherds, Simeon, and Anna the prophetess loved and worshiped the Baby Jesus. And with these, casting a sacred and holy light on the dark picture of wicked, godless men despising the Light of the world, are the Wise Men from the East.

WHO WERE THE WISE MEN?

The Scripture simply reads, "Wise men from the east." Take a map of Bible lands and trace east across the desert to the first great land, which is Babylonia or Assyria. Evidently from there these Wise Men came. Babylon many years before had been influenced by Daniel, carried captive there when but a boy. He had been the most important minister and wise man in the reign of several great emperors. The book of Daniel was written there, and most of it in the Chaldaic or Syriac language!

We naturally believe that these Wise Men were spiritually minded, saved men acquainted with the book of Daniel and from that, knew about the holy city Jerusalem and about the promised "King of the Jews."

Tradition says there were three Wise Men, but the Bible does not give any number. Perhaps most of us get our ideas from the novel, *Ben Hur*, but that good book is not inspired. Or because there were three kinds of gifts—gold, frankincense and myrrh. Perhaps there were only three men, though we are not told.

The word translated "wise men" is the Greek "Magi," which Young's Analytical Concordance defines as meaning "Persian astronomers or wise men." At least we know that these Wise Men were spiritually minded, saved men who knew that the Saviour was to be born and so came to worship Him. At enormous expense and trouble, they traveled from the East to see Jesus, to worship Him and to offer gifts.

Perhaps they rode camels. They had to cross a great desert or go around it. It would take many weeks to make the journey. It took Ezra and his companions four months to come from Babylon back to Jerusalem (Ezra 7:9). These men may have taken as much time.

THE STAR

The Wise Men said about Jesus, "We have seen his star in the east" (Matt. 2:2). And later the same star appeared to them again at Jerusalem and went before them till it stood over where the Baby Jesus was (vs. 9). The word "star" in ancient languages might have meant star, planet, comet or meteor. Astronomers have tried to pick out the star but have not been able to agree upon it. Why should they? If God sent a star to hearten the Wise Men, He could easily work a miracle about it, and I believe He did.

He prepared a star, just as in the book of Jonah He prepared a fish. The appearance of the angels was a miracle. The birth of the Saviour Himself, with no human father, was the greatest miracle of all. Why should not God work a miracle and prepare a star especially for the occasion, or move it out of its course in the heavens to signal the birth of the Son of God, the Creator of all the fiery hosts of the heavens! It is best to take the facts as mentioned in the Bible with the same simple, unquestioning faith that the Wise Men had. They were astronomers, I have no doubt, and their keen minds must have been thrilled; but with simple and childlike hearts they accepted the supernatural token and went to seek the King of the Jews!

THEY FOLLOWED THE BIBLE

How did these men of the East know that there was to be a King of the Jews? Do you suppose God revealed to them supernaturally the facts about the coming Saviour without any human agency? Not likely. Remember that the Bible says, "How then shall they call on him in whom they have not believed? and how shall they believe in him of whom they have not heard? and how shall they hear without a preacher?" (Rom. 10:14).

It is God's plan that men shall learn through His revealed Word. God uses signs and dreams and wonders and impressions and leading by the Holy Spirit, but He uses them to back up the teaching of His Word. We know from the Scripture that it is God's plan that men should hear the Word of God from other men, or read the Word of God as men have written it down.

Cornelius, a devout and prayerful man, could not be saved until God sent him Peter to preach the Gospel. Abraham would not send Lazarus from the dead to preach the Gospel since they already had the Bible, "Moses and the prophets." God honors His Word and demands that men hear His Word.

When you follow what light you can get from the Bible, you may be sure that the Holy Spirit will lead you. He never leads contrary to the Bible and usually does not lead those who will not take the Bible.

So these Wise Men must have heard, either through the Scriptures or some man of God, of the coming Saviour.

They probably read in Daniel 9:25 of "the Messiah, the Prince," that is, the King, and the immediate context mentions the holy city of Daniel's people, which is Jerusalem. And in the same verse the Wise Men found a plain promise of the time when the Saviour would come—sixty-nine weeks of years, that is, 483 years, after the royal command went out to restore Jerusalem in the days of Ezra and Nehemiah. These men probably knew about the records.

Then they must have known that the time was at hand for the Saviour to be born! It is not surprising that they knew—it is more surprising that everybody else did not know. In fact, when you read the Gospels with this in mind, it becomes evident that multitudes did believe the time was at hand for the Saviour to appear.

When John the Baptist came, many people "mused in their hearts of John, whether he were the Christ or not" (Luke 3:15; John 1:20-22).

God had revealed to Simeon that he should not die until he saw the Saviour (Luke 2:26).

When Jesus worked miracles, the people said, "When Christ cometh, will he do more miracles than these which this man hath done?" (John 7:31; Matt. 12:23).

Even a poor half-breed Samaritan woman with all her false ideas was looking for the Messiah and said, "I know that Messias cometh, which is called Christ: when he is come, he will tell us all things" (John 4:25).

The scribes and Pharisees must have known about this promise, for all Jerusalem was troubled when the Wise Men asked where the King of the Jews would be born.

It is important that we recognize here that God honored His Word. It seems almost certain to me that these men studied their Scriptures, that is, what Scriptures they had (evidently the book of Daniel) and therein learned when the Saviour was to be born.

God gave the star for a witness, but it was a witness to verify the infallible Word of God.

Psalm 19 shows that the Word of God is greater and more perfect than the heavenly bodies. The first six verses speak about the heavens, the firmament, the sun, etc., but verse 7 brings in the contrast that "the law of the Lord is perfect, converting the soul: the testimony of the Lord is sure, making wise the simple."

Nature is not perfect, but the Bible is! Nature bears witness that there is a God, but only the law of the Lord can convert a soul! Do not give the star all the credit for revealing to the Wise Men about Jesus. It was given, surely, as a token, an encouragement, a witness, but they doubtless got the clear teaching, upon which they based their faith, from the Word of God itself! Oh, that we would magnify the Word of God!

If Wise Men from the East would travel hundreds of miles on the single testimony of one verse—Daniel 9:25—how we ought to serve God and live for Him, with the multiplied thousands of promises in our Old and New Testaments!

WHY THEY CAME TO JERUSALEM

Why did they come to Jerusalem to inquire for the Saviour? Jesus was not born in Jerusalem. But they followed what light they had. They acted in faith on the Scriptures that were given them. We know the book of Daniel was written in that Eastern country, and that part of it— from Daniel 2:4 to Daniel 7:28—was in Aramaic or Chaldaic (practically the same language), the language of the Babylonians. God must have intended for the Babylonian people and their descendants to especially learn a lesson from this book of Daniel.

But Daniel does not tell where Jesus would be born. It mentions the holy city, Jerusalem, but does not mention Bethlehem. Micah the prophet tells us in chapter 5, verse 2, that the Saviour would be born in Bethlehem.

The Wise Men from the East came to Jerusalem. They could go no further until they got further light from the Bible! The Bible led them to the Holy Land and to Jerusalem, then to Bethlehem and to the Saviour. We should follow the Scripture as explicitly as did they. The Bible always leads men to Christ when they follow it. Whether Old Testament or New, the Bible is a signboard pointing to Jesus Christ.

Another interesting lesson is that if you want to understand more of the Bible, then act on what Scripture you already know.

THE STAR DID NOT LEAD THE WISE MEN

There is a popular misconception about the star. The story is generally told that the star led the Wise Men to Jerusalem, then to Bethlehem. No—the star simply appeared in the East and then without the star, these men followed the Scripture to Jerusalem. Later, after they had gone to Jerusalem and had inquired and learned that the Saviour would be born at Bethlehem, after they had "departed" (vs. 9), then the star appeared to them again, and went before them! The Scripture says, "Lo, the star"! It was a great surprise. And verse 10 says, "When they saw the star, they rejoiced with exceeding great joy."

When a servant runs before the king to clear the road, he is not leading the king. When the star went before the Wise Men, it was not leading them. They were following God's Word and God simply added the testimony of His approval by the star. The Word of God is much more important than a star.

I can imagine that, as the men plodded long mile after long mile across sandy, burning deserts, up rocky hills and across rivers, they must have had their doubts: *Are we making a mistake? Is all this time and money and sacrifice wasted in following a vain hope? Have we played the fool to go so far with such little evidence to back up the Word of God?* Faith does have doubts; knowledge has none.

When I first believed in Christ, that was faith. After I had the joy in my heart and He had proved Himself in so many ways, my faith grew stronger and my doubts grew weaker. But when I get to Heaven my faith will be made perfect and will turn into perfect knowledge. "Faith will be lost in sight" until faith is completed. We may expect some doubts on the journey.

Some people believe that the happiest day of one's life should be when he is converted, but the way should grow brighter as you serve God and know Him better. "The path of the just is as the shining light, that shineth more and more unto the perfect day" (Prov. 4:18).

So the Wise Men had their doubts, their fears, their misgivings. Then, thank God, after they had gotten all the light they could from the Word of God and were acting in faith upon that light God had given them, the token of His favor; lo, the star appeared again! They had seen it in the East. Now, to see it again and to have it proved that they were on the right track was joy unspeakable. "And when they saw the star they rejoiced with exceeding great joy."

Christian friend, it is joy further on! Fear not to take up your cross and follow Jesus. Fear not to leave houses and land, father, mother, brother, sister—all things for Jesus' sake. Fear not to take Him at His Word and believe all He said, and believing, risk everything that God will do even what He has promised. God will give you all the evidence you need if only you will follow His Word by faith.

Do not depend upon feeling, for feeling is fickle. It ebbs and flows. Feeling may make a lost man feel that he is saved. It has many times made a saved man feel that he is lost. Feeling is often a dreadful liar! Your feelings are deceiving since they may picture your own heart and not the heart of God. They are based too often on your own deeds, worthy of destruction, and not on the marvelous grace of God.

Someone asked Luther, "Do you feel that you have been forgiven?"

He answered, "No! but I'm as sure as there's a God in Heaven."

> **For feelings come and feelings go,**
> **And feelings are deceiving;**
> **My warrant is the Word of God,**
> **Nought else is worth believing.**
>
> **Though all my heart should feel condemned**
> **For want of some sweet token,**
> **There is One greater than my heart,**
> **Whose Word cannot be broken.**
>
> **I'll trust in God's unchanging Word**
> **'Til soul and body sever:**
> **For though all things shall pass away,**
> **His Word shall stand forever.**

The Wise Men had their joy. They saw the star. But this joy came after obedience and faithful following of the Word of God. If they had not been on the road to Bethlehem, I doubt whether these men would have ever seen the star again.

THE WISE MEN WERE SAVED

These men did not come to cuddle a baby, to toss Him in the air, to tickle Him under the chin. Instead, they came to give gifts unto the King, to worship the Son of God. When they saw the Baby Jesus, they "fell down and worshipped him."

Their gifts tell a wondrous tale. These men opened their treasures and gave gifts of gold and frankincense and myrrh. They were fitting gifts. By faith, these godly men gave the things that would best picture that which was due Jesus.

They gave Him GOLD. Gold is the tribute for a king and fit for the worship of a God. The holy place or holy of holies in the Temple had only golden vessels. Gold, the universal money, as brought to Jesus, symbolizes that He is the Creator and Owner of all things. To Him tribute is due.

At Christmastime we should offer gifts to Jesus, but all the year our tithes and offerings, given out of loving and surrendered hearts, should picture our humble submission to Him as Lord.

FRANKINCENSE is a type of prayer and praise offered to Christ as God. They knew about the virgin birth of Christ in spirit—at least they knew this Child was the Son of God. In some way, God had made it clear to them that they should offer the kind of incense which was forbidden by the Mosaic law to any secular use. I do not suppose they knew the Mosaic law, but in their hearts they knew that Jesus was the very Son of God, and they worshiped and praised Him as such.

Take away the tinsel and trappings of our modern drinking, eating, carousing and a commercial Christmas and give us instead a Christmas with a virgin-born Christ, announced by angels and received with faith! Jesus is God!

They brought also MYRRH, the bitter spice which reminds us of those with which they wrapped the body of Jesus when He was buried. The myrrh reminds us of the bitter spices with which the roasted Passover lamb was eaten. It speaks of death, of suffering, of the price of sin!

These men from the East were wise indeed, with spiritual wisdom, revealed by the Spirit of God. They knew that this Baby Jesus some way must suffer for man's sins and, dying as the Lamb of God, would take away the sins of the world. Perhaps all this was clear in their minds, but I believe God put the essence of it into their believing hearts.

So the Christ Child is pictured at Christmas as the King who will reign, the King of the Jews at His second coming, the very God to whom men must give an account, the dying Saviour who made atonement for the sins of the world!

My friends, may this message lead you with humble hearts to search the Scriptures that will lead you to find the Christ. If you do not know and love Him, I trust that you, like the Wise Men, will find Him at any cost, then finding Him, that you will open your treasures and give Him all the love and devotion of your heart! Trust Jesus as your Saviour this Christmas, love Him with all your heart, claim Him openly as Saviour as did the Wise Men of the East!

LEE ROBERSON
1909-

ABOUT THE MAN:

When one considers the far-reaching ministries of the Highland Park Baptist Church and pauses to reflect upon its total outreach, he has cause to believe that it is close to the New Testament pattern.

In the more than forty-one years—from 1942 when Roberson first came to Highland Park until his retirement in April 1983—the ministry expanded to include Camp Joy, reaching some 3,000 children annually; World Wide Faith Missions, contributing to the support of over 350 missionaries; 50 branch churches in the greater Chattanooga area; Union Gospel Mission, which feeds and sleeps an average of 50 transient men daily; a Sunday school bus ministry, which covers 45 bus routes; a deaf ministry; "Gospel Dynamite," a live broadcast held daily over 2 radio stations, now in its 44th year; a church paper, THE EVANGELIST, being mailed free twice monthly to over 73,000 readers; and Tennessee Temple University, Temple Baptist Theological Seminary, and Tennessee Temple Academy.

He is an author of many books.

Preaching to thousands, training preachers, supporting the mission cause, Dr. John R. Rice called him the Spurgeon of our generation.

VII.

Royalty in a Stable

LEE ROBERSON

"And she brought forth her firstborn son, and wrapped him in swaddling clothes, and laid him in a manger; because there was no room for them in the inn."—Luke 2:7.

Three times in this chapter we are reminded of the manger—in verses 7, 12 and 16. Christ Jesus, the King of kings, was born of a virgin and laid in a manger. Here is royalty in a stable.

Isaiah gives a glowing picture of this One who was born in such a lowly place:

"For unto us a child is born, unto us a son is given: and the government shall be upon his shoulder: and his name shall be called Wonderful, Counsellor, The mighty God, The everlasting Father, The Prince of Peace."—Isa. 9:6.

Oh, the greatness of this little One born in a stable and laid in a manger! Isaiah said, "His name shall be called Wonderful." And surely He is the world's great wonder. No one else has ever approached Him. He is in a class all by Himself. He has no second.

No man ever spoke as did Jesus. "The common people heard him gladly," but His teachings were so profound that no philosopher has ever sounded their depths. He never wrote a sermon; He never published a book; He never founded a college; yet His teachings have endured for almost two thousand years.

Only the great, eternal, infinite God should conceive such a stupendous plan! Jesus, born of a virgin, was born in a stable and laid in a manger.

I do not believe the plan was without purpose—the Bible reveals that God does nothing foolishly. The God of the heavens makes no mistakes.

The scene of the stable gives encouragement to the lowliest to come to Christ. We are invited to come "without money and without price" (Isa. 55:1).

I repeat, that scene in the stable gives encouragement to the lowliest, and that reminds us of the verse in II Corinthians 8:9,

"For ye know the grace of our Lord Jesus Christ, that, though he was rich, yet for your sakes he became poor, that ye through his poverty might be rich."

The scene of the stable gives humility to the proud. The haughty must pause and think—Christ born in a manger! Salvation does not come to anyone unless he bows down before God in repentance and faith. The self-righteous will never come unto salvation unless there is a forsaking of that self-righteous spirit.

Now give thought to this manger scene—think about the royalty in the stable.

I. THE COMPASSION OF GOD

Do not try to explain the love of God—just receive it. I can't explain the love of a mother for a wayward son, but there it is. Nor can I understand God's love, but I can certainly receive it.

As you look at the scene in the stable, then you are reminded that God was working. The birth of Christ, the life of Christ, the death of Christ can be explained in only one way—the love of God.

From the cradle to the cross, just one word explains it all, and that word is *love*.

When Jesus came into the world, He revealed the love of God. He showed to us the compassion of the eternal God for the worst of sinners. Who can measure it? Who can fathom it?

I like the great portion given unto us in Romans 8, which begins,

"Who shall separate us from the love of Christ? shall tribulation, or distress, or persecution, or famine, or nakedness, or peril, or sword?... Nay, in all these things we are more than conquerors through him that loved us. For I am persuaded, that neither death, nor life, nor angels, nor principalities, nor powers, nor things present, nor things to come, Nor height, nor depth, nor any other creature, shall be able to separate us from the love of God, which is in Christ Jesus our Lord."

The love of God reaches down to the poorest sinner and brings him unto salvation. The love of God changes and transforms the worst of men.

There is a touching story about John Callahan of New York City. He had gone the limit in sin and had done time in Joliet Penitentiary. When the day of his release came, he promised the keeper that he would let the bottle alone, but he was drunk in less than twelve hours.

Then John Callahan became a bartender. He struck a man in a drunken brawl and landed behind bars again. The police knew him only as a criminal and a man to be watched.

One night he found his way into a rescue mission. He heard the story of Jesus Christ. He said, "I want to be free from the shackles of sin."

John Callahan went down to the front and fell on his knees and asked God to forgive him, and received Jesus Christ as his own personal Saviour.

One of his old pals asked him to take a drink and John said, "No, I don't want any. I've been saved." That was a stunner for his pal. He couldn't understand why he didn't want it. John told him that Jesus had come into his life and the desire for drink had been destroyed.

John had four photographs in the rogue's gallery, and it troubled him. He got three of them from the Chicago police through a friend, but one was in Joliet and he couldn't get it.

One day he spoke at the Battlecreek Sanitarium with Harry Monroe, and among the guests at the meeting was the governor of Illinois. John Callahan told his story. He told how he had gotten the pictures from the rogue's gallery in three of the prisons, but he still had a picture left in Joliet.

When he finished, the governor of Illinois came up to him, wiped his eyes and said, "Mr. Callahan, I'll see what I can do for you."

In a few days, John Callahan received a letter from the governor saying, "It gives me pleasure to enclose your photograph from the penitentiary of Joliet and to tell you that your record of crime has been destroyed. There is no record except in your memory that you were ever here." The governor signed his name.

For many years John Callahan did a mighty work for God on the Bowery in New York City.

My friend, there is no way to explain a story like that outside of the love and compassion of the Almighty God and Saviour, Jesus Christ.

Let me turn to the practical side for just a moment. I read this statement the other day from a Christian writer, "If I have not compassion on my fellow servant even as my Lord had pity on me, then I know nothing of Calvary love."

What a blow that statement is to our haughty minds! How this strikes at our selfishness! How this breaks into our carelessness!

As God has had compassion on us, so must we have compassion upon others.

First, we must pray for others. Samuel said, "Moreover as for me, God forbid that I should sin against the Lord in ceasing to pray for you: but I will teach you the good and the right way" (I Sam. 12:23). We must pray much. We must pray fervently for others.

Second, we must tell sinners of Christ and His death for them. This means that we are to be witnesses. Jesus said, "Ye shall be witnesses unto me." Compassion for sinners will drive us to speak to them. One of the striking verses in the Gospel of Matthew is this one in 9:36:

"But when he saw the multitudes, he was moved with compassion on them, because they fainted, and were scattered abroad, as sheep having no shepherd."

Third, we must plead with men to repent and believe. We must "compel them to come in." This means that we must urgently present our testimony and lay before men their need of the Saviour.

The manger scene speaks of the compassion of God.

II. THE COSTLINESS OF OUR SALVATION

"For I delivered unto you first of all that which I also received, how that Christ died for our sins according to the scriptures."—I Cor. 15:3.

"Who his own self bare our sins in his own body on the tree, that we, being dead to sins, should live unto righteousness: by whose stripes ye were healed."—I Pet. 2:24.

Perhaps no word is more needed than this one: We must see the cost of our salvation.

He was born of a virgin. He walked among men and died on the cross. His death gives us salvation. The Bible tells us, "Without shedding of blood is no remission."

Our salvation is free to us, but, oh, what it cost Him!

Listen to Hebrews 9:26: ". . . but now once in the end of the world hath he appeared to put away sin by the sacrifice of himself."

I was reading the story of Kazainak, the robber chieftain of Greenland. He came to a cabin where a missionary was translating the Gospel of John. He wanted to know what he was doing, and the missionary told him he was making letters and that with letters words were made and that by the use of those words the book he had before him could speak.

Kazainak thought that was very wonderful and asked that the book might speak to him. The missionary read the story of Christ's sufferings and His death on the cross, and immediately the robber chieftain said, "What has this man done? Has He robbed anyone? Has He murdered anyone?"

"No," was the reply. "He has robbed no one, murdered no one. He has done nothing wrong."

"Then why does He suffer? Why does He die?" asked the robber chieftain.

"Listen," said the missionary—and then he told him the story of the cross, the story of the atonement and the meaning of the sufferings of Jesus. When he finished, the hard-hearted man, weeping as a child, turned to Christ for salvation.

Christ died for your sins. He paid the price of Calvary's cross.

We have seen evidences of revival in our church for many years. From whence does it come? I believe that it comes from the consistent, constant preaching of Jesus Christ, the Saviour.

We have spoken much about the death of the Son of God upon the cross.

We have consistently and persistently pressed upon men the invitation to be saved.

If God has moved this way in the past, then He will continue to move this way in the future.

God grant that more churches will get a vision of the needs of man and will present the message of redemption.

Now, when we look into the stable and witness the birth of Jesus Christ, we are made to think of the costliness of our salvation. God's Son came down from Heaven's glory to save us.

III. THE OPENNESS OF THE DOOR TO LIFE

In what part of the Bible shall I begin with a description of the open door to life everlasting? Perhaps it is best to begin in the last chapter of the Bible and let you hear these words again:

"And the Spirit and the bride say, Come. And let him that heareth say, Come. And let him that is athirst come. And whosoever will, let him take the water of life freely."—Rev. 22:17.

The way is open unto all—whosoever will may come. This is God's amazing plan whereby men can be saved.

Christ died for all—but this doesn't mean that all men will be saved. Some will not repent and believe. I could have a building full of sick people and offer a cure to anyone who would walk down the aisle and take the medicine that I would prescribe; but you know, there would be some who would not believe what I was saying. They would doubt and turn away and rot in their disease.

So it is with the open door to life. The door is open—but you must enter in.

Christ came down from Heaven's glory and "took upon him the form of a servant, and was made in the likeness of men: And being found in fashion as a man, he humbled himself, and became obedient unto death, even the death of the cross" (Phil. 2:7,8).

What was the reason for our Saviour's coming? What was the purpose of God in sending His Son? The answer is found in the Word of God.

First, He came to take away sin. In John 3:5 we read, "And ye know that he was manifested to take away our sins; and in him is no sin."

This means pardon for the past. For the man who suffers under the oppression of a guilty conscience, to the man who knows his sin and hates the memory of it, here is the sweetest message of all. Jesus came to take away sin.

Second, what was the meaning of the Incarnation? Look now at I John 3:8. In this verse we are told that **He came to destroy the works of the Devil:**

"He that committeth sin is of the devil; for the devil sinneth from the beginning. For this purpose the Son of God was manifested, that he might destroy the works of the devil."

This portion tells us that we have help for the present. We can be overcomers. We do not have to be conquered by the evil one. We can be victorious through Jesus Christ. Christ is able to reach down and snap the fetters of sin and set a man free.

Third, we are told in John 10:10 that **He came to give us life**—"...I am come that they might have life, and that they might have it more abundantly."

Here is hope for the future.

WILLIAM KENNETH MCCOMAS
1929-

ABOUT THE MAN:

William Kenneth McComas was born just prior to the Great Depression. Denied a formal education largely due to poverty, he completed only eight grades of school in Wayne County, West Virginia. A physical breakdown at fourteen was followed by a disease diagnosed as incurable.

He felt, at an early age, that God had called him to preach, so he entered the ministry and became remarkably successful as a pastor, author and evangelist.

God has given this self-educated man an incredibly retentive and photographic memory. His sermons are spiced with colorful, illustrative language. And he writes the way he preaches.

Dr. McComas began the Calvary Baptist Church, Rittman, Ohio, in 1960 with eight members; today it boasts a membership of several thousand.

Before going into full-time evangelism in 1976, in addition to pastoring this large church, he conducted revival campaigns, preaching in many great churches. Also, he often spoke on college campuses and to civic organizations.

His prolific pen has produced many books. Somewhere on his agenda, he also found time to record twenty long-play stereo albums of his messages. Two of his patriotic sermons have been read into the *Congressional Record*. He holds an honorary Doctorate of Divinity and an LL.D. degree for outstanding achievements.

Dr. John Rawlings said of him: "I consider Dr. McComas one of the strongest men spiritually I have ever known. He lives and practices what he believes with a dedication to God that sets him apart from others."

VIII.

Don't Just Star-Gaze in Bethlehem This Christmas

KENNY MCCOMAS

"Then shall ye return, and discern between the righteous and the wicked, between him that serveth God and him that serveth him not. For, behold, the day cometh, that shall burn as an oven; and all the proud, yea, and all that do wickedly, shall be stubble: and the day that cometh shall burn them up, saith the Lord of hosts, that it shall leave them neither root nor branch. But unto you that fear my name shall the Sun of righteousness arise with healing in his wings; and ye shall go forth, and grow up as calves of the stall."—Mal. 3:18; 4:1,2.

Astronomy is the oldest science known to man. Like many other sciences, it had its origin in the occult and superstitious; the mythology and mythical. Chemistry, for instance, was first alchemy. The primary purpose of the early chemist was to transmute the baser metals into silver and gold. Their secondary purpose was to prolong physical life indefinitely. Unfortunately, both were a stupendous failure.

Metallurgy is obviously an ancient scientific skill. Apparently it played an important economic roll prior to the Flood. "And Zillah, she also bore Tubalcain, an instructor of every artificer in brass and iron..." (Gen. 4:22).

Astronomy was known at first as astrology. It was literally pregnated with all sorts of superstitious ideas. Many sincere folk today, even in our affluent society, think the stars somehow affect their personality. Modern psychiatry has contributed to this theory by reporting a drastic personality and emotional change in people they have studied under the dark and light moon changes. The Bible, however, gives a clear warning against the necromancers, fortunetellers and star-gazing prophets.

The heavenly bodies were first observed by men with only the naked eye. Curiosity mounted and drew men to the heavens like a mighty magnet. The beauty of the heavens caused men to invent and develop powerful mechanical eyes. Space visibility has been increased a thousand times over.

For centuries now men have closely observed the heavens. A lonely vigil is kept night after night at various strategic points of the world from sundown to sunup. Man has been watching the stars intently in modern times in hopes he can find a place out there to go. They hope to find something better than what this money-mad, materialistic, mundane world has provided. Our space agents are desperately searching for a new landing field out yonder somewhere beyond the wild blue among the heavenly bodies.

Some time ago a group of scientists spent the night in a gondola fourteen miles above the surface of the earth. Their powerful scopes were zeroed in on the morning and evening star known as Venus. They descended to the earth with what they considered astounding news. There are vapors and possibly bodies of water on the surface of Venus. Unfortunately, these dedicated scientists stay in a state of frustration because their discoveries are so few and far between.

The Word of God repeatedly turns man's eyes toward the heavens. The psalmist said, "The heavens declare the glory of God; and the firmament sheweth his handywork. Day unto day uttereth speech, and night unto night sheweth knowledge" (19:1,2). The language of the heavens knows no barriers. They do not speak English, German or French, but they speak to all Englishmen, Germans and Frenchmen.

The Bible raises a very interesting question relative to the glory of God's celestial handiwork. "When I consider thy heavens, the work of thy fingers, the moon and the stars, which thou hast ordained; What is man, that thou art mindful of him?" (Ps. 8:3).

When I consider the beauty of God's heavens, I too want to raise the same question the inspired writer asked in the long ago. When God made a great promise to Abraham and convinced him he would make good, He did so by turning his attention toward the heavens. After having asked Abraham to calculate the number of stars and after his having admitted his inability to do so, God promised him his seed would be as numberless as the stars.

When the Old Testament closes, God is directing men to look to the heavens for hope. Thank God, He did because the Old Testament curtain falls to the stage with a frightening thud. Four hundred years of impenetrable darkness and anxious silence follows without the twinkle of a star or a ray of light.

When the Old Testament curtain falls, it does so at the end of the first act in the drama of human life. Only part of the story has been told. The play stopped at a point of tragedy, leaving the anxious audience to stare at an empty stage. When the lights of the Old Testament went out, sin was sweeping over the world like a belligerent tidal wave. The last words are, "Lest I come and smite the earth with a curse" (Mal. 4:6).

What a fearful, frightening and final word, without a postscript! If you don't fix your eyes upon the heavens, you'll find the Old Testament the most disappointing book ever written. It comes to no conclusions. It offers no solution to sin, sorrow and suffering.

Thank God, He promised a sunrise at the end of a long dark night! "But unto you that fear my name shall the Sun of righteousness arise with healing in his wings..." (Mal. 4:2). The Old Testament repeatedly calls God a Sun. And now Malachi, before stepping off the scene of action, calls Jesus a Sun. This, of course, adds to the scriptural proof of His deity.

When man sinned and rebelled against God, this old world became a disaster area. God withdrew, as it were, and pulled in His glory. The universe became dreadfully and fearfully dark. Except for a few candles God placed in the heavens, the darkness would be unspeakable and unthinkable. When the Sun of righteousness arises with healing in His wings, we won't have need of those little candles we call stars. "And there shall be no night there; and they need no candle...for the Lord God giveth them light..." (Rev. 22:5).

Man has never seen real light in all its beauty and glory. We can't even look at our little sun with its intense ultraviolet rays. Our eyes are too fragile now to focus upon the searing quasar beams. "Now we see through a glass darkly," according to Paul the apostle, but God has promised us new eyes someday.

When Sky Lab was anchored out yonder in the vast regions of space, our astronauts reported to space headquarters in Houston that an explosion was taking place on the sun. When asked to describe what they were seeing, one astronaut replied, "It looks like a million blast furnaces thrown out into space." That was only a Roman candle or Chinese firecracker compared to the light believers will someday see.

The Old Testament presents Jesus as a Sun and the New Testament as a Star. Human reasoning says, *Why don't you boys get together? Is He a Sun or Star?* Malachi closes out the Old Testament by saying, 'Watch for the sunrise.' Matthew makes no mention of the Sun in relation to the birth of Christ. "Now when Jesus was born in Bethlehem of Judaea in the days of Herod the king, behold, there came wise men from the east to Jerusalem, Saying, Where is he that is born King of the Jews? for we have seen his star in the east, and are come to worship him" (Matt. 2:1,2).

The Old Testament is "expectation," and the New Testament is "realization." The New Testament does not open where the Old Testament closes. The Old Testament closes with a public proclamation; the New Testament opens with private revelation.

Gabriel appeared first to Zechariah the Priest, then to Mary and still later to Joseph. When Jesus was born, His birth was not announced to the world from tel-star nor did a megaphonic voice declare it from a transmitter on a satellite. I would suppose a matter of such magnitude deserved a proclamation by every created being in the infinitudes of Heaven. Such was not the case, however, since God chose to privately announce the event of the ages to lowly, insignificant shepherds on those Galilean slopes in the stillness of the night while the world slept.

Simultaneous with the coming of Jesus to Bethlehem, Wise Men converged on Jerusalem from all over that mysterious oriental land. The same words are falling from each of their lips, "Where is he that is born King of the Jews, for we have seen his star. . . ." These men are astrologers. They have spent their lives studying the stars. But they readily confess they have never seen a star like this one.

How did these wise men associate the coming of Jesus with a star? They sure didn't get a hint in that direction from Malachi. His instructions were, 'Watch for the sunrise.' To investigate their source of information, we must climb into a gondola and go aloft traveling backward over hundreds of years. We must visit the tent of a heathen prophet by the name of Balaam. This prophet made four interesting prophecies relative to the future of the nation Israel, the last of which concerns us.

"I shall see him, but not now: I shall behold him, but not nigh: there shall come a Star out of Jacob, and a Scepter shall rise out of Israel. . ."

(Num. 24:17). Balaam, looking through prophetic binoculars, saw one who was not then present. His coming was not nigh but rather distant. He then clearly identified Him as being a Star.

Jesus happens to be both a Sun and a Star. The Star identifies His first coming, and the Sun identifies His second coming.

Let's be careful not to just star-gaze in Bethlehem this Christmas. Let's go on to Gethsemane where the great drops of agony distilled upon the Saviour's brow. Let's go on to Calvary where from the cross He said, "It is finished." Let's go on to Olivet where the angelic beings said, "This same Jesus shall so come in like manner."

Before the inspired word comes to a close, Jesus declares Himself to be "the root and offspring of David, and the bright and morning star" (Rev. 22:16). We must not lose track of the fact, however, that the Sun of righteousness is going to rise with healing in His wings. What hope, what promise and what encouragement in this impenetrable dark midnight hour of appalling apostasy! We need to bear in mind, the darkest hour of the night is just before the sunrise.

My heart goes out with pity to our space agents. They are spending their entire lives peering out into empty blackness, inky and void. They're looking into a frigid, lifeless atmosphere that shivers the mind. Looking for a Utopia, they have been chasing pots of gold at the ends of receding rainbows. They study those little candles burning so far, far away with dreamy anxiousness, without the faintest notion how to get there. Even worse, they realize if they ever find a way, they may discover they are still as far away from what they are searching for as when they began.

Don't put your hopes in the stars this Christmas. Science can only fill your stocking with dry atomic ashes. Turn your eyes toward the heavens and fix them firmly upon Him who said, "Look unto me, and be ye saved, all the ends of the earth."

Young Charles Haddon Spurgeon, as a teenager, was crossing London one Sunday morning on his way to church when a blinding snowstorm forced him to take shelter in a Wesleyan chapel. Due to the inclement weather, the pastor was absent. As a matter of fact, one layman was there besides young Spurgeon. The lay preacher took his text from Isaiah where God invited all the ends of the earth to look to Him and be saved. Spurgeon for a long while had been searching for the formula to eternal life. That morning he said to himself, *Any fool can look.* So with the eye of faith he looked to Jesus and instantaneously received eternal life.

John Newton said, "With a powerful telescope I can see thousands of miles out into the heavens, but on my knees in prayer I can see more of Heaven through the eye of faith than any telescope could ever reveal."

For the unregenerate I urge a look to Jesus for salvation. For believers I urge you to "look up, for your redemption draweth nigh."

WILLIAM EDWARD BIEDERWOLF
1867 - 1934

ABOUT THE MAN:

Presbyterians produced some of the most noteworthy evangelists of the late 1800's and early 1900's—and a notable among them was William E. Biederwolf.

After his conversion, he continued his education at Princeton, Erlangen and Berlin universities, and at the Sorbonne in Paris.

Biederwolf's first church was the Broadway Presbyterian Church of Logansport, Indiana, the state where he was born. Then he became a chaplain in the Spanish-American War and then entered evangelism— a ministry he was to serve for 35 years.

In conjunction with his evangelism, Dr. Biederwolf was associated with the world-renowned Winona Lake Bible Conference for 40 years.

In 1929, he became pastor at the storied Royal Poinciana Chapel in Palm Beach, Florida, a position he held until his death.

Biederwolf's ministry was mighty. Perhaps his greatest campaign was in Oil City, Pennsylvania, in the bitter winter of 1914. Thousands thronged the tabernacle. Twice it was enlarged. His messages were pungent and powerful.

His kind of preaching brought men and women from every walk in life coming in deep contrition for their sins—the mayor of the city, physicians, lawyers, and men from the factories, young people from the schools; and the whole city and county were mightily stirred in deep concern about the things of God.

He was the author of several books.

IX.

If Christ Had Not Been Born, What Then?

WILLIAM E. BIEDERWOLF

"For unto you is born this day in the city of David a Saviour, which is Christ the Lord."—Luke 2:11.

If Christ had not been born—What? It would be interesting to go through the Bible and see how often this little word *if* occurs.

"If thou wilt." "If I be lifted up." "If I go not away." "If Christ be not risen." "If in this life only we have hope." Whichever page you turn, there you will find it written, "If...."

If is everywhere—like stars in a dark night of uncertainty...like red lights on a pleasant road of unsuspected peril...like oases in a waterless desert of death...like invitations to a feast where no good thing is withheld! *If* is everywhere!

That little word takes you up Himalayas of hope, carries you over Pacific Oceans of peace, leads you through Yosemites of delight. But it leads you as well, if you thwart the will of God, through Saharas of despair, across wild seas of sorrow, into infernos such as no Dante ever described.

If Christ had never been born—What? Such an assumption rings with the hopelessness of the grave. It sounds like a muffled drum beating the sad funeral march of despair through the darkened chambers of a lost soul. If Christ had never been born!

It's a wonderful text which is ours this morning. How we ought to thank God for it: "For unto you is born this day in the city of David a Saviour, which is Christ the Lord."

No wonder that a wonderful message like that was accompanied by an angel host singing, "Glory to God in the highest." And really it is quite as strange as it is wonderful—angels singing before shepherds!

We have read of the rustic fiddler from Maine playing before the commercial princes of America; of Jenny Lind, of Adelina Patti, of Caruso, of Galli Curci and others like them singing before the crowned heads of the world. But here are the exalted beings of a celestial world coming down from the dazzling courts of Heaven to sing before a group of humble shepherds, men who came out of obscurity and went back into obscurity, and of whom the only record is that "there were... shepherds abiding in the field, keeping watch over their flock by night."

And what a message it was they sang!

"Fear not; for, behold, I bring you good tidings of great joy, which shall be to all people. For unto you is born this day in the city of David a Saviour, which is Christ the Lord."

Of all the days of the year, we look forward to Christmas most of all. What is back of it? Why all the lighted trees sparkling with tinsel? the children's stockings bulging with love-gifts of others? the holly in the window? the store, the office, the schools all closed, as we rest from the strenuous rush and metallic clinking of our modern life and the dear ones come back home and together we explore the kingdom of love and good will, led on by the mystic influence of the hallowed season known to us as Christmastime?

What is there about this season that casts a mellowing spell over us and finds us all in a mood where meanness is out of place, where selfishness is outlawed and where kindness, with the giving of gifts, is the order of the day?

It is all because of the song the angels sang. As Milton puts it in his hymn, "On the Morning of Christ's Nativity":

> **This is the month and this the happy morn**
> **Wherein the Son of Heaven's eternal King**
> **Of wedded maid and virgin mother born,**
> **Our great redemption from above did bring.**

But what if there had been no such song to sing! What if Christ had never been born!

IF CHRIST HAD NOT BEEN BORN, ALL THE PROMISES GIVEN BY GOD OF A COMING REDEEMER WOULD HAVE BEEN BROKEN; all the prophecies that foretold the glad event would have failed, and all the bright hopes of the ages would have been blasted.

In bitter disappointment and despair, the world would be living and walking in ever-deepening shadows today; for if He who was to bring life and immortality to light had never come, what had men to live for more than beasts?

They of Old Testament times had been taught to believe He was coming, He who the prophet had called "the Desire of all nations"; and in this expectancy they had lived, worked and died. It was in this faith their hands had been stretched out down through the thousands of years. It was in this hope the fires were kept burning on human altars while their hearts beat high with the thought of coming glory.

But had He not come, those hands would have been stretched out in vain; those lives would have been lived in vain and closed without one ray of light to illumine the darkness and the night into which they went. And what would have been true of them would equally be true of us.

IF CHRIST HAD NOT BEEN BORN, WE NEVER WOULD HAVE KNOWN THE REAL CHARACTER OF GOD.

We must not overlook the fact that there is such a thing as a progressive revelation of God in His dealings with the sons of men. Certainly in the God of the New Testament we find an advance over the concept of God as set forth in the Old Testament.

Jesus said, "He that hath seen me hath seen the Father."

Among the masterpieces of Thorwaldensen, the Danish sculptor, there is perhaps none more artistically executed than that of Hector's farewell to his wife and child. It was at the gates of Troy through which Hector was about to pass to his last battle, for in the encounter that ensued he met the mighty Achilles and went down before his far-shadowing spear.

Andromache had accompanied him to the gates and with her came the nurse bearing in her arms their infant child, Astyanax. The moment came when the father must say "Goodby." As he reached out his hands to take the little one in his arms, his burnished helmet and waving plume so terrified the little one that he turned and clung crying to his nurse.

Surmising the ground for the little one's fear, Hector took off the fierce and shining armor from his head and laid it on the ground. Instantly, laughing through his tears, the child leaped into his father's arms.

Is it not so that when men think of the majesty of God, of His divine splendor and awfulness, they are afraid and taken back? If God revealed

Himself only as the Almighty One and men were forced to contemplate only His resplendent glory, the terrors of His justice and the terribleness of His throne, these things would strike them deep with awe, and from such a God men naturally shrink.

But what was it Jesus said? "He that hath seen me hath seen the Father." And just as the father of the little child of our story laid aside his fierce armor and revealed himself in all the tenderness of paternal affection, so, as another has said, "God veils His glory and splendor and awfulness and reveals Himself in Jesus Christ to His children in the sweetest aspects of His love."

The only perfect revelation God ever made of Himself, He made in Jesus Christ, and if you look at Him through Jesus Christ, you will know what kind of God He really is. Read the story of Christ's wonderful life—full of compassion, tenderness and forbearance. And if you want a single word to characterize it all, you will have to take four letters and write over it, from the cradle to the cross and from the beginning to the end, the word "love." That is God. And that, too, by the way, is the spirit of love and good will.

The late Morgan Cook of the *Philadelphia Inquirer* told us one time in his editorial column of a tiny little fellow who was saying his prayers one Christmas Eve. He had finished his childish petition and had gotten up from his knees. Then he said, "I forgot something," and kneeling down again he closed his eyes and said, "Dear Jesus, I hope You have a happy birthday." The prayer of this little lad leads us into the very heart of God.

IF CHRIST HAD NOT BEEN BORN, THE WORLD WOULD STILL BE WAITING, BUT IN VAIN, FOR A SAVIOUR, AND YOU AND I WOULD BE, AS ALL OTHERS, "WITHOUT HOPE AND WITHOUT GOD IN THE WORLD," as we are told in Paul's letter to the Ephesians.

It is related that the eldest son and heir of the Duke of Hamilton was an earnest Christian. He was stricken with a malignant disease which ended in his death. As the hour of his departure from the world drew near, he took his Bible from under his pillow and read the passage,

"I have fought a good fight, I have finished my course, I have kept the faith: Henceforth there is laid up for me a crown of righteousness, which the Lord, the righteous judge, shall give me at that day: and not to me only, but unto all them also that love his appearing."

As death approached, he called his younger brother to his side and, addressing him with deepest affection and seriousness, closed with these remarkable words, "And now, Douglas, in a little time you'll be a duke, but I shall be a king."

This is the Christian's hope. Compared with it, this world and all it holds is as a grain of sand compared with a sparkling diamond from the Transvaal, or a flawless emerald from Muzo.

The man of the world, of course, does not know it, but hope is the best part of our riches. And if we have the wealth of the Indies in our pockets and have not the hope of Heaven in our souls, we are poor beyond the power of language to describe. "For what shall it profit a man, if he shall gain the whole world, and lose his own soul?"

Hope! Oh, the music of that word! The charm of it! It is a rainbow that spans the cloudy sky of our storm-swept lives. It comes to the sick on the couch of suffering and whispers of returning health. It comes to the poor toiler bending over his task telling him of the better days to come. It comes to the bewildered traveler, lost in the night, suggesting a light he will surely see in some friendly cabin. It comes to the ocean-liner whose SOS has gone out on the air, bidding its imperiled passengers not to despair, for the curling smoke on the distant horizon comes from the answering steamer on its way to the rescue.

But, alas, such hopes are often disappointing and end in despair. But when hope comes to the believer in his dying hour it is, as Paul said in II Timothy 1:12, "I know whom I have believed, and am persuaded that he is able to keep that which I have committed unto him [my soul] against that day."

But oh, to be "without hope and without God in the world"! To express adequately what that means one would have to have in his voice the moan of all heartaches, the groan of all distress, the shriek of all torment, the scream of all terror, the agony of all despair, the weeping and wailing and gnashing of teeth of all the damned forevermore.

I can think of no picture more nearly describing what in reality would have been true if Christ had not been born than that suggested by the thirty-four men who died many years ago in the submerged submarine S-4. There had been a wreck, and they were imprisoned in the bottom of the sea off Provincetown, Massachusetts. Rescuers were coming from all directions in response to the SOS call which had been signaled abroad. The rescue work was placed in charge of an Admiral of the U.S. Navy, and the government was doing all in its power to save the men.

The only means of communications was by the method of signal tapping. The one message that was tapped out again and again by the doomed men was, "How long will it be now?" "How long will it be now?" Oh, the infinite pathos, the heart-breaking despair of it all! "How long will it be now?"

One by one they died. Then came painfully the last despairing tapping, "How-long-will-it-be-now?" and the signals ceased. The rescuers did their best, but the doomed men died because help did not come.

And so it would have been with the whole world if Christ had not come; for if He had not come, if He had not trodden the winepress alone, when "of the people there was none to help him," if He had not risen again from the grave after the death of the cross, then, truly, as Paul says, 'They who have fallen asleep in him are perished, and we of all men are most miserable.'

But "thanks be unto God for his unspeakable gift," by reason of which the herald angel could say, "Fear not: for, behold, I bring you good tidings of great joy, which shall be to all people. For unto you is born this day in the city of David a Saviour, which is Christ the Lord."

If Christ had not been born! But He was born—born of a humble virgin mother. If Christ had not come into the world! But He did come—come from the bosom of God and the breast of a woman. "Lo, I come to do thy will, O God," He said, as together before the Father's throne they conferred over the sad plight of the world because of sin.

How much the angels have felt when they learned that He, when out of nothing made all that was made—who threw into space, as though they were tiny balls of cotton, whirling worlds and racing planets and burning suns and the shining stars which for multitude no man could ever number; who stretched out the skies with the wonders thereof— the deep-voiced thunder, the flash of lightning and the bewildering beauty of the rainbow; that He who laid the foundations of the earth, filled it with its myriad wonders of teeming life, of glassy seas, rushing rivers, tumbling cataracts, towering mountains, sparkling diamonds, laughing rivulets and fragrant flowers—that He who was in the form of God was to take upon Himself the form of a servant—that the Infinite was to become an infant and that He upon whose mighty shoulders the whole universe did hang was to become so helpless as to hang on a woman's breast.

Yes, how the angels must have felt! How they must have felt as they saw Him take one lingering look at His home in Glory, heard Him say goodby to His Father's house and its many mansions, to the thrones and to the angels and saw Him start for the outer gate, look down into it out of a bright and starry Heaven, knowing full well that the end must come in the cross, the crown, the nails, the soldiers and the spear.

Yes, He came, and it was a mighty purpose that brought Him. He did not come to save us from sorrow, for "He . . . is a man of sorrows, and acquainted with grief." He did not come to save us from temptation, for He "was . . . tempted in all points like as we are." He did not come to preach or to teach or to be a worker of miracles. He did not come to show us how to live as no other has ever done. He had in His coming but one supreme, stupendous and all-mastering objective. The angel said to Joseph, "Thou shalt call his name JESUS: for he shall save his people from their sins." It was for this that He came, and it was purposed in the mind of God before the foundation of the world.

> **O listen to our wondrous story,**
> **Counted once among the lost;**
> **Yet, One came down from the Heaven's glory,**
> **Saving us at awful cost.**
>
> **What did He do?**
> **He died for you!**
> **Where is He now?**
> **In Heaven interceding.**

Someone has reminded us that it is one thing to say "Jesus," but quite another thing to say, "My Jesus." Can you say it?

It was Elisha Hoffman who sang,

> **What a wonderful Saviour is Jesus, my Jesus!**
> **What a wonderful Saviour is Jesus, my Lord!**

Is this wonderful Saviour yours?

Oh, why should men want to rob the world of the Christian faith so long as they have no better faith to give it! It was Joseph Parker who said this, and he was right when he said it:

> If Christ the Lord will not do, get some other man; but do get a Saviour. We do not want you to be finding fault with one Saviour if you can get another. They take a mean course—selfish, dishonorable, inhuman—who simply say Christ is not the Lord. . . . Oh, why hold a controversy on the shore when one of you should plunge into the sea and save the drowning man!

Why not take Him for yourself this Christmas morning and then enter into His passion to see a world redeemed and brought back to its birthplace in the heart of God?

"For unto you is born this day in the city of David a Saviour, which is Christ the Lord."

DWIGHT LYMAN MOODY
1837-1899

ABOUT THE MAN:

D. L. Moody may well have been the greatest evangelist of all time.

In a 40-year period, he won a million souls, founded three Christian schools, launched a great Christian publishing business, established a world-renowned Christian conference center, and inspired literally thousands of preachers to win souls and conduct revivals.

A shoe clerk at 17, his ambition was to make $100,000. Converted at 18, he uncovered hidden gospel gold in the hearts of millions for the next half century. He preached to 20,000 a day in Brooklyn and admitted only non-church members by ticket!

He met a young songleader in Indianapolis, said bluntly, "You're the man I've been looking for for eight years. Throw up your job and come with me." Ira D. Sankey did just that; thereafter it was "Moody will preach; Sankey will sing."

He traveled across the American continent and through Great Britain in some of the greatest and most successful evangelistic meetings communities have ever known. His tour of the world with Sankey was considered the greatest evangelistic enterprise of the century.

It was Henry Varley who said, "It remains to be seen what God will do with a man who gives himself up wholly to Him." And Moody endeavored to be, under God, that man; and the world did marvel to see how wonderfully God used him.

Two great monuments stand to the indefatigable work and ministry of this gospel warrior—Moody Bible Institute and the famous Moody Church in Chicago.

Moody went to be with the Lord in 1899.

X.

Good News!

D. L. MOODY

"And the angel said unto them, Fear not: for behold, I bring you good tidings of great joy, which shall be to all people. For unto you is born this day in the city of David a Saviour, which is Christ the Lord."— Luke 2:10, 11.

We are about to celebrate one of the grandest, if not the grandest, event that ever took place in this world—the birth of Jesus Christ—Immanuel, God with us—and the text I want to call your attention to is the 10th and 11th verses of chapter 2 of Luke that I have just read.

That was the announcement of the angels. They came to bring the good tidings to us, and if the angels cannot look into the future, I have no doubt in my own mind that they thought the world would rise up and receive Him as one man. But instead, we find that not only Herod in Jerusalem but all Jerusalem was troubled when the Wise Men brought tidings in that city. If the shepherds had brought it, they probably would not have received it—wouldn't have believed it—but because some Wise Men from a distant country brought the tidings that they had seen His star in the East, we are told that Herod and all Jerusalem was troubled by the thought that He had come.

What God calls good news, man thinks is bad news.

It was so then; it is so at present. When we preach the Gospel of Jesus Christ, very few believe it. I will venture to say half this audience today do not believe that the Gospel is good news. The moment you begin to proclaim the glad tidings, many will put on a long face as if you had brought a death warrant, or as if you had brought them an invitation to attend a funeral, or to go out and witness the execution of some man, or to go to some hospital where there was some plague. They do not look upon the Gospel as good news. Do you think that ministers would have to stand in pulpits Sunday after Sunday to proclaim that Gospel if people believed it?

No one has to urge men to believe good news. We like to believe it but do not. People think it is bad news that Christ came into the world to redeem it. John testified that God sent Christ into the world to save it. He came to deliver men from sin, He came for the recovery of sight to the blind, He came to set at liberty those who were bound, and to proclaim the acceptable year of the Lord, He came to bring salvation into this world; yet men do not believe it.

But the moment a man's eyes are opened and he sees really Christ's mission in its true light and he begins to realize what Christ came to do and that truth dawns upon him, then it is the best news that ever fell upon his ear.

No better news ever came out of Heaven than the Gospel of Jesus Christ. No better news has ever fallen upon the ears of men than the Gospel of Jesus Christ. No news like this—and there never will be any like it—a Saviour is born unto you.

Good News of Death Conquered

Now I want to tell you why the Gospel is good news—that is, why it is good news to me. It has taken out of my path the very bitterest enemies I have ever had. Now, you may talk as much as you are a mind to about death not being an enemy, but death is an enemy, and death is a bitter enemy to the human race; and while we are gathered in this meeting today it may steal into our dwellings and take away the dearest friend we have on earth. It may take the wife of your bosom; it may take the children who are now full of glee and full of joy at the anticipation of Christmas coming; and you may go home and find that death has entered into your dwelling and thrown a dark shadow across your path and a blight across your threshold. Death is an enemy. But the Gospel of Jesus Christ tells me that that very enemy has been conquered.

When Christ came into the world, He met Death and conquered him. When I was a boy, I remember I used to look upon death as the most horrid monster that ever was in the world. The first time I put my hand on the forehead of a corpse, how quick I drew it back. What a cold chill went right to my heart!

In the town where I was brought up, it used to be the custom, when a man or woman was buried, to toll out their ages. If they were seventy or eighty years old, there would be seventy or eighty strokes of the bell. I always counted the strokes of that bell, and I used to think when an aged person died, *Death is a good way off, and it will be a long while before it will take me.* But then sometimes it came among the teens and took a child of my age—that would bring death a little nearer home, and I would think: *It may come and take me in my childhood.* Many a time I have lain awake thinking of death. I used to think it was a horrid enemy; but as a believer, that is all gone now.

As you go on through life you may shout, now, "O death, where is thy sting? O grave, where is thy victory?" And you hear a voice coming down from the cross of Christ—rolling down through the centuries—"Buried in the bosom of the Son of God." He took the sting of death into His own bosom. He tasted death for every man.

What is it that makes death so bitter? Sin. And if Christ has borne the penalty of death, if He has taken our sins on Himself and borne them away on the tree, we have the victory over death. Death is a conquered enemy, a conquered foe.

The Grave Is Robbed of Victory

Well, then, I used to think I could not go to the grave and lay away a loved one. It seemed as if I hadn't the power, that I hadn't grace enough to go to the narrow house appointed us to die in and lay away a loved one. But as I look into the grave now, I can think that Jesus Christ has been down in that grave and has measured its depth, that He has lain there Himself.

It was not that death took Christ into the sepulcher, but He went down into the sepulcher Himself after death. He went down there to conquer death and the grave, and to rob the grave of its victory. That is what Paul meant when he shouted, "O grave, where is thy victory?"

The Son of God had robbed the grave of its victory. He went down into the grave, and Jesus bound death hand and foot and came up out of the grave and brought up a few released captives to be the witnesses of the victory He had won. Or, as Christmas Evans said, He took possession of the whole territory when He went into Joseph's sepulcher, and so the grave now is conquered. It may have this body—this house that I live in, but I am going to gain something even by the grave. If it is sown in dishonor, it shall be raised in glory. If it is sown in weakness, it shall rise in power. If it is sown in corruption, it shall be raised in incorruption. If it is sown a mortal body, it shall be raised an immortal.

We are going to gain something by death. We are going to get the victory over death and the grave. That is what the Gospel brings us. Isn't that good news?

It is astonishing how men go to sleep over the Gospel. It is astonishing how little some men care for it, when these enemies are in the path of every man who treads this earth. He knows it is only a little while, only a few shadows, and it is gone. Only a few breaths, and it is gone. It is but a vapor, life is; it is but a shadow, but a cloud, but an inch of time, then the eternal ages roll on.

But then if we are in Christ, we have the victory. Death has had his hand on Christ once; he will never have his hand on Him again. "I am he that shall live. Behold, I live forevermore."

He lives; and if I have Christ, Death cannot touch that new life. "He that hath the Son hath life; and he that hath not the Son of God hath not life." If I have Christ formed in me, the hope of glory, Death cannot touch that. He may have the old Adam life—I don't care for that. It is not worth having. It is forfeited; it is gone anyway, but we have a new life, and that is the good news.

Good News of Sins Forgiven

Well, then, the other enemy is sin. I used to think it would be an awful time when a man had to render an account of his sins; but the Gospel tells me that if I believe on the Lord Jesus Christ, out of love to me He has taken all my sins and cast them behind God's back. It is a safe place, isn't it, to have our sins? Not behind our backs, because the Devil would get behind us and bring them all out again to torment us with our sins; but God has taken them and cast them behind His back.

How is the Devil to get at them? You may challenge the Devil to find your sins if God has put them away. If God has washed them away, they are clean gone. If God has buried our sins, they are buried so deep that they will never have a resurrection. No fiend of Hell, no Devil can find our sins when God buries them. When God forgives a man, when God justifies a man, he is justified. If God puts away our sins they are put away forever, the Gospel tells me. Isn't that worth hearing? Isn't it good news to be told you have had your sins put away, that you have had them blotted out for time and eternity? God says, "I will blot them out as a thick cloud."

During the past month we have seen a good many clouds, but suppose we get up tomorrow morning and there isn't a cloud to be seen. Can you see one after it has vanished? We have seen a good many during the past month, but when once a cloud is blotted out, is there a philosopher on earth who can find it?

God says, "I will blot them out as a thick cloud"; and if God has blotted out our sins, who is going to find them? To think that they are blotted out! And not only that, but God says, "I won't remember them." God forgets them. Wonderful!

Now, you know some men say, "Oh, I—I—I will forgive you, but I won't forget." But God not only forgives—He forgets.

Do you know what forgiveness is? It is putting a thing away as if it had never happened. Do you know what justification is? It is putting man back as if he had never sinned. It's a great thing for God to justify a sinner, and it is the best news a man can hear. Do you know any better news than to have all the sins that you have committed from the cradle up, blotted out and put behind God's back, out of sight—put away and have God never remember them?

Well, that enemy is gone. Sin is out of the way—and what an enemy it is. How it has cursed this earth! How it has broken up families! How it has ruined households! But God came down to the earth and out of love to your soul He says, "I forgive you, if you will believe on My Son; if you will take Him."

Glad Tidings of Judgment Removed

Well, the next enemy is judgment. I used to think it would be a terrible hour when we would stand before God and have all the sins that we had committed from childhood up all blazoned out before the assembled universe; sins that we had committed in secret; sins that we committed in childhood—all of them.

But that blessed Gospel tells me that Jesus Christ went into judgment for me, and I don't have to go there for sin! Says Paul, 'Know ye not that He shall judge the world?' We are going to be brought to judgment for rewards and stewardship, and every man is to give an account for the deeds done in the body. That is written to the church and to believers, but we are not going to be brought to judgment for sin. Why? Because

Christ was judged for us. "He was wounded for our transgressions, he was bruised for our iniquities: the chastisement of our peace was upon him; and with his stripes we are healed"; and "who his own self bare our sins in his own body on the tree."

If Christ bore them, I don't have to bear them. Is God going to demand payment twice? If I owe a man $500 and I am poor and can't pay him a dollar, and Dr. Ganse comes and pays that $500 and gets a receipt in full and hands it to me, can that debtor collect that money from me? Is there any court in Christendom that will make me pay that if another has paid it for me?

Jesus Christ has paid the debt. He took my place when He died on Calvary. He was the sinner's Substitute. He died in our stead. He who knew no sin became sin for us, and upon the sacrifice of Himself has put away our sins.

Now you see we are not going to come to judgment for sin. That is passed. That is behind us. Grave, sin and judgment are all behind us. So we can enjoy Christmas if we have Christ. And one who does not have Him—how can he enjoy it? It seems to me like mockery for a man to rejoice over a rejection of the Son of God; rejecting Him who came into the world to save it; rejecting a Saviour who came into the world to bless it; rejecting a Saviour who came into the world to blot out our sins and iniquities.

How Simple the Way of Salvation

Now there may be some here who would like to know just how you can become a Christian and enter into the joy of a Christian life so that you may have a real true Christmas gift. It is very simple, so simple that I am afraid you will stumble over it.

I have sometimes wished that I could make the plan of salvation as simple as it really is. If I could only command language to make it as simple as it really is, I sometimes think I would preach but one sermon, and I would just go up and down Christendom and tell it to the world. It seems to me that we sort of mystify it when we explain it, and that we cannot make it as plain as it really is, and the world stumbles over the very simplicity of it.

Now it is said, "The wages of sin is death, but the gift of God is eternal life. . . ." It is a gift. Is there a person in this audience who does not know how to take a gift? I venture to say there is not a man or woman in this audience who will not receive a gift in the near future. Do you know how you will take it? You will just take it—that is all. It would be an absurd thing for me to stand here and undertake to explain to you how you would take a Christmas gift, wouldn't it? I see some of you smiling in contempt. Now you think I am talking as though I were talking to little children; but we have to get down and preach to men like little children, because we just mystify the plan of salvation.

A teacher in a Sunday school one Sunday took out his watch and said to one of the scholars, "I will give you that watch if you will take it." The first boy grinned but wouldn't take it. He thought the other boys would make fun of him if he did. Then the teacher offered it to the next boy in the class. Neither would he take it. He offered it to every boy in the class but one. When he came to the very last boy and offered it to him, the little fellow at the foot of the class reached out, took the watch and put it in his pocket. The teacher said, "It is yours."

The rest said, "You didn't really mean it; you didn't really mean to give it to us, did you?"

The teacher said, "Yes."

"Did you really offer it to us?"

"Yes."

"Well," they said, "we didn't believe it; if we had, we would have taken it."

When we offer the gift of Christ, we find people act just that way— "You don't really mean what you say, do you—that we are saved at once; that all we have to do is take it—just to take the gift; just to take Christ and be saved?"

"Oh, yes, I mean that."

"Do you mean that? Well, I don't think we can be saved that way. I don't think a man can be saved that easy." So people go off without the gift.

Now, you can take God's gift before you go out of this house, and it is worth more than all the Christmas gifts that you will get, worth more than all the gifts the world can give. Think of eternal life, a life without end! Think of God offering that! Yet He just comes down and offers it to everyone who will take it. Don't say that you can't take it. God does not offer a man a gift, then not give him the power to take it. That would be an unjust God. But with the gift comes power, and when God commands you to believe on His Son and receive Him as His gift to you, He gives you the power to take Him, and you can take Him if you will. Christ says, "Ye will not come unto me that ye might have life." It is not because men can't come, but because they won't! It is this "will." The battle is fought on that one word—"will." "Ye will not come unto me that ye might have life."

Just Take Him

Now, take Him; as you sit in that pew say, "Lord Jesus, I take Thee as God's gift to me." Paul says, 'He gave him up freely for us all.' God gave Christ to me as much as to Paul. He gave Christ to this reporter as much as to any minister on this platform. He gave Him freely for us all. It is a universal Christ to a universal world. It is Christ offered freely to the whole world, and we have either to receive or to reject.

Now, if a man offered me a gift, I would have to do one of two things: reject the gift or receive it. I couldn't do both, receive and reject it—could I? I must do one of two things. The mind must be brought into play, into action. And I don't see why it doesn't take the same will power to reject Jesus Christ that it does to receive Him. And people who reject Him every day, why are they not bringing the will power to bear on that very thing?

Now, instead of willing tonight that you will not receive Him as God's gift to you, as your Saviour, just will that you will have Him. You say, "What is the first step?" The first step is to make up your mind that you will have Him. "What is the second step?" It is to take Him. Just thank God for sending Jesus Christ to this world. That is a way to spend Christmas—to thank God for sending Christ into the world.

As I got up this morning the first thought that came to my mind was, *O God, I thank Thee for sending Christ into this world.* How it has lit up my little home. How my children are filled with joy that Christ came. And the best thing you can do today is to receive Christ and then thank God for sending Him; and then light, peace and joy will come right into your heart.

You say, "What am I going to do with all the sins I have committed?" The only thing that you have that God does not have is your sins, and the only thing that God wants is your sins and the moment you give them up to Him God will take your sins.

One of the hardest things that men find to do in this life is to become Christians, and yet it is one of the easiest. You say that is a plain contradition. I mean what I say. It is one of the hardest things men have to do to become Christians, and it is one of the easiest things.

A Matter of the Will

A few years ago I was in Chicago. My sister-in-law had a little child—my nephew. One day he took my Bible and threw it upon the floor. His mother said, "Charlie, you go pick up Uncle's Bible." The little two-year-old said, "I won't." His mother looked at him with amazement. "Charlie, where did you learn that naughty word?" No one had to teach him; it sprang up in his heart. You don't have to teach a child those kinds of things.

She thought at first that he didn't know what she meant, but she soon found out that he knew very well. Not only that—but he had made up his mind that he wouldn't pick up the book. Now she said, "Charlie, you will have to pick up that book. If you don't, Mama will punish you." The little fellow looked at her to see if she really meant it. "Yes," she says, "Mama will punish you."

I was interested in the fight. I knew if she didn't break his will, he would break her heart. It was only a question of time. It was her first child, and I wanted to see that young mother conquer that will. I watched the progress of the conflict. Finally he looked at her and when he saw that she was going to punish him, then he got up and looked very serious. When he saw that she was really going to punish him, then he said that he would like to do it but couldn't.

Don't laugh at it, for that is yourself. You say you would like to become a Christian, but you can't.

You can if you will. I don't know why, but the little fellow reasoned himself into the belief that he couldn't pick that book up. Finally he got down and put both arms around the book and this healthy boy said he couldn't lift it. He would like to, but he couldn't lift it, and got up without it.

Finally his mother said, "Charlie, you must pick up that book." It was hard for him to do it, but the moment his will was broken, he bent his back and picked up the book as easily as I could.

When one makes up his mind to come to Christ, it is easy enough then, when you *will* to do it.

Oh, my friends, will to do it tonight. Let this be your last night in this dark world without God and without Christ. Take the gift of God as you take other gifts, and tonight and tomorrow morning as you receive gifts and give them to others, rejoice that you have that gift, the only gift God has—the gift of His Son; a gift as free as the air, an unspeakable gift.

Let us bear in mind that it was all He could do when He gave up Jesus Christ. He gave up the richest jewel Heaven had. He gave liberally all He had. And what an insult for you not to take God's gift. What an insult for you to spurn the gift of God. "God so loved the world that he gave his only begotten Son, that whosoever believeth in him should not perish, but have everlasting life."

T. T. SHIELDS
1873-1955

ABOUT THE MAN:

Dr. Shields was born in Bristol, England, 1873, the son of a Baptist minister.

Converted in his youth.

Received early education in England.

Ordained to the Baptist ministry in 1897.

Held Ontario pastorates in Florence, Delhi, Hamilton and London.

In 1910 was called to Jarvis Street Baptist Church, Toronto.

Elected to the Board of Governors of McMaster University 1920-28.

Received Doctor of Divinity degrees from Temple and McMaster Universities.

Founded *The Gospel Witness*, a weekly magazine, in 1922.

Was author of several books and booklets.

Was president of Baptist Bible Union from 1923-1930.

Founded Toronto Baptist Seminary in 1927.

For many years was president of Union of Regular Baptist Churches of Ontario and Quebec.

In 1948 was elected vice-president of International Council of Christian Churches.

Passed on to be with Christ April 4, 1955.

XI.

A Christmas Message

T. T. SHIELDS

"But when the fulness of the time was come, God sent forth his Son, made of a woman, made under the law, To redeem them that were under the law, that we might receive the adoption of sons. And because ye are sons, God hath sent forth the Spirit of his Son into your hearts, crying, Abba, Father. Wherefore thou art no more a servant, but a son; and if a son, then an heir of God through Christ."—Gal. 4:4-7.

If I were to give you that text alone, surely we should have the sum of the Christmas message. Let me read it again. What God Himself says is far more important than any comment we may make upon it. This is the Word of God:

"But when the fulness of the time was come, God sent forth his Son, made of a woman, made under the law, to redeem them that were under the law, that we might receive the adoption of sons."

I think perhaps there has never been a day when religious life was more superficial than it is today. People are content to dwell upon the surface of things. Perhaps that is especially apparent at this Christmas season.

To great multitudes of people, Christmas means little more than a time for the ringing of bells, the singing of carols and for general merrymaking. It ought to be a time for ringing of bells and singing of carols. Those of us who know the true significance of Christmas ought to be able to make merry in our hearts. Of all seasons of the year, it ought to be an occasion of gladness to the believing soul.

The message of the angels was especially, explicitly said to be for "all people." We all need it. I should like this company this evening to enter into the true spiritual significance of this season.

I read an editorial in one of our evening papers last night. Hall Caine was the principal authority quoted in the discussion of Christmas! We were told that nowhere in the world do the stars shine quite so brightly as in Palestine! It is not difficult to "imagine" anything there! Quite possible to persuade one's self that he can hear heavenly music, not difficult to imagine one is beholding a company of angels! Why not utterly abandon the Christmas story—or else accept it on the basis of the only authority we have for the story, namely, the Bible, the Word of God?

We believe there was a star, that the angel did actually speak to the shepherds and that they did really hear the angelic choir, that when they went to Bethlehem they actually found the Babe "even as it was told them." Let us try to understand something of the significance of that great event.

I. IT OCCURRED "IN THE FULNESS OF THE TIME"

God never works haphazardly. He is the Source and Center of all law and order. He is the greatest of all clockmakers. His clock has never needed repair.

Astronomers tell us they can so accurately predict the movements of the heavenly bodies as to be able to tell the exact second at which an eclipse of the sun or moon will take place, a hundred years in advance, so regular, undeviating, are the courses of the stars.

God does not change. There was a time appointed for this great event. There was a time ordained from the foundation of the world. Let it ever be remembered that the scheme of redemption was not a divine afterthought. It was not some method of repair originating in the divine mind after the great catastrophe effected by the advent of sin. "Known unto God are all his works from the beginning of the world." Therefore the precise time of the coming of Messiah was predetermined from the very beginning. The time to which reference here is made was a time which prophetically was foretold: all the prophets spoke of One who should come. His coming was no accident, and every prophet spoke of the coming of Messiah, even to the very day.

I read to you tonight of what should take place until a certain time appointed had been accomplished. God is never in a hurry: He is never behind His time. He is never surprised by the machinations of men or of devils. He knows the end from the beginning. The Old Testament predicted the coming of the One whose birth we celebrate. He did not come a moment before the time that was determined: He arrived exactly as the prophets had said He would arrive.

How we ought to be comforted—turning aside from the specific subject for a moment—by such a reflection, that we worship a God of order and of infinite resource, who is not only able to make His plans but to make them effectual! He speaks with His mouth, as David said, and performs with His hand. Not one word of anything that God has spoken shall fall to the ground. How it ought to inspire us with confidence in the dependability of the Word of God! How we ought to rely upon it!

At the time of the siege of Jerusalem in the days of Hezekiah—he was the human medium through whom God spoke to the people; he told them what God would do—the record says that "the people rested themselves upon the words of Hezekiah king of Judah."

I lean upon this pulpit; I stand with confidence upon this platform. We sit in this building without disquietude of any sort. You do not fear that the roof will fall in or that the floor will open beneath you, that the seat upon which you sit will collapse under you. With perfect composure you rest.

But the Word of the Lord is more enduring than any material substance. It is a record of God's dealings with His human creatures from the beginning until now, written by inspiration for the confirmation of our faith. God, having never failed His people yet, will not fail them in the future.

Just as surely as the Lord Jesus came the first time—when "the fulness of the time was come," and every prophecy which predicted His coming was fulfilled—so every word which tells of His coming again may be relied upon with the same stedfast faith. As He came once, He will come again. "For verily I say unto you, Till heaven and earth pass, one jot or one tittle shall in no wise pass from the law, till all be fulfilled."

Christmas ought to be a time of settlement and establishment in the faith, to believers. We celebrate another anniversary of the divine faithfulness manifested in the fulfillment of His Word. "The fulness of the time" marked the fulfillment of those principles and precepts which were symbolically set forth; for we have not only a plain and specific, an unmistakable prophetic Word, but there were symbolic teachings in the Old Testament.

As for example, the offering of the passover lamb and all the subsequent dealings of God with His ancient people. It is said in the Book,

"Now all these things happened unto them for ensamples [types]: and they are written for our admonition, upon whom the ends of the world are come."

You remember how the Lord Jesus, born in Bethlehem, fulfilled throughout His earthly career all that was predicted, dying at the exact hour of the offering of the Passover and fulfilling to the letter, as well as in the spirit, all that had been written respecting the sufferings of Christ: "When the fulness of the time was come."

Write it down in your hearts, cherish it in your memory, that our covenant-keeping God never faileth. Time is an element in this contract. You will find in any contract you make, you promise to do a certain thing, not at any time, but at a particular time; and God thus fulfilled His Word to a waiting world.

II. WHAT DID GOD DO?

He "sent forth his Son." Let us settle it in our minds that the life of the Babe in Bethlehem did not begin there. The Child that the Wise Men worshiped was the Ancient of Days. In fact, as I said to you, I know not how long ago, the Jehovah of the Old Testament is the Jesus of the New. God has never spoken to men at any time, in any dispensation, save through His Son. All the communications of God in the Old Testament are just as truly divine communications given to men through the second Person of the Trinity as is the full-orbed revelation of grace in the New Testament.

How blind they are who would put a difference between the Old and New Testaments, as though we were dealing with one God in one and with another in the other. The Babe of Bethlehem was none other than the Son of God, Immanuel, God with us.

We know nothing at all of Christmas until we have learned that the birth of Mary's Child was the advent to this earth in visible human form of the Creator and Preserver of it. "All things were made by him; and without him was not any thing made that was made."

Of whom is that said? Of the Word which was in the beginning with God, which was God and which was "made flesh, and dwelt among us." We shall never understand the Lord Jesus if we fail to keep clearly in mind that He is from everlasting to everlasting God. He was as we read this evening, from old, from everlasting, "Without father, without mother, without descent, having neither beginning of days, nor end of life," the Son of God and God the Son.

Some of you sent Christmas cards to your friends or commissioned someone to carry a gift of some sort to a friend; you left an order at the store or sent someone with it.

Not so did God the first Christmas morning. He did send angels, but only to herald His coming; for God was "in Christ." He came Himself to this world for its everlasting enrichment. With hands full of blessing He came. "God sent forth his Son" into the world. Have nothing to do with men who say He was anything other than the Son of God and God the Son.

I passed a church this morning that is dedicated to the proposition that Jesus Christ was not God, a church that exists to deny His Deity but to admire and praise His humanity. I saw a little group of people coming out and remarked as I passed, *Poor souls! I wonder what they have to say this Christmas morning.*

Who was He who came to Bethlehem? An ordinary child? Or merely an extraordinary human being, a genius, a kind of super-man but not the God-man? They have no Christmas who so regard Him. That is the fundamental message of Christmas, that God "sent forth his Son." None other. And "when he bringeth in the first-begotten into the world, he saith, And let all the angels of God worship him."

III. HOW DID HE COME?

He was "made of a woman." "He took not on him the nature of angels; but he took on him the seed of Abraham." He became bone of our bone and flesh of our flesh, our fellow, one with us in nature. He clothed Himself with our human nature. He became incarnate. God wrapped Himself with human flesh, made Himself visible, "made of a woman."

Again, it was so predicted. As I read that passage this evening, perhaps some of you may have said in your minds, *That is rather a strange Scripture for a Christmas day, a Scripture which describes One who is mighty, One who will destroy certain things and triumph over all evil.*

I am glad that, wrapped up in this Scripture, is the promise that we need at this hour; for it was said that the Seed of the woman shall bruise the serpent's head. There is enough of the serpent manifest in this old world today. His slimy trail, his fatal hiss, the venom of his fangs, are everywhere apparent; and who is equal to the task of dispossessing him, of bruising his head and at last destroying him and casting him into the abyss? None other than He who was "made of a woman."

Born as the "gentle Jesus," I know. "Meek and lowly in heart," it is true. And yet the irresistible Conqueror, the Mighty One against whose strength and prowess even all the forces of darkness are helpless. He was "made of a woman."

Further, *the miracle of the Incarnation is here set forth,* namely, that Jesus Christ had a human mother but no human father. Begotten of the Holy Ghost, the God-man; a union of Deity with humanity. That is the miracle of Christmas.

I know there are those who deny it, but the same record which tells of His coming tells us of the manner of His coming. The angel said, "The Holy Ghost shall come upon thee, and the power of the Highest shall overshadow thee: therefore also that holy thing which shall be born of thee shall be called the Son of God." He was "made of a woman"; and He has magnified and glorified womanhood and childhood by His coming.

Hold fast to the truth of the virgin birth of Christ. I count it part of my duty always to warn people against error. There may be much of truth mixed up with the most fatal error. The Gospel may be so diluted as to be robbed of its power; and sometimes so polluted, corrupted as to have poison at its heart, notwithstanding certain elements of truth.

Let us be on our guard. There are certain plain principles which will help us always to distinguish between the precious and the vile. My counsel to you is that if ever you hear any man cast doubt even upon the truth of the virgin birth of Christ—much more if you hear anyone positively deny it—you cannot safely expose your soul to the influence of that teaching. To deny the miracle of the virgin birth—the truth enshrined in these four words—is to deny that which is fundamental to the whole Christian revelation. You had better give such teachers a wide berth.

IV. "MADE UNDER THE LAW"

He had to enter into human life, amid conditions similar to those under which His creatures lived. He subjected Himself to all the limitations of our human flesh. He was tired; He was hungry; He was thirsty; He needed sleep. His was a perfect human nature.

By that miracle of the virgin birth, human nature was lifted up to the divine; and it became possible for human nature to be joined to the divine. He was "holy, harmless, undefiled, separate from sinners, and made higher than the heavens." Notwithstanding, He was "made under the law"; subject to the requirements of the moral law of God.

You remember how beautifully He exemplified that perfect obedience which the holy law of God required when but twelve years of age. Missed by Mary and Joseph for some time, He was found in the Temple talking with the doctors of the law, asking them questions and hearing questions from them. When Mary gently rebuked Him, He said, "How is it that ye sought me? wist ye not that I must be about my Father's business?"

At twelve years of age He recognized His obligation to the first requirement of the law, to love God supremely, with all His heart and soul and mind and strength. He put God first, even before Mary His mother. Then He went down to Nazareth and "was subject unto them," to His mother and His reputed father. "Honour thy father and thy mother: that thy days may be long upon the land which the Lord thy God giveth thee."

The first of the second table of the law found its complete obedience in the person of the Child Jesus. Made under the law, He loved God with all His heart, and His neighbor as Himself; thus He wrought out for us a righteousness.

I fear that evangelical Christianity fails often properly to emphasize the vicariousness of the righteousness of Christ as well as the substitutionary character of His death. Jesus Christ was "made under the law." He was our Fellow, our Representative, the second Adam; and by His perfect obedience to the law, He wrought out a flawless righteousness which He might impute to those who believe. But Jesus lived vicariously just as truly as He died vicariously, in order that He might be "touched with the feeling of our infirmities." Tempted in all points, yet without sin. He was "made of a woman, made under the law."

V. AND HE WAS SO MADE THAT HE MIGHT "REDEEM THEM THAT WERE UNDER THE LAW"

He came to be a Redeemer to redeem an alienated province of the universal kingdom of God, an alienated world, a sinful earth, a lost inheritance; for Adam and all his seed had forfeited their right to the divine favor—and the whole earth was corrupted for their sake.

I know our evolutionary friends—I mean those who hold to the greatest of all delusions that ever afflicted the human mind, the evolutionary hypothesis—I say, they would be disposed to question that scriptural doctrine. But I cannot understand how any man in his senses can, in the face of the present world situation, doubt the saying of Scripture that "the whole creation groaneth and travaileth in pain together until now." Surely some kind of curse has fallen upon this world of men—not only upon the earth, but upon the inhabitants thereof.

Jesus Christ came to be a Redeemer, to "redeem them that were under the law." He could only redeem them by fulfilling the requirements of the law; to put it plainly, by paying the penalty of the law. Only thus could He redeem us and our forfeited inheritance. But He came just to do that.

Did He come only to let us hear the angels sing? To teach us to ring the bells at Christmas—and sometimes to find a good deal of difficulty in ringing them? I declare to you that it is very difficult for me to be merry this Christmastime if I take the large view and look out upon this sinful world. When I think of the bondage of those who live in Russia, the serfdom of those who were trodden under the heel of Hitler, the experience of those who trembled under the shadow of Mussolini, the unspeakable atrocities committed in Spain and the appalling blindness of our own people—and I must say it, the utterly wicked, yes, the shameful compact of Munich, surely it proves beyond peradventure that the whole earth lieth in the wicked one and that it is not in vain that the Bible says the Devil is "the god of this world."

Millions of men died in the World War, died, as they supposed, for the maintenance of the world's liberties. They might just as well have stayed at home, for Mr. Chamberlain handed over to Hitler, without his having to fire a shot, far more than the Kaiser ever asked. After twenty years of unspeakable sorrow and suffering, the loss of a generation of millions of men in all nations, we came back to conditions far worse than that which prevailed before the Great War. What blindness, what fatal blindness, has come upon the world's statesmen?

I remember that one Sunday during the Great War, I announced as my subject, "Does 'Killed in Action' Mean Gone to Heaven?"; and one of my deacons—for there were some of them who presumed to be kindly censors—came to me in fear and trembling and said, "Pastor, I am awfully afraid of that subject. People are very sensitive." I replied, "I do not care. I shall proclaim the Gospel of the grace of God."

One Saturday I was called on the telephone and told that a certain distinguished man was in town, that he had a great message, and was asked if I would like to have him preach for me Sunday morning. I said, "I know him personally, and he is a great man; but are you sure he has a great message?" "Yes, he has a great message."

He stood in my pulpit, in Jarvis Street Church, and said, "I will take my chances with the eternal salvation of any man who dies for his country." He preached salvation by the supreme sacrifice. He was my guest, but I rose afterward and said, "There was one great Sacrifice which has made the sacrifice of all other bloods superfluous. I want to disassociate myself entirely from the doctrine preached by this distinguished gentleman this morning and to say I do not believe a word of it. We shall sing for our closing hymn, ' There is a Fountain filled with blood.' I did not like to do it, but was compelled.

Tell me that the blood of the Great War redeemed this earth? No! The blood of millions was not of sufficient value. But there was One who came "to redeem them that were under the law," in whom "are hid all the treasures of wisdom and knowledge." If I may dare to say so, one drop of His precious blood had more merit in it, more redeeming power, than the blood of all the millions who ever died. He died, this Child of Christmas! He came, not for an easy life, but to suffer, and at last to die. He counted down the ruby drops. He paid the price of the world's redemption. He not only redeemed every individual who will believe on Him, but He died for the redemption of the whole world.

God is not going to be driven out of this earth.

"I saw a new heaven and a new earth: for the first heaven and the first earth were passed away; and there was no more sea. And I John saw the holy city, new Jerusalem, coming down from God out of heaven, prepared as a bride adorned for her husband."

This earth is to be redeemed, and we who believe on the Lord Jesus, who were under the law, have been redeemed by His precious blood. I trust you can sing it:

> **Dear dying Lamb! Thy precious blood**
> **Shall never lose its power,**
> **Till all the ransomed church of God**
> **Be saved to sin no more.**

"To redeem them that were under the law." He paid the penalty.

We read in the paper sometimes of a man who has got into trouble—very often, in fact. And the first thing the authorities do is to take his fingerprints to find out whether he has been in trouble before, whether he has a record with the police.

We all have a record, but God does not need a fingerprint bureau. He made our fingers! He can read our hearts. "All things are naked and opened unto the eyes of him with whom we have to do." He can find people. Often have I known Him to find a wandering boy or a wayward girl, when all the detective agencies combined could not find them.

He came "to redeem them that were under the law." And what a record! Do you not wish you could blot it out? Do we not all wish we could blot out some things? This great Redeemer blots out the handwriting of ordinances that was against us, "which was contrary to us, and took it out of the way, nailing it to his cross; and, having spoiled principalities and powers, he made a show of them openly, triumphing over them in it."

He took the record of your sinful life and put it on file where His precious blood was shed—it is a figure of speech, I know—blotting it out, redeeming you—

VI. WHAT FOR?

"That we might receive the adoption of sons." "God sent forth his Son"—what for? That He might have many sons. "For it became him, for whom are all things, and by whom are all things, in bringing many sons unto glory, to make the captain of their salvation perfect through sufferings."

He did not come to give a little Christmas present: He came to redeem you, to make you a child of God, a member of the divine family. He came to lift us up to His own level, making us, by a new birth, to be partakers of His nature; even as by His miraculous birth into this world He became partaker of ours. Deity stooped to humanity, to lift humanity up to Deity.

Then He put the Spirit of adoption into our hearts so that we might cry, "Abba, Father." "After this manner therefore pray ye: Our Father which art in heaven." "Wherefore thou art no more a servant, but a son; and if a son, then an heir of God through Christ." That is the meaning of Christmas.

A CHRISTMAS MESSAGE

Someday we are going Home for Christmas.

I remember when I was away from home in my early manhood how I longed to be home for Christmas. I am old enough now not to be ashamed of it, but I lived in a town through which the railroad ran; and as Christmas drew near, I used to go out and stand on the tracks and look up those two converging lines of steel, knowing that they reached toward home. I envied every inch of steel in the railroad—I wanted to go home.

We used to have a great time at home during Christmas. We do not anymore. That home has long since passed away. Father and Mother have gone.

But someday we are going to have a great Christmas gathering. Our Heavenly Father will see to it that all His children come Home.

What presents we shall have then! He is good to us now. He gives us a great deal to go on with, but someday when the family are gathered Home and when "unsearchable riches" are spread out to our wondering view, then we shall understand the meaning of Christmas. Then we shall know why Jesus Christ came into the world.

May you all know this evening, ere you leave this place, that you have been born again. Believe the truth, receive Christ, be made a child and heir—and who knows, perhaps by this time next year some of us—almost certainly some of us will be in Heaven. But it will make no difference. Some will go first, and the rest by and by.

Late in the evening, I wish you a Merry Christmas. The only kind of Merry Christmas that can be lasting, and that fadeth not away—that merriment which springs from a consciousness that all is well between the soul and God, that we are children of God and heirs of glory.

THOMAS L. MALONE
1915-

ABOUT THE MAN:

Tom Malone was converted and called to preach at the same moment! At an old-fashioned bench, the preacher took his tear-stained Bible and showed Tom Malone how to be saved. He accepted Christ then and there. Arising from his knees in the Isbell Methodist Church near Russellville, Alabama, he shook the circuit pastor's hand; and this bashful nineteen-year-old farm boy announced: "I know the Lord wants me to be a preacher."

Backward, bashful and broke, yet Tom borrowed five dollars, took what he could in a cardboard suitcase and left for Cleveland, Tennessee. Immediately upon arrival at Bob Jones College, Malone heard a truth that totally dominated his life and labors for the Lord ever after—soul winning!

That day he won his first soul! The green-as-grass Tom, a new convert himself, knew nothing of soul-winning approaches or techniques. He simply asked the sinner, "Are you a Christian?" No. In a few minutes that young man became Malone's first convert.

Since that day, countless have been his experiences in personal evangelism.

Mark it down: Malone began soul winning his first week in Bible college. And he has never lost *the thirst* for it, *the thrill* in it, nor *the task* of it since. Pastoring churches, administrating schools, preaching across the nation have not deterred Tom Malone from this mainline ministry.

It is doubtful if young Malone ever dreamed of becoming the man he is today. He is now Doctor Tom Malone, is renowned in fundamental circles for his wise leadership and great preaching, is pastor of the large Emmanuel Baptist Church of Pontiac, Michigan, Founder and President of Midwestern Baptist Schools, and is eagerly sought as speaker in large Bible conferences from coast to coast.

Dr. John R. Rice often said that Dr. Tom Malone may be the greatest gospel preacher in all the world today!

XII.

The Infinite Christ

TOM MALONE

"For unto us a child is born, unto us a son is given: and the government shall be upon his shoulder: and his name shall be called Wonderful, Counsellor, The mighty God, The everlasting Father, The Prince of Peace."—Isa. 9:6.

How much we could say about the whole book of Isaiah, a book that has sixty-six chapters! It has many times been called the "Gospel of Isaiah" because, as in all parts of the Bible, Jesus is the theme. Someone has said that Isaiah is a miniature Bible, as the Bible also has sixty-six books. It was written seven hundred years before Christ was born in Bethlehem.

This book prophesies so much about the ministry of the Lord Jesus Christ! Our text has to do with His incarnation, with His coming. It has to do with Christmas, the coming of Christ into the world, born of a virgin, the incarnation of the Son of God. Now Jesus was born in a manger. He died on a cross, and had no room to lay His head during those thirty-three years between. This verse speaks of the condescension of Jesus Christ.

One of the most wonderful things about the Bible to me is the prophetical part. Someone has said that three-fourths of the Bible is prophetical. It could easily be true. Stop and think for a moment how much of the Old Testament contains prophecy which has already been fulfilled. Think of the Old Testament prophecies that have to do with Israel as a nation which have already, hundreds and hundreds of years ago, been fulfilled. If three-fourths of the Bible is prophetical, there is little of it actually left to be fulfilled, mainly—the second coming of our Lord Jesus Christ.

I have heard people deny that this Bible is a miracle Book, an inspired Book. There are lots of proofs about the inspiration of the Bible, but I will just name one. We mention them often as we preach from the pulpit.

Suppose we put a target back on that back wall in this room. Suppose we pick ten men and women from this audience who have no experience whatsoever in marksmanship with a bow and arrow. We tell each one that we want him to shoot an arrow in the heart of the target some eighty yards away. To complicate it even more, we turn out all the lights so that these ten people will be in utter darkness when they let the arrow go from the bow.

We hear the arrows fly through the air. We turn the lights on, and back yonder in that target are ten quivering arrows right in the very heart of the bull's-eye on the back wall!

Everyone in this room says, "That's a miracle. That's extraordinary. That's unusual." Every one of us says, "There must have been some miraculous power, some guiding hand, or that would not have been possible."

Think of all the hundreds of prophecies in the Word of God, and, my friend, not one of them has ever gone astray. Like the Bible says, every one has her mate. Every prophetical utterance has its fulfillment. Anyone must admit that in back of all of this is a Mastermind, a Guiding Hand, or it could not be possible.

If I had no further proof of the inspiration of the Bible than its prophetical utterances, this history pre-written, I would be satisfied. You explain how that even the course of the age in which we live was declared hundreds of years beforehand.

So this is a prophetical verse. It points forward to the coming of Christ and His incarnation.

1. MICAH 5:2 tells us where He would be born.
2. ISAIAH 7:14 tells us how He would be born.
3. HOSEA 11:1 tells us how He would flee into Egypt.
4. ISAIAH 7:14 tells us what His name would be.

Now, the incarnation of Christ—deity being confined within the body of a little baby—is the greatest mystery of all mysteries. Let us read: "And without controversy great is the mystery of godliness: God was manifest in the flesh..." (I Tim. 3:16). That is what took place in the womb of the Virgin Mary when Christ was born. "And the Word was made flesh, and dwelt among us, (and we beheld his glory, the glory as of the only begotten of the Father,) full of grace and truth" (John 1:14).

A child is born—that speaks of His humanity; a Son is given—that speaks of His deity.

THE CHRIST OF CHRISTMAS

**Five names were given Jesus Christ
Long centuries before
He came down from His throne above
To open Heaven's door.
Isaiah calls Him "Wonderful,"
How well this prophet knew
His person and the works of love
That He on earth would do.
And next He calls Him "Counsellor."
Ah, this He is indeed!
And, oh, how blest we are today
When we His counsel heed.
"The mighty God," yes, He alone
Has conquered death and sin,
And faith in His atoning blood
Will Heaven for us win.
"The everlasting Father"—this
May seem a little odd—
But with the Father Christ is one,
Redeemer, and true God.
"The Prince of Peace," how true this is,
The angels knew it, too.
He brought a heavenly peace when He
Was born for me and you.
May we remember these five names
And never once forget!
The Saviour who was thus portrayed
Is here among us yet.**

—Marie C. Turk

Notice these four truths tonight.

I. HE IS THE WONDERFUL COUNSELLOR

He is the Wonderful Counsellor, which means He is infinite in wisdom.

The Lord Jesus Christ is omniscient, that is, He is all-knowing. He knows everything. That is what this verse is talking about. He is the Wonderful Counsellor. He is infinite in wisdom. In Matthew 13:54, there was a question asked, a good question. They listened to Jesus speak. They heard Him explain the mysteries of life. He spoke of the future.

He spoke of death. He spoke of eternity. He made it all clear; then they asked this question, "Whence hath this man this wisdom, and these mighty works?"

I'll tell you why. He is the all-knowing God. My friend, you are dealing with a Saviour of infinite wisdom. He knows every heartbeat. He knows every thought. He knows every sin. He knows every step you take. He knows your tomorrow—something you don't know. You do not know whether you will leave this building alive tonight, but Jesus knows. He knows the date of your departure from this earth. He knows the date that will be on your tombstone. He is infinite in wisdom.

Speaking of the Queen of Sheba, Jesus said, ". . . for she came from the uttermost parts of the earth to hear the wisdom of Solomon; and, behold, a greater than Solomon is here" (Matt. 12:42). Solomon knew 3,500 proverbs and 1,500 songs. He had sayings of wisdom by the scores. But Jesus said, ". . . a greater than Solomon is here"—One who is wiser by far than Solomon ever was! We read again in Luke 2:40, "And the child grew, and waxed strong in spirit, filled with wisdom: and the grace of God was upon him."

Friend, Jesus knows you tonight. He knows whether you are saved or lost. He knows whether you are on your way to Hell. He knows all about you. There is not one thing about you and me right now that the Son of God does not already know.

I have always been so glad that the Lord, being infinite in wisdom, could impart wisdom to His own. That is what I Corinthians 1:30 teaches us: "But of him are ye in Christ Jesus, who of God is made unto us wisdom, and righteousness, and sanctification, and redemption."

There are two verses that I claim from the Bible. One is James 1:5, "If any of you lack wisdom, let him ask of God, that giveth to all men liberally, and upbraideth not; and it shall be given him." You know, our Saviour, who is infinite in wisdom, gives leadership, direction and guidance to the lives of those who belong to Him.

It is like the man who came home after a storm. He must walk across a bridge high over a deep chasm. He walked safely across the bridge that night, to his home. It is said that the day after the storm, when he came back to view the damage, he saw how the bridge had been almost entirely destroyed, with the exception of a narrow little path. But in the darkness that night he had walked safely across. Standing now in the light, he said, "Thank God for the guiding hand of Christ in the darkness last night!"

THE INFINITE CHRIST

My friend, I don't care who you are or what you have, if in your life you have not the guiding hand of the Son of God, you are lost. You need the guidance of Christ, the wisdom He can give to lead you out of darkness into light.

I heard a story one time, which comes to mind when I think of the guidance of God, the wisdom of the Lord imparted to those who belong to Him. An awful fog had gripped the city of London, England, known for its fog. It is said that one night, groping along the streets, a man stumbled over another. He begged his pardon and said, "I'm lost. I cannot find my way."

The man over whom he stumbled said, "Where do you live?"

He gave him a number and a street.

The man said, "I will guide you there."

He reached and took his hand on that dark and foggy night. He led him along the streets and without missing a step, took him to his home.

When they got there and after the man had thanked him, he said, "I don't know how you do it."

The man said, "Sir, I'm blind. I have no sight at all. But I have had to learn my way along these streets."

I am saying to you now, there is One who knows the way through life, and that is Christ. I say to you now, there will come mysteries, riddles, questions in life for which there is no answer, unless it comes from the Son of God. He is infinite in wisdom. He is the Wonderful Counsellor.

"For unto us a child is born, unto us a son is given: and the government shall be upon his shoulder: and his name shall be called Wonderful, Counsellor, The mighty God, The everlasting Father, The Prince of Peace." —Isa. 9:6.

II. HE IS THE MIGHTY GOD

In the second place, He is infinite in power, for it says He is the mighty God. Oh, think of it! Sweet little baby lying in that manger and to all those who observed with uninstructed minds, He was like any other baby. The mother that night sat and watched over Baby Jesus. But think! He is the mighty God! That little baby a span long, out there in the cattle's stall that night, was Almighty God!

The most foolish thing that anyone ever believed is that the birth in Bethlehem's manger was the beginning of Jesus Christ. Why, He just changed addresses for thirty-three years. He was in the beginning. The Bible says, "All things were made by him; and without him was not any thing made that was made" (John 1:3). There He is—a little Baby in a manger. "The mighty God" means that He is infinite in power.

Oh, what we could say right now about the power of Christ! Romans 1:4 says, "And declared to be the Son of God with power, according to the spirit of holiness, by the resurrection from the dead."

Paul says in Philippians 3:10, "That I may know him, and the power of his resurrection, and the fellowship of his sufferings, being made conformable unto his death."

His words even have power.

Think of Jesus walking along, speaking to the diseased. They were made well.

He walked along and spoke to demons. They had to flee.

He came to where the dead were and spoke to them. They came back to life.

His presence has power. I thank God for His presence in this church. I thank God for His presence in my life and in yours.

The presence of Christ means power. That is what Paul is talking about in Ephesians 1:19,20:

"And what is the exceeding greatness of his power to us-ward who believe, according to the working of his mighty power, Which he wrought in Christ, when he raised him from the dead, and set him at his own right hand in the heavenly places."

The mighty God is infinite in power.

III. HE IS THE EVERLASTING FATHER

Our text tonight says He is the everlasting Father. That means that He is infinite in love. *"Father"* is the term of relationship. And there is only one way that that can come to you and that is to be born in a man's family. And "The everlasting Father" means that He is infinite in love. Aren't you glad tonight that you can look up toward God and say, "My Father," through Jesus Christ the Lord? He is the everlasting Father, infinite in love.

IV. HE IS THE PRINCE OF PEACE

Now in the last place, He is the Prince of Peace. That means that He is infinite in redemption.

When He was born that night the angels said, "Glory to God in the highest, and on earth peace, good will toward men" (Luke 2:14).

He is the Prince of Peace. And that is why we can have peace when He is in our lives. "Therefore being justified by faith, we have peace with God through our Lord Jesus Christ."

When I heard a missionary tell one of the sweetest, most wonderful stories of the redeeming grace of Jesus, I was moved to tears of joy. He said that he had been working among the lepers (the most pitiful people I have ever seen. That Bible disease is typical of the disease of sin. Facial features eaten away, the nose and ears gone, maybe part of the mouth, facial features twisted almost beyond the look of a human being. Instead of hands with fingers, just little stubs of their hands. I have seen them with their feet almost gone, with just little stubs left to walk on like a cripple.)

This missionary said that one of the greatest blessings he ever had was when one of these poor lepers came to the leprosarium where he was working. Not only was his body eaten almost away, but his soul was in darkness and in sin. He came for physical help. The missionaries told this untouchable about One who loved him. Because he was untouchable, when he came to the public well, he couldn't drink. When people approached him, he had to put his hand to his mouth and cry, "Unclean! Unclean!" He could not sleep on the same bed with his dearest loved ones, could not eat with them.

But the missionary said, "We know One who will touch you. He is Jesus. He loves you."

This missionary told of this poor leper who got saved and the leprosy was arrested. While he was getting ready to come home on furlough, the missionary heard this leper singing in his native tongue: "There's a land that is fairer than day. . . ." That is the hope that Christ had put in his life.

My friend, that's what the Prince of Peace can do for all. He is infinite in redemption, because He is the Prince of Peace.

"For unto us a child is born, unto us a son is given: and the government shall be upon his shoulder: and his name shall be called Wonderful, Counsellor, The mighty God, The everlasting Father, The Prince of Peace." —Isa. 9:6.

THE PRINCE OF PEACE

To us a Child of hope is born,
To us a Son is given;
Him shall the tribes of earth obey,
Him, all the host of Heaven.

His name shall be the Prince of Peace,
Forevermore adored;
The Wonderful, the Counsellor,
The great and mighty Lord.

His power, increasing, still shall spread;
His reign no end shall know;
Justice shall guard His throne above,
And peace abound below.

To us a Child of hope is born,
To us a Son is given;
The Wonderful, the Counsellor,
The mighty Lord of Heaven.

—Author Unknown

WILLIAM SUNDAY
1862-1935

ABOUT THE MAN:

William Ashley (Billy) Sunday was converted from pro baseball to Christ at twenty-three but carried his athletic ability into the pulpit.

Born in Ames, Iowa, he lost his father to the Civil War and lived with his grandparents until age nine when he was taken to live in an orphanage. A life of hard work paid off in athletic prowess that brought him a contract with the Chicago White Stockings in 1883. His early success in baseball was diluted by strong drink; however, in 1886 he was converted at the Pacific Garden Mission in Chicago and became actively involved in Christian work.

Sunday held some three hundred crusades in thirty-nine years. It is estimated that a hundred million heard him speak in great tabernacles, and more than a quarter million people made a profession of faith in Christ as Saviour under his preaching. His long-time associate, Dr. Homer Rodeheaver, called him "the greatest gospel preacher since the Apostle Paul."

Billy Sunday was one of the most unusual evangelists of his day. He walked, ran, or jumped across the platform as he preached, sometimes breaking chairs. His controversial style brought criticism but won the admiration of millions. He attacked public evils, particularly the liquor industry, and was considered the most influential person in bringing about the prohibition legislation after World War I.

Many long remembered his famous quote: "I'm against sin. I'll kick it as long as I've got a foot, and I'll fight it as long as I've got a fist. I'll butt it as long as I've got a head. I'll bite it as long as I've got a tooth. And when I'm old and fistless and footless and toothless, I'll gum it till I go home to Glory and it goes home to perdition!"

Those who heard him never forgot him or his blazing, barehanded evangelism.

The evangelist died November 6, 1935, at age 72. His funeral was held in Moody Church, Chicago, the sermon by H. A. Ironside.

XIII.

"Wonderful"!

BILLY SUNDAY

". . . . And his name shall be called Wonderful, Counsellor, The mighty God, The everlasting Father, The Prince of Peace." —Isa. 9:6.

In olden times a name meant something, and that is still the case with the Indians. Kill Deer, Eagle Eye, Buffalo Face, Sitting Bull, Sleepy Eye, Blackhawk, Red Cloud, Rain-in-Face are all names that tell something of the facial expressions and characteristics of the Indians. This habit of using names expressive of some tendency of an individual crops out in the mining, military and lumber camps, in colleges, among baseball players and in every field of sport. Most nicknames indicate some peculiarity or trait of character and frequently are more nearly right than the given names.

All family names have their origin in something and in olden times meant something. All Bible names have a meaning. There are 256 names given to Jesus. He was infinitely more than any one name could express; and of the many names, I propose to consider this one: "His name shall be called Wonderful."

Let us look and see if He is true to the name given Him by the prophet Isaiah eight hundred years before He was born.

Wonderful—that is something transcendently above the common.

Wonderful—that is something away above the ordinary.

Wonderful—that is something in a class by itself.

The Yellowstone Park, Niagara Falls, the Grand Canyon, the Statue of David, the Taj Mahal—all are wonderful.

David killing Goliath the way he did was wonderful.

When the Red Sea opened for the children of Israel and they crossed over on dry land, it was wonderful.

The sun standing still for Joshua was wonderful.

Let us see if Jesus is true to that name.

Jesus Wonderful in His Birth

Two thousand years ago a star poised above a lowly manger in Bethlehem. The shepherds watched their flocks on the plains. Rome then ruled the world. Italy, Spain and Greece held the human culture of the then known world. France and England were barbarian. America was nothing but an unknown wilderness.

When Christ was born, His birth was greeted by angels, singing, "Glory to God in the highest, and on earth peace, good will toward men."

Today Rome is a memory, while the manger of Bethlehem is exalted in the thoughts and affections of the world far above the lofty place once held by the occupants of the throne of the Caesars.

The birth, character and life of Christ were all wonderful. His birth was wonderful; no other ever occurred like it. He had only one human parent. He inherited the nature of God and of man. He came to be the Prince of princes and the King of kings.

The birth of Christ was not looked forward to with glad expectation. There was no room for Him at the inn. He was born in a manger, yet the angels proclaimed His birth with joy and aroused the sleeping shepherds who guarded their flocks.

Mark how He might have come—in all the pomp and glory of the upper world. It would have been a condescension had He been born in a palace and rocked in a golden cradle with angels for nurses; yet He gave up all that glory, was born of a poor woman and cradled in a manger.

Think what He came to do! To bless, not to curse; to lift up, not to drag anyone down; to save drunkards, thieves, blasphemers; to dry the tears, bind up the wounds; to give rest for the weary; and yet there was no room for Him at the inn.

The Wise Men led by His star soon made His birth known, and the king sought His life. The babies were the first martyrs.

Wonderful Character

His character was wonderful. No other ever approached it in its perfection. It was wonderful that the greatest character in all history came from such obscurity and became the most famous. It was wonderful that at such a time and in such a country such a people could produce Jesus.

It can be accounted for on no other ground than that of His deity.

When a famous man was asked what impressed him most during his trip to the Holy Land, he immediately replied, "Nazareth; for such a people could not have produced Jesus except for His deity."

His life was wonderful in its sinlessness, usefulness and unselfishness. His enemies could bring no greater charge than,

(1) He claimed God as His Father;
(2) He received sinners and ate with them;
(3) He let a sinful woman come near enough to touch Him;
(4) He would do good on the Sabbath day.

There was no evidence of selfishness or self-interest. He was always helping others; He never did anything to help Himself. Jesus had the power to turn stones into bread, yet He fasted forty days. While escaping from His enemies, He saw a blind man and, at the risk of His own life, stopped and opened the eyes of the man. He never sought His own; He lived only for others.

The first miracle was not performed before a great multitude, but to save a peasant's wife embarrassment. He had compassion on the multitudes. He wept over Jerusalem. His teaching was wonderful in its simplicity, clearness and adaptation to the individual. He never sought the multitudes; He never avoided an individual.

We read that "the common people heard him gladly." He put the jam and the cookies on the lower shelf. No one needed to lug an unabridged dictionary along to find out what He meant. He illustrated His thoughts and made plain His teachings in wonderful word pictures. "Without a parable spake he not unto them." He made people see things clearly.

This wonderful Galilean peasant never taught school, yet the pedagogy of today is modeling after the pattern Jesus gave.

His originality is proof of His deity. Human mind cannot create absolutely, but must build out of the material already created, such as lumber, wool, cotton, hides, steel. There is no such thing as out-and-out originality. We cannot imagine anything that does not resemble something we have seen. Everything is the outgrowth of something else.

The first railway cars looked like the old stage coaches; the first automobiles, like carriages.

No one ever made a book unlike all other books.

The stories on the Dutch and Irish are older than the Dutch and Irish nations. There are stories in early literature like them; but you cannot find stories in any literature that even resemble the parables of Jesus. The parables of the Good Samaritan, the Prodigal Son and the Ten Virgins are new. They proclaim Him divine. He could create.

His teachings were wonderful in what He taught and the way in which He taught. He said He was greater than Moses. Think of His audacity in making that claim to a crowd of Jews! He declared He fulfilled the law of Moses and the prophets. The only effort He ever made to prove His claims was to point to His works. The first thing an impostor does is to over-prove his case. Jesus never turned His hand to convince His enemies. You've got to explain the oil in a lamp, but not the sun nor spring.

Jesus taught that all who did not believe on Him as the Son of God were lost. There never was a saved person who did not get salvation from Jesus. Some try to save themselves by culture, by philanthropy and by charity. You find me the place on earth the nearest like Heaven, and I'll find men and women who are followers of Christ. You find me a place nearest like Hell, and I'll find men and women who despise His wonderful name.

Jesus taught He was equal with God. He said, "He that hateth me, hateth my Father also." He said, "Come unto me...I will give you rest." He said, "I am come that ye might have life." He said, "I am the resurrection and the life. No man cometh unto the Father but by me."

Has anyone ever made such claims? No wonder they got after Him for heresy! No wonder it made them shriek, "Away with him!"

Wonderful Death and Resurrection of Christ

His death was wonderful! He prophesied it. He foretold how and when He would be betrayed by a trusted disciple.

It was wonderful that He should be sold so cheap—thirty pieces of silver. He was tormented, tortured cruelly before His crucifixion. He was put to death in a brutal manner.

The time was wonderful! It was during the Passover Feast. The great publicity given to His death was wonderful. Hundreds of thousands were there for the Passover.

The events accompanying His death added to the wonder. The sky was darkened; the sun hid its face; the city was shaken as by an earthquake. The graves opened, and many appeared to their friends.

The veil of the Temple was rent from top to bottom.

His resurrection was wonderful! He foretold to His disciples, "... the third day I will arise." All appeared to forget that He said this. No one thought of going to the sepulchre except some women, and they to prepare the body for burial. Some of the disciples had left the city; two were on their way to Emmaus.

The manner of His resurrection was wonderful! No human mind could have ever imagined the scene. If someone had attempted to describe it, there would have been earthquakes, thunderings and commotion. See how different it really was! An angel rolled away the stone as quietly as the opening of a spring flower. When the women came, they found no disorder; the linen clothes were neatly folded.

Wonderful were His recorded appearances, and so different from what man would have them. He appeared only to His friends, and His best friends. Not one of His enemies saw Him.

I know the story is true! No one but God could have had it happen in the order it did. Had the story been false, it would have had Jesus appearing to Pilate, to the high priest and to the Pharisees.

How Wonderful Were Christ's Teachings

His teachings were wonderful! He left no colleges to propagate His ideas. He committed them to a few humble fishermen. He never wrote a sermon; He never published a book. Nothing Jesus ever said was engraven on stone or scrolled on brass; yet His doctrines have endured for two thousands years, have gone to the ends of the earth, have lifted individuals and nations out of degradation and have made the wilderness of sin to bloom like paradise.

When Jesus began to teach, Rome ruled the world. Her invincible legions went everywhere. Rome's power, her armies and her religion are gone. The Temple of Diana lies in ruins; not one worshiper can be found.

When Jesus fed the five thousand and healed the woman who touched the hem of His garment, there wasn't a church, a hospital, an institution for the blind, an insane asylum nor a poorhouse. There was no Red Cross, no Christmas trees. Now they are as countless as the sands on the seashore.

When the cloud received Him, the only record of His sayings was written on the hearts of His disciples. Now our libraries groan with the weight of books concerning Him and His teachings. The scholarship of the world sits at His feet.

We are told, "Never man spake as this man." His utterances are translated into every tongue. His thoughts run through all literature. If some discoverer could find twelve words spoken by Jesus, heretofore unpublished, they would be on the front page of every newspaper and magazine on earth.

There may be another Homer, another Virgil, another Dante, Milton, Alexander, Caesar, Shakespeare, another Raphael; but there will never be another Jesus.

We have watched over His cradle, amidst the malodors of the stable.

We have seen Him in the Temple at the dawning of His mental powers.

We have watched Him in the wilderness when the forces of Hell bombarded Him.

We have stood by His side on the Mount of Transfiguration.

We have gone with Him to the Temple when He drove out the money-changers.

We have walked beside Him in His triumphal entry.

We have heard the mob cry, "Away with him!"

We have knelt with Him in the Garden of Gethsemane.

We have stood weeping beside the cross.

We have seen Him when He burst asunder the bands of death.

We have seen Him as the clouds received Him out of our sight.

And we shall see Him when He comes to receive His own.

This Wonderful Jesus Is God's Son, the God-Man

We see in Jesus a priest greater than Moses, a king greater than David, a commander greater than Joshua, a philosopher greater than Solomon, a prophet greater than Elijah.

We talk about the great of earth—Alexander the Great, Caesar the Great, Frederick the Great, Alfred the Great, Peter the Great, Napoleon the Great—but there has been only one truly and supremely great One—*Jesus!*

Jesus Christ is the greatest character in all history. There are others for whom men have died in order to show their loyalty, but He is the only One worshiped among all peoples and in all ages.

The most glorious geniuses of all ages will be obscured, whether men have sought to remember them in monuments or palaces, whether in obelisks or tombs, whether in written encomiums, papyrus, parchment, brick or medallions. Only reminiscences of them remain.

Faith in Jesus is the foundation of all faith in God. Everything rests upon our faith in Him.

If Jesus were indeed the wretch despised by pagans, how has He carved on earth such a glorious pathway? How has He founded a religion that dominates the world?

If Jesus were merely human, the achievements would be impossible. They are proof that He is what the Bible and church affirm—the Son of God.

If Christ were only a man, just as others of the human race, only more highly developed spiritually, then good-night, Gospel! and good-by, Christianity! The Bible *is* the Word of God! Jesus *is* the Son of God!

Children cluster at His knee.

Womanhood places a crown on His brow.

The enthusiasm of youth forsakes all to follow Him.

Culture whispers, "We know thou art a teacher come from God."

Empires fling their crowns and scepters at His feet.

The seething seas throw their dripping arms around Him when they hear Him say, "Peace, be still!"

The dead waken into life, the lame leap for joy, the deaf hear, and disease slinks away like a wolf in a den at the sound of His voice.

The name "Jesus" stands alone! We can link Caesar and Alexander, Napoleon and Wellington, Fox and Pitt, Longfellow and Tennyson, Wesley and Whitefield, Cromwell and Lincoln. Jesus has a name which is above every name.

True to His name, this wonderful Saviour saves now.

What influence sent the Red Cross to bind up the wounds?

What influence sent the Y.M.C.A., the Y.W.C.A., the Salvation Army, and the Knights of Columbus into the front trenches?

Spurgeon said a doctor who could save ninety percent of his patients would be a wonder. The disciples were constantly finding hopeless cases and bringing them to Jesus. A word, a touch, and the trouble was gone, and peace again flowed like a river.

It is just the same today. It is wonderful that He can save so quickly, almost quicker than you can speak, as quickly as you can receive a present.

This wonderful Saviour has saved me; that's why I am speaking to you. Nothing is so convincing as our own experience. I do not know that I am the son of my mother any more certainly than I know that I am a child of God. I do not know that I was born in a natural way any more convincingly than I know I have been born of God.

Has this wonderful Saviour saved you? When the proof is so overwhelming and He has been saving for centuries, why will you not accept Him? No one will ever be saved unless Jesus saves him.

I imagine when God was about to create man He called to the ministering ones who wait constantly before His throne and said, "Justice, shall we make man?"

And Justice replied, "No, Lord, do not make man. He will trample on Your laws, profane Your name and pollute Your sanctuaries. I would never make man."

I hear Him ask, "Truth, shall we make man?"

And Truth replied, "O God, make him not. He will controvert Thy word, insult Thy gracious Spirit and turn away from His Creator with heartless ingratitude."

Again I hear Him say, "Mercy, shall we make man?"

Mercy dropped to her knees and, looking up through her tears, said, "Yes, Lord. I know all that Justice and Truth have said is true, but I will watch over him. When he forgets Thee, I will whisper to him of Thy love, and in all the sins of his life I will tell him of Thy forgiveness. Though he be vile and utterly undone by wickedness, I will follow him through all the dark days and will woo him in tenderness back to Thee."

We have gone to the farthest limits of sin, down to the lowest depths. We have profaned God's name, violated His Sabbaths, lived in adultery, drunkenness and debauchery, trampled beneath our feet the atoning blood of Jesus; yet God is still waiting for us. His mercy has followed us all our days.

Mercy is still looking through those tears and calling.

> **All through the depths of sin and loss**
> **There drops the plummet of the cross;**
> **Never yet abyss was found**
> **Deeper than the cross could sound.**

(From WONDERFUL AND OTHER SERMONS, Zondervan Bros.)

LOUIS T. TALBOT
1889-1976

ABOUT THE MAN:

Born in Sydney, Australia, Louis, as he grew up, assisted his father in the brewing business, becoming a distributor of alcoholic beverages.

But with the help of his mother's prayers, he, now in his manhood and still unsaved, became restless, dissatisfied, disillusioned at the business he was in. He dreamed of America and a new life. His brother Jim, in Moody Bible Institute, was to be a preacher: "Why couldn't there be two preachers in the family?" So "Louie" followed Jim to Moody, now cut loose from the liquor evil and ready for a fresh adventure.

He was far along in his studies at Moody when, under the preaching of John Harper of London, he was genuinely converted.

After Moody Institute, this young Australian went from pastorate to pastorate in the United States and Canada until he received a call to the great Church of the Open Door in Los Angeles, the very church the mighty R. A. Torrey had founded. Dr. Talbot was also president of the Bible Institute of Los Angeles (BIOLA).

He met and married Audrey Hogue while pastoring a Congregational church in Paris, Texas.

The story of Dr. Louis Talbot's activities in Los Angeles make a fiction tame. He found a church of 1,200 discouraged members; he left it with 3,500 and the future bright. He came to a debt of over a million dollars; he left the church free from debt and thousands of dollars raised on new promotional enterprises. He extended the missionary program to where literally hundreds of American missionaries and native workers circle the globe, supported by this great church. He came to 300 students in the Bible Institute; he left it with more than a thousand. His ministry over the air was phenomenal.

Few men in this generation achieved success as Dr. Talbot did. He had tremendous faith and was absolutely loyal to the Bible, and he loved the Lord with all his heart.

XIV.

The Names of Our Lord

LOUIS T. TALBOT

One of the most beautiful of the Christmas choruses which we shall hear over the radio and in our churches during the season when we commemorate our Lord's birth will be that from Handel's *The Messiah*, entitled "For Unto Us a Child Is Born." Even as we think of it, the music rings in our ears:

"For unto us a child is born, unto us a son is given: and the government shall be upon his shoulder: and his name shall be called Wonderful, Counsellor, The mighty God, The everlasting Father, The Prince of Peace."

It is as beautiful in its way as the awe-inspiring "Hallelujah Chorus"—majestic, worshipful, sublime! Handel must have been a devoted Christian as well as a close student of the Bible, or he could never have composed this most beautiful of all oratorios, *The Messiah*.

If you have never seen a copy of it, go to a public library and get one; read its pages; and you will find a masterful compilation of Old Testament prophecies of the coming Saviour and King; the story of His suffering, death, resurrection and ascension into Heaven; and the prophecy of His coming again in power and great glory. Seldom do we hear the entire oratorio presented at one time, in all three parts. It would be the most eloquent of sermons if we could only hear it all again and again; for every word is a quotation from the holy Scriptures, set to music that defies description.

A careful reading of Handel's *The Messiah* will show that the musician not only was a master of his art, but that he also loved the One of whom he wrote, remembering that "his name shall be called Wonderful, Counsellor, The mighty God, The everlasting Father, The Prince of Peace."

This one chorus alone is filled with "Christmas Chimes" which we would echo around the world!

A Message to a People at War

When Isaiah wrote this remarkable prophecy, he addressed it to a people at war. Judah's wicked, idolatrous King Ahaz was on the throne; "He did not that which was right in the sight of the Lord" (II Chron. 28:1); and when trouble came in the form of a confederacy between Samaria and Syria, designed against Judah, the children of Judah and their faithless king were sore afraid. But God had a faithful prophet in Judah, the mighty Isaiah; and to him the Lord said, "Go forth to meet Ahaz...and say unto him, Take heed, and be quiet; fear not, neither be fainthearted.... It shall not stand, neither shall it come to pass" (i.e., this attempt on the part of Judah's enemies; see II Chron. 28:1-15; Isa. 7:1-9:7).

Ahaz did not deserve this goodness from God; neither did those in Judah who had departed from the Lord. But God does not deal with His people according to what they deserve! If He did, "who could stand" before His holy Presence?

And the abundance of His grace was revealed in a special way to Judah's wicked King Ahaz; for it was in connection with this prophecy of Isaiah to the children of Judah that the Holy Spirit uttered two of the most wonderful promises concerning Israel's promised Messiah and the world's Saviour and King. To the "house of David"—not to Ahaz alone, but to David's "house"—the prophet promised the virgin-born Immanuel, saying, "Therefore the Lord himself shall give you a sign; Behold, a virgin shall conceive, and bear a son, and shall call his name Immanuel" (Isa. 7:14; cf. Matt. 1:22,23).

And to the people in Judah who would heed His warning and obey His command God spoke again in this time of crisis during the reign of Ahaz, saying that the divine Child was "Israel's only hope." And this is what the inspired prophet said:

"For unto us a child is born, unto us a son is given: and the government shall be upon his shoulder: and his name shall be called Wonderful, Counsellor, The mighty God, The everlasting Father, The Prince of Peace. Of the increase of his government and peace there shall be no end, upon the throne of David, and upon his kingdom, to order it, and to establish it with judgment and with justice from henceforth

even for ever. The zeal of the Lord of hosts will perform this."—Isa. 9:6,7.

Today, after nearly twenty-seven hundred years, Isaiah's message comes down from God to a world far free from war. Even at Christmastime, when we remember the birth into the world of "The Prince of Peace," some nations are arming with all the fierceness and cruelty known to man. All over the world there is pain, there is anguish, there is sin! Yet down the centuries still echoes the voice of the prophet of God, pointing fallen man to "Israel's only hope," even the Lord Jesus Christ, the Saviour of sinners.

If only the nations would look back to the manger where the divine Child was born; back to the cross of the eternal Son of God who was "given" to a lost world; and forward to His coming again to be recognized by all men everywhere as the One whose name shall be called "Wonderful, Counsellor, The mighty God, The everlasting Father, The Prince of Peace"! If only the nations would read and understand God's Word, which foretells "wars and rumors of wars," even until the King of kings and Lord of lords is back on earth to reign!

But the nations will not heed the warning. Thank God, millions of individuals do look back to the Christ of the cross, and forward to the Christ of Glory as the only solution to this world's problems! It is to such as these, to all who will be born again, that the "Christmas Chimes" of Isaiah's glorious prophecy can give light and hope and peace, even in a disturbed world. For such as these—all who will love the Lord Jesus Christ—His own reassuring message offers comfort and blessing, "I will come again"!

Communists may think they can overthrow the nations of the world where Christ is named, think they can stamp out Christianity—but no confederacy formed against God's people can stand. Christ shall one day sit upon "the throne of his father David"; and "of his kingdom there shall be no end." The message of Isaiah to Judah in the days of Ahaz comes down the centuries to all of God's children, "Fear not, neither be fainthearted.... It shall not stand, neither shall it come to pass."

"Unto Us a Child Is Born, Unto Us a Son Is Given"

The birth of the Child Immanuel is here distinguished from the giving of the Son of God. The Child was indeed the Son of God; but the language used by the Holy Spirit is significant. As a Child, in human flesh, Immanuel, that is, "God with us," was born in Bethlehem's manger; but as the Son of God, He had no birth, no beginning or end; as the Son He is eternal!

As the Second Person of the Holy Trinity, our Lord wanted to die for sinners. But God cannot die; therefore, in order to "taste death for every man," the eternal Son of God was "made flesh, and dwelt among us" (John 1:14). Because He was born of the Virgin Mary, without a human father, because God was His Father, and He was born of the Holy Spirit, He was the sinless God-man. Because He was perfect Man, He could suffer and die for us. Because He was eternal "God manifest in the flesh," He was sinless, all-powerful, divine.

Let us never fail to recognize the clear teaching of all the Scriptures, that, as the Child, He was born into the world on that first Christmas, but as the Son of God, He was "given" to become the world's Saviour and Israel's Messiah.

Satan has ever sought to get rid of Christ; yet today all over the world there are those who are remembering the Saviour's birth. It is true that Christmas has been commercialized; it is true that many will sing the Christmas carols who do not know the Lord. Yet the carols are sung! All the civilized world is constantly reminded of the Christian's Christmas. Surely that fact alone is a silent testimony to the deity of our Lord! Then there are the multitudes of God's redeemed children who observe this sacred season because they love the Child of Bethlehem, who is the only Saviour and the coming King of kings!

There is another silent testimony to God's value upon the birth of Christ in Judaea nearly two thousand years ago: All secular history dates from His birth. Even the infidel has to bear testimony to His birth every time he writes a check, every time he dates a letter. The historian—whether he be Christian or not—must write of the Caesars who lived "before Christ," and of Napoleon and Shakespeare and all the world's great men who lived "in the year of our Lord" at such and such a time. Every teacher of history must tell his pupils that the birth of Christ stands in the center of the ages, whether he wants to honor the Christ of the cross or not. It is an irrefutable fact, which God Himself so ordered, to let all men everywhere know that honor is due His eternal Son.

The Virgin's Son

Matthew and Luke, guided by the Holy Spirit, have written the beautiful story of the birth of the Christ Child, born of the Virgin Mary. Poets have sung of the Wise Men and the star, of the shepherds and the angels, of the manger and the faithful care given by Joseph to the Infant Jesus. Luke has told us also of how Joseph and Mary fulfilled the Law of Moses, and took the Child to the Temple when He was eight days old, to fulfill every single command given to godly Jews. Luke has told us of the adoration of Simeon and Anna in the Temple, as well as of Mary's song of praise when she rejoiced in God, her Saviour. To the first two chapters of Matthew and Luke we turn for this beautiful story. Over the radio and from our churches we hear it re-echoed— this song the angels sang on the Judaean hills, this song that still rings out its Christmas Chimes to a sin-weary, troubled world. "There's a song in the air" at this Christmas season; and it makes our burdened hearts glad. Josiah Gilbert Holland has sung it in the words of his beautiful hymn, "There's a Song in the Air":

> **There's a song in the air!**
> **There's a star in the sky!**
> **There's a mother's deep prayer**
> **And a Baby's low cry!**
> **And the star rains its fire while the beautiful sing,**
> **For the manger of Bethlehem cradles a King!**
>
> **There's a tumult of joy**
> **O'er the wonderful birth,**
> **For the virgin's sweet Boy**
> **Is the Lord of the earth.**
> **Ay! the star rains its fire and the beautiful sing,**
> **For the manger of Bethlehem cradles a King!**
>
> **We rejoice in the light,**
> **And we echo the song**
> **That comes down through the night**
> **From the heavenly throng.**
> **Ay! we shout to the lovely evangel they bring,**
> **And we greet in His cradle our Saviour and King!**

"And the Government Shall Be Upon His Shoulder"

Beautiful as the Christmas story is, it would hold no abiding meaning for a world in sin had the Christ Child not lived a sinless life on earth, had He not gone to the cross to pay the penalty of sin for a bankrupt humanity, had He not risen from the dead and ascended into Heaven, there to intercede for His own, had He not promised to return in glory to usher in everlasting peace and righteousness. It is the prophet's reassuring promise that "the government shall be upon his shoulder" which gives hope to a world in darkness and despair at this Christmas season.

Moreover, this promise of that prophet is but one of hundreds of like prophecies by God's other prophets. It is but the foretelling of similar promises by our Lord Himself when He was on earth, and by His inspired apostles after He went back to Heaven.

"The government shall be upon his shoulder.... Of the increase of his government and peace there shall be no end, upon the throne of David, and upon his kingdom, to order it, and to establish it with judgment and with justice from henceforth even for ever. The zeal of the Lord of hosts will perform this."

When Jesus comes, when "the government shall be upon his shoulder," then there will be justice for all: the poor will not be oppressed; minorities will not be persecuted; poor suffering Israel will not be hunted and treated with contempt and cruelty; the wicked shall be "cut off," immediately compelled to obey the righteous laws of the King!

Today "the dark places of the earth are full of the habitations of cruelty" (Ps. 74:20). In that coming day God's righteousness shall cover the earth "as the waters cover the sea" (Isa. 11:9). As we think of our Lord's rule over this troubled world, we can but pray, in the words He taught His disciples: "Thy kingdom come. Thy will be done in earth, as it is in heaven.... For thine is the kingdom, and the power, and the glory, for ever. Amen."

"His Name"

The names given in the Scriptures to our Lord are highly significant. There are many of them, because one or a dozen or very many names could never tell the wonders of His person and work. Someone has said that there are more than five hundred proper names and descriptive terms used in Scripture to portray the Holy Trinity. And names in Bible times had much significance.

Today the names of men have ceased to distinguish them, or to signify their characteristics or their mission in life.

I heard of a man who named his child *Dora* simply because a rich kinsman had promised to give the child a rich gift if she were called by that name. Had the father inquired, he would have learned that *Dora* is an abbreviated form of *Theodora*, which means "the gift of God."

Again, *Henry* is a name common enough; it means "home ruler, ever rich," one who manages his home affairs wisely and well. Yet all of us have known many Henrys who have not exemplified the meaning of the name.

James means "superior"; yet how many bearing that name have not lived up to its meaning? History is filled with the stories of very inferior men named *James*.

In Bible times, however, it was not so. Among the Hebrews, names had very definite significance. Abraham, the father of the Hebrew nation, left the idolatry of Chaldea and erected altars to the true and living God. And it was the Lord Himself who changed the patriarch's name *Abram,* which means "high father," to *Abraham,* which means "the father of many nations." Abraham did become the father of the Israelites, of the Ishmaelites, of the Midianites, and of other nations of history. And, in a wider, spiritual sense, he became "the father of us all" who believe in the Lord Jesus as the only Saviour of sinners.

Pharaoh's daughter gave Moses his name because she "drew him out" of the water.

Jacob's name, signifying "supplanter," one who takes the place of another, was changed by the Lord to *Israel,* meaning "a prince with God." When he saw the ladder which reached to Heaven, Jacob called the place where he saw the Lord *Beth-el,* even "the house of God." When he wrestled with the angel, he called that place *Peniel,* meaning "the face of God." All twelve of Jacob's sons were given names suggestive of certain conditions existing at their birth. *Samuel* means "asked of God." *David* signifies "beloved." We might go on endlessly, illustrating from the Hebrew names the significance attached to them. But these few suffice to illustrate the importance the Hebrews gave to their proper names. Therefore, they were deeply impressed by the many beautiful names which God gave to them concerning Himself.

For example, when He spoke to Moses from the burning bush, He called His name "I AM THAT I AM," indicating both self-existence and eternity. When the Lord Jesus was on earth, He applied this name of deity to Himself many times, saying: "I am the light of the world"; "I am the bread of life"; "I am the good shepherd"; "I am the door"; "I am the resurrection and the life"; "I am the way, the truth, and the life"; "I am the vine." And when He said to the unbelieving Jews, "Before Abraham was, I am," they sought to stone Him for claiming to be God (John 8:58).

His name *Jesus* means "Saviour." *Messiah* is the Hebrew for the Greek word *Christ*. *The Lamb of God* speaks to us of His sacrificial work on the cross. *Lord* is a name for deity; *Jehovah* is the Old Testament word often used for *Lord;* and *Jehovah* means "the self-existent One who reveals Himself." *Son of God* emphasizes His deity; *Son of man,* His humanity. As the eternal *Word* who was "made flesh, and dwelt among us," He told forth the very thoughts of God toward us—never-dying love. *The Holy One of God* tells us that He was without sin. *Redeemer* speaks to us of how He bought us from the penalty of everlasting condemnation.

Then He is called "The King of glory"; *Shiloh,* which means "Peacemaker"; "The Good Shepherd," "The Great Shepherd," "The Chief Shepherd"—these three names signify His atoning work on the cross, His intercessory work at "the throne of grace," and His kingly glory. He is called "the rose of Sharon," "the lily of the valley," "the chiefest among ten thousand," the One "altogether lovely"—all reminding us of His beauty and perfection. "The Nazarene," "the Carpenter," "the Servant of Jehovah"—these tell us of His humble, lowly obedience to His Father's will.

Whole volumes have been written on the many beautiful names given to the Triune God; but these will suffice to illustrate the importance which the Scriptures attach to the names of our Lord. They will serve to prove to us that the Prophet Isaiah and the people to whom he wrote realized something of the far-reaching implication associated with the names given to the promised Messiah in the message we are considering today—the message which we have chosen to call "The Names of Our Lord." Verily they did ring out "good tidings of great joy" to a people who sat in darkness; for they heralded the coming of "a great light," even the One whose name shall yet be called, by all men everywhere, "Wonderful, Counsellor, The mighty God, The everlasting Father, The Prince of Peace." Like the ringing of a bell, they send their chimes down the ages, promising a kingdom "wherein dwelleth righteousness," promising a golden age yet to be ushered in by Him whose promise never fails! As these chimes of Christmas echo down the centuries, let us listen to their clear, unmistakable message of righteousness and peace and "good will" yet to cover the earth.

"His Name Shall Be Called Wonderful"

Our Lord Jesus has always been "Wonderful." Before the heavens and the earth were created, He was wonderful in His Being—in His glory and beauty. In Old Testament times He was wonderful in His patience and love with His sinning creatures. How faithfully He led and taught and chastened them throughout all the centuries!

He was wonderful in His birth; for He was born as no other human being was ever born. God was His Father; He was "conceived by the Holy Ghost"; He was the "only begotten Son of God." A beautiful star led Wise Men to His crib; angels filled the sky on the night when He was born. Humble shepherds and learned scholars worshiped Him in His lowly manger. He was wonderful in His birth!

Our Lord Jesus Christ was wonderful in His life. He lived a holy, sinless life on earth. His Heavenly Father spoke more than once from Heaven, saying, "This is my beloved Son, in whom I am well pleased" (Matt. 3:17; 17:5). Jesus Himself could say, "I do always those things that please him" (John 8:29). And His apostles ever spoke with authority in such terms as this: He "was in all points tempted like as we are, sin apart." He is "holy, harmless, undefiled, separate from sinners, and made higher than the heavens" (Heb. 7:26).

Our Lord Jesus Christ was wonderful in His life!

He was wonderful in His works. Only because He was God could He perform His mighty deeds. Moreover, because He always was, is now, and ever shall be the God of love, He had compassion on the multitudes, He healed the sick, opened the eyes of the blind, raised the dead, cast out demons, comforted the brokenhearted, forgave sins. Only God can do those things!

As the Creator, He manifested His power over nature, turning the water into wine, stilling the tempest, walking upon the sea, multiplying the loaves and fishes. Thus He showed His power over nature, sickness, demons, death and sin. He was wonderful in His works, in order to prove that He had every right and all power to become our Sin-Bearer, Lord and King.

Christ Jesus was wonderful in His words. Even the officers who were sent by the Pharisees to take Him prisoner could only reply, "Never man spake like this man" (John 7:46). He always spoke the truth—the truth about the Triune God and His plan of salvation; the truth about things to come; the truth about man's moral and ethical obligation to God and to his fellowman.

The Lord Jesus was wonderful in His death. No one else ever died as He did—a propitiatory sacrifice for sin. He died that we might live. He died willingly, gladly for lost, never-dying souls!

Our Lord was wonderful in His resurrection. In His glorified, yet very real, body Christ bore the keys of hades and the grave (Rev. 1:18). He broke the bands of death, robbing Satan of his mightiest weapon. Because He lives, we too shall live!

He was wonderful in His ascension into Heaven. Angels attended His return to His eternal, uncreated glory, reassuring His loved ones that He would come again (see Acts 1:11). The Father in Heaven greeted Him with those marvelous words of, "Welcome Home," foretold by David a thousand years before David's Son was born in Bethlehem: "The Lord said unto my Lord [i.e., God the Father said to God the Son; for David's Son was David's Lord], Sit thou on my right hand, until I make thine enemies thy footstool" (Ps. 110:1).

Our greatest High Priest, even Jesus, is wonderful in His present ministry at the right hand of the Father, for there He "ever liveth to make intercession" for His blood-bought children (Heb. 7:25). He is our "Advocate with the Father" (I John 2:1). When we sin, He prays for us, chastens us and restores us to fellowship with Himself. He guards and cares for us—and how patiently He deals with His own! He is wonderful in His authority, power and love!

"And his name shall be called Wonderful" when He comes in glory to reign. The whole world will be filled with His glory. From all eternity He has been wonderful in the eyes of the Father and the Spirit, in the eyes of angels, and in the eyes of His saints—separated ones. But when He rules over the earth, all men will call Him "Wonderful." And His glory shall cover the earth "as the waters cover the sea."

All that mankind has ever desired that is worthy and true; all that is good and righteous and just; all that godly men have dreamed about and more—these will all be realized when Jesus comes again. Longevity will be restored to men. Even the animal kingdom will live at peace: for birds and beasts and cattle will be subject unto Him. The wolf shall dwell with the lamb; the leopard shall lie down with the kid; the calf and the young lion shall feed together—and a little child shall lead them. There will be no more thorns; "the desert shall blossom as the rose." Every man shall sit under his own vine and fig tree; the poor and needy shall be enriched; and the lame man shall leap as the hart. Our Lord will be wonderful in His reign of glory upon earth!

"His Name Shall Be Called... Counsellor"

We may not even attempt to say that, in ages past, the world of men has accepted Christ as "Counsellor." Today the unbelieving world still rejects His counsel. Instead, "The kings of the earth set themselves, and the rulers take counsel together, against the Lord, and against his anointed..." (Ps. 2:2; Acts 4:26-28).

The godless world crucified the "only wise God our Saviour" (Jude 25). Even those of us who love Him and truly want His counsel all too often fail to go to Him for wisdom and guidance! We are self-willed, impatient, forgetful of our utter dependence upon Him who "doeth all things well."

But in the ages to come it will not be so. All men shall call Him "Counsellor." In His inherent worthiness, He has always been the only safe and true Counsellor; but never yet has the sinful world accepted Him as such. Six thousand years of human history are but the record of failure and sin on the part of frail humanity; and the nations are rushing headlong to eternal doom—all the nations that forget God. But when Christ sits upon the throne of David, then all men everywhere will ask, "Who hath been his counsellor?" He shall judge in righteousness and equity; and "...the spirit of the Lord shall rest upon him, the spirit of wisdom and understanding, the spirit of counsel and might, the spirit of knowledge and of the fear of the Lord" (Isa. 11:2).

The Lord will be the righteous Judge as well as King of kings. He will satisfy the afflicted soul; He will guide His people continually and be to them as "a watered garden." "Sorrow and sighing shall flee away." And there "shall be no more curse."

"And His Name Shall Be Called... The Mighty God"

The Lord Jesus Christ was the Almighty God throughout the past eternity. He was "God with us" in His incarnation. As the God-man, He moved among men, performing mighty miracles. Then, in His death, it looked to the world as if His claims to deity had proved false. The world thought He was a failure. But His resurrection, foretold in the Old Testament and by the Man of Galilee Himself, proved for all time and for all eternity that Jesus of Nazareth was the Almighty One, the One into whose hands had been committed "all power in heaven and in earth." For forty days He showed Himself alive to those who loved Him; then in His ascension He added further proof that all His claims to deity were forever established. Yet it will not be until He takes the reins of government in His omnipotent hands that the whole wide world will acknowledge Him as "The mighty God." But that day will come just as surely as were all His prophecies fulfilled in His death and resurrection and ascension into Heaven. "The word of God can not be broken."

This name of our Lord takes us back to the days of Abraham when the patriarch first told that the God in whom he had put his trust was *El Shaddai*—"the God who is enough." It was when Abram was ninety years old and nine that *El Shaddai* appeared unto him to say, "I am the Almighty God—*El Shaddai*—; walk before me, and be thou perfect" (Gen. 17:1).

At this meeting of the Lord with Abram the latter's name was changed to Abraham; the token of the Abrahamic covenant was established; and the birth of the son of praise was foretold for the ensuing year. "Walk before me, and be thou perfect," *El Shaddai* said unto Abram; and for such a walk the Almighty God promised strength and companionship by the way.

Almighty! What a word! It symbolizes the source of all power, all majesty, all might. Christ's almighty power shaped a world into being. His voice brought order out of chaos, light out of darkness, life eternal out of everlasting condemnation and death.

By the power of the risen Christ all nature fulfills its mission. Every flower, every tree, every mountain, every valley, every bird-song, every flash of lightning—all of God's universe speaks to us of His omnipotence.

As a school boy I learned to sing, and still love to repeat the words,

> **I sing the mighty power of God**
> **Which made the mountains rise,**
> **That spread the flowing seas abroad,**
> **And built the lofty skies.**

But how does this manifestation of power help me? Simply because I know that the Almighty God is able to keep my soul which He has redeemed by His own precious blood. Since He has "all power in heaven and in earth," I may trust Him with all that concerns me, knowing that Satan and all his hosts cannot pluck me out of His all-powerful hands!

On my pilgrimage to Heaven I often stumble and fall; but underneath are the "everlasting arms" of the Almighty God, *El Shaddai*, the God who is enough!

"And His Name Shall Be Called... The Everlasting Father"

The name, "The everlasting Father," foretold the coming of the One who was always one with the Father, even our Lord and Saviour Jesus Christ. When He was upon earth, He told men that He did the works of the Father, that He was worthy of equal honor with the Father, that He was in the Father and the Father in Him. Chapter 5 of John makes these claims very clear and unmistakable. Our Lord came to fulfill the Father's will, to speak the words of the Father's love for lost mankind, to "declare" or "manifest" the Father. To Philip's request that He show to the disciples the Father, Christ said:

"Have I been so long time with you, and yet hast thou not known me, Philip? he that hath seen me hath seen the Father; and how sayest thou then, Shew us the Father?"—John 14:9.

"No man hath seen God at any time; the only begotten Son, which is in the bosom of the Father, he hath declared him" (i.e., 'led him forth into full revelation'; see John 1:18).

"The everlasting Father" is a comforting name! Everything about us is fleeting, changing, temporary. The world is ever seeking, yet never finding, that which will abide, apart from the message brought down to earth by the Son of God, whose "name shall be called The everlasting Father." It is no wonder that Napoleon, while reviewing his army before the pyramids of Egypt, said, "There is nothing lacking here"; then, catching his breath, he added, "...except permanence."

It is startling to us to see how the things of earth come to naught. Where are the Pharaohs today? Where are the men who built one of the most wonderful kingdoms the world ever saw? They are withered old mummies in a glass case in the British Museum. Where are the Caesars today? They are a handful of dust that helps to make up old Rome. Where is Nebuchadnezzar today? The exact site of his palace of splendor cannot even be identified.

When some years ago I stood in the British Museum and saw helmets of brass, breastplates and swords and all the armor that knights once wore, I wondered whose eyes had flashed through those helmets, whose beating hearts those breastplates had once protected.

Today we carry in our pockets coins bearing the image of a past President of the United States of America. Where is he now? Even the metal of the coin is wearing away.

Today you and I sit in the pews of our churches; we who are ministers stand behind our pulpits. Tomorrow, if the Lord tarries, we shall be gone. Yet, in the midst of all this change, you and I long for life. We want to live, and rightly so.

We bury our loved ones in the graves; and one asks us, "If a man die, shall he live again?" (Job 14:14). The infidel has no answer of hope. The worldly-wise say, "We do not know." But God's living Word tells us that He whose name is "The everlasting Father" reassures us, saying:

"I am the resurrection, and the life: he that believeth in me, though he were dead, yet shall he live: And whosoever liveth and believeth in me shall never die."—John 11:25,26.

As we rejoice in the name of "The everlasting Father," we sing also in the words of the much-loved hymn:

> **Change and decay in all around I see;**
> **Oh, Thou who changest not, abide with me!**

"And His Name Shall Be Called...The Prince of Peace"

When Christ was born in Bethlehem, the angels appeared unto the shepherds as they watched their flocks by night; and this is what they said: "Glory to God in the highest, And on earth peace among men in whom he is well pleased" (Luke 2:14, A.S.V.).

It was Christ Himself who said to His own, "Peace I leave with you, my peace I give unto you: not as the world giveth, give I unto you. Let not your heart be troubled, neither let it be afraid" (John 14:27). The peace that Christ gives to the redeemed includes "peace with God," "the peace of God" and "peace on earth."

"Being justified by faith, we have peace with God through our Lord Jesus Christ."—Rom. 5:1.

"Having made peace through the blood of his cross...he is our peace."—Col. 1:20; Eph. 2:14.

The sad truth is, my Christian friend, that many of God's born-again children do not know what it means to have "the peace of God" in a restless, troubled world. They are saved by His grace for all eternity;

yet they worry and fret and fear what tomorrow may bring, while all the while God loves them and longs for them to rest in His sure promise of grace sufficient for every need. Through the Apostle Paul He bids us, every one who has been redeemed, to heed His admonition:

"Be careful ['anxious'] for nothing; but in every thing by prayer and supplication with thanksgiving let your requests be made known unto God. And the peace of God, which passeth all understanding, shall keep your hearts and minds through Christ Jesus."—Phil. 4:6,7.

And in that coming day, which seems to us to be even at our doors, the Lord Jesus, "The Prince of Peace," will come in glory to establish "peace on earth" which will be literal, world-wide and abiding. The day will come when our Lord Jesus "... shall judge among the nations, and shall rebuke many people: and they shall beat their swords into plowshares, and their spears into pruninghooks: nation shall not lift up sword against nation, neither shall they learn war any more" (Isa. 2:4).

Christmas chimes! And what chimes these are! They peal out the "good tidings of great joy" which the angels sang to the shepherds on the Judaean hills that first Christmas night. They echo in our hearts at this Christmas season, bidding us think upon Him who was the virgin's Child, born of the Holy Spirit, the eternal Son of the Father in Heaven. They tell us that He was "the only begotten Son" of the Father, "given" to a world lost in sorrow and sin. They point us on to that yet future day when all men everywhere shall call His name "Wonderful, Counsellor, The mighty God, The everlasting Father, The Prince of Peace." With the psalmist of many centuries ago we sing, with hearts of joy and peace: "They that know thy name will put their trust in thee" (Ps. 9:10).

"And he shall judge the world in righteousness, he shall minister judgment to the people in uprightness. The Lord also will be a refuge for the oppressed, a refuge in times of trouble. And they that know thy name will put their trust in thee: for thou, Lord, hast not forsaken them that seek thee."—Ps. 9:8-10.

When Sankey Sang the Shepherd Song on Christmas Eve

The beautiful story of a song that gave glory to God on a Christmas Eve many years ago has been printed in a little tract entitled, "When

Sankey Sang the Shepherd Song on Christmas Eve." We quote it here in full, because it gives honor and glory to the Christ of Bethlehem and the Christ of the cross.

* * *

It happened that on Christmas Eve of the year 1875, Ira D. Sankey, to whom God had given wonderful power to sing the Gospel as he worked with Dwight L. Moody, was traveling by steamboat up the Delaware River. It was a calm, starlit evening, and there were many passengers gathered on the deck. Mr. Sankey was asked to sing; and, as always, he was perfectly willing to do so. He stood there leaning against one of the great funnels of the boat, his eyes raised to the starry heavens in quiet prayer. It was his intention to sing a Christmas song, but somehow he was driven to sing "The Shepherd Song":

> **Saviour, like a shepherd lead us:**
> **Much we need Thy tend'rest care;**
> **In Thy pleasant pastures feed us;**
> **For our use Thy folds prepare.**
> **Blessed Jesus, blessed Jesus,**
> **Thou hast bought us; Thine we are.**
>
> **We are Thine, do Thou befriend us;**
> **Be the Guardian of our way:**
> **Keep Thy flock, from sin defend us;**
> **Seek us when we go astray.**
> **Blessed Jesus, blessed Jesus,**
> **Hear, oh, hear us when we pray.**
>
> **Thou hast promised to receive us,**
> **Poor and sinful though we be;**
> **Thou hast mercy to relieve us,**
> **Grace to cleanse and power to free.**
> **Blessed Jesus, blessed Jesus,**
> **We will early turn to Thee.**
>
> **Early let us seek Thy favor;**
> **Early let us do Thy will,**
> **Blessed Lord and only Saviour,**
> **With Thy love our bosoms fill.**
> **Blessed Jesus, blessed Jesus,**
> **Thou hast loved us, love us still.**

There was a deep stillness. Words and melody, welling from the singer's soul, floated out over the deck and the quiet river. Every heart was touched. After the song was ended, a man with a rough, weather-beaten face came up to Mr. Sankey and asked, "Did you ever serve in the Union Army?"

"Yes," answered Mr. Sankey, "in the spring of 1860."

"Can you remember if you were doing picket duty on a bright moonlight night in 1862?"

"Yes," answered Mr. Sankey, very much surprised.

"So do I," said the stranger; "but I was serving in the Confederate Army. When I saw you standing at your post, I thought to myself, *That fellow will never get away from here alive.* I raised my musket and took aim. I was standing in the shadow, completely concealed, while the full light of the moon was falling on you. At that instant, just as a moment ago, you raised your eyes to Heaven and began to sing. Music, especially song, has always had a wonderful power over me, and I took my finger off the trigger.

"*Let him sing his song to the end,* I said to myself. *I can shoot him afterwards. He's my victim at all events, and my bullet cannot miss him.*

"But the song you sang then was the song you sang just now. I heard the words perfectly,

We are Thine, do Thou befriend us;
Be the Guardian of our way.

"Those words stirred up memories in my heart. I began to think of my childhood and my God-fearing mother. She had many, many times sung that song to me. But she died all too soon; otherwise, much in my life would no doubt have been different. When you had finished your song, it was impossible for me to take aim at you again. I thought, *The Lord who is able to save that man from certain death must surely be great and mighty*—and my arm of its own accord dropped limply at my side.

"Since that time I have wandered far; but when I saw you just now, standing there praying, as on that other occasion, I recognized you. Then my heart was wounded by your song. Now I wish you would help me find a cure for my sin-sick soul."

Deeply moved, Mr. Sankey threw his arms about the man who in the days of the war had been his enemy. And this Christmas Eve the two went together to the manger in Bethlehem and to the Christ of the cross. There the stranger found Him who is the only Saviour, the One of whom the angel and the prophet sang many centuries ago:

"*And the angel of the Lord . . . said unto them* [the shepherds], *Fear not: for, behold, I bring you good tidings of great joy, which shall be to all people. For unto you is born this day in the city of David a Saviour, which is Christ the Lord.*"—Luke 2:9-11.

"*For unto us a child is born, unto us a son is given: and the government shall be upon his shoulder: and his name shall be called Wonderful, Counsellor, The mighty God, The everlasting Father, The Prince of Peace.*"

XV.

Should a Christian Observe Christmas?

JOHN R. RICE

"One man esteemeth one day above another: another esteemeth every day alike. Let every man be fully persuaded in his own mind. He that regardeth the day, regardeth it unto the Lord; and he that regardeth not the day, to the Lord he doth not regard it...."—Rom. 14:5,6.

I love the Christmas season. I find great joy in preaching on the Christmas themes of the angels, the shepherds, the manger, the virgin birth, the Wise Men. I get a great thrill when I hear Christmas carols. I love the gathering together of loved ones, the giving of gifts. And I rejoice to be remembered by those I love.

Perhaps my own feeling is colored somewhat by the fact that for many years I have been away from home most of the year; but at the Christmas season, I can be with my family.

How sad that many do not enjoy Christmas! Even some devoted Christians feel sour, are cantankerous and full of objections about the season. To you I would say in the words of Scripture—if you regard the day, regard it unto the Lord. And if you do not regard the day, then be sure you act Christian about it. Let nobody judge or criticize others for an honest, worshipful, spiritual and loving attitude about Christmas.

SOME OBJECTIONS ABOUT CHRISTMAS ANSWERED

1. "December 25 Is Not Really Christ's Birthday"

The Bible does not tell us exactly when Christ was born, and there are no other trustworthy sources from which we can learn the time. Therefore, some think it wrong to observe Christmas.

I know a little girl who was born on February 29—leap year. Now, is it wrong for her to observe her birthday on February 28 when there is no leap year? In other words, is it wrong for her or others to observe her birthday anytime except leap year? The precise date—February 29—is not the important factor, but that another year had gone by and the little girl had grown a year older; and that fact should be recognized by loved ones.

Would you say it is wrong to observe Thanksgiving on a certain Thursday in November, when not all our blessings have come on that day? Or would it be wrong to set a more convenient day if all agreed on a national day of thanksgiving? Whatever the day, it is still right to have a time when we publicly thank God and as a nation officially express our gratitude to the Father of Mercies for all His bounty, for all His goodness, for all His blessings. The important thing is not what day of the calendar, but that we give praise to the One who loadeth us with benefits.

Although I do not know of any scholar who believes that Jesus was born on December 25, it just could be the date on which the angels announced His birth. We love the dear Lord Jesus. We want everyone to remember His birth. We want to teach our children about the Babe in the manger, about the Wise Men from the East who came to worship Him, about the angels' announcement to Mary, about the angel chorus that told the shepherds of His birth. And December 25 is as good a day for that as any other day. It is not wrong to remember the birth of Christ on the day which is as close as we can come to His birthday.

2. "Christmas Means Only 'Christ's Mass' —a Catholic Holiday"

We are told that Christmas comes from Christ's Mass, that it was instituted by Catholics; therefore, good Protestants ought not observe it.

That objection seems a little foolish. Nearly all the names we have, we inherited from the heathen. Many cities, towns, counties, rivers in America have Indian names. But when we see the Susquehanna River or read of Shawnee, Oklahoma or Comanche, Texas, we are not thinking about the Indians. And the names have no connotation of heathendom. Names mean what they mean, no matter what the origin.

Sometimes Seventh-day Adventists make much of the fact that the name of our day "Sunday" comes from the worship of the sun. I reply that their "Saturday" is named from the god *Saturn*. But no one has reference to the sun when he uses the word "Sunday" or when he worships on Sunday; and no one has any reference to the god *Saturn* when he works or serves on Saturday.

So it seems foolish to make an artificial distinction when none exists in the minds of people who observe Christmas.

January was named for the Roman god *Janus*. Are Christians, therefore, wrong to call the month by that name? To every sensible person, Christmas means simply Christmas, not some kind of *mass*. Catholics may observe it with a mass, but not Protestants.

It will be good to keep these things in mind.

3. "Christmas Was a Former Heathen Holiday"

It is true that before the birth of Christ, December 25 was a pagan holiday. The Encyclopedia Brittanica says this date was a "Mithraic feast day" to celebrate the unconquered Son of Philocalus.

Evidently many new converts were tempted to keep the pagan feast celebrated on December 25. Probably it was to counteract this pagan influence that caused Christian leaders to decide to observe "Christmas" on this day, which means "Christ-sent," hoping this would help new converts resist the temptation of partaking in the pagan feast. (Following the same reasoning, many churches have a special banquet and program for high school seniors on the night of the annual Senior Prom.)

At any rate, the celebration of Christmas is definitely not a continuation of a pagan custom. It is a unique Christian holiday to counteract the influence of a pagan holiday. Pagans did something on every day, and we cannot do away with all the days they used, whether for worship or for ceremonies about sowing or reaping or about the solstices or the new moons. We use the same sun heathens worshiped, and we love the sun rising and setting, though we do not have the heathen ceremonies about that.

In 1936 I held a blessed revival campaign in the Binghamton Theatre in Binghamton, New York, sponsored by eight churches. The fact that in this theatre people had seen lewd movies or burlesque shows or legitimate theatre productions did not change the fact that now the building was used for the glory of God and souls were saved.

I myself am under new management, too. Once the Devil lived within; now Jesus Christ does. So if heathen used December 25 for idolatry, why should Christians not use it now to honor Jesus Christ and His birth? If we set aside any day to honor Christ, it will be a day somebody else has used for bad purposes.

But now all the days belong to Christ and none to heathen gods. No Christian should be grieved if we think about the birth of Christ on December 25. Is that a worse sin than working to make money on that day? Why should anybody object if we sing Christmas carols, have a happy celebration with a feast and go over the Bible story of His birth and teach it to our children, on Christmas Day? We would not honor God more by having less Scripture, less singing, less of the spirit of giving, less manifestation of love for others. All the days belong to Christ; and December 25 should be used to honor Him, too.

4. "Christmas Trees and Decorations Are an Abomination"

Many people believe Jeremiah 10:1-4 is talking about Christmas trees; therefore, it is a sin to put up one. Notice verses 3 and 4:

"For the customs of the people are vain: for one cutteth a tree out of the forest, the work of the hands of the workman, with the axe. They deck it with silver and with gold; they fasten it with nails and with hammers, that it move not."

This is a description of an idol made of wood and covered with silver and gold. Notice that God tells Israel not to be afraid of these idols because "...they must needs be borne, because they cannot go. Be not afraid of them; for they cannot do evil, neither also is it in them to do good."

As a matter of fact, the Christmas tree has a distinctive Christian origin. In the 8th century an English missionary named Boniface went to Germany to preach Christ. The Germans, at that time, were heathen and worshiped idols. One of their objects of worship was the oak tree. But Boniface told them God was more like the evergreen tree which did not lose its leaves and appear to be dead in the winter.

So gradually, as people were converted to Christ, the evergreen tree became a symbol of the Eternal God in whom they had learned to trust. Eventually the evergreen tree was used for decoration at the Christmas feast. And because God had shown His love to us through the gift of His Son, it became customary for Christians to give gifts to those whom they loved at Christmastime.

The decorations on a Christmas tree could not possibly be called heathen nor have any idolatrous significance. Who thinks that heathens worshiped their gods with paper chains? that popcorn on a string is a form of idolatry? that electric lights on it for the joy of little children to brighten the home, are sinful?

I love Christmas and its decorations, which are but an expression of joy in my heart as I think how God became man, how the Creator became a Babe, how "though...rich, yet for [our] sakes he became poor, that [we] through his poverty might be rich."

It is sad that the world as a whole does leave Christ out of Christmas. But for those of us who love the Lord, it can be a blessed time of fun and feasting and fellowship.

5. "There Is Too Much Revelry During the Christmas Holidays"

It is true that many do not honor Jesus Christ at Christmas. Some drink more liquor during Christmastime than at any other time. That is a sin. Many business people think of Christmas only as a time to make money. In this they are wrong. Sometimes even Christians lie about Santa Claus and deceive little children with a heathen legend, when they could tell about the dear Lord Jesus. That is wicked. Deceit is the poorest possible way to honor the birth of our Lord.

I do not believe in having a Santa Claus at Sunday school or in the church service unless all understand that it is only a little parody, only play-acting. Certainly to deceive little ones with a lie is a sin. No Christian ought to condone it. The truth is so much better than a lie. We should tell them how the dear Lord came into the world to save sinners.

Yes, people often dishonor God at Christmas. I am sorry they do. I hope you will not grieve God by such a sin.

But we should not turn Christmas over to Satan and wicked people because some misuse the Christmas season.

Should we abandon Sunday because it is often misused?

On the Lord's day there is more drinking, more revelry, than on any other day of the week. Should Christians, therefore, count the Lord's day the Devil's day and give it up? Certainly not.

A great many teach that baptism is essential to salvation. They give more honor to the water than to the blood. That is wrong. But should we, therefore, disobey Jesus Christ about baptism because some others have overstressed baptism and made it a false doctrine?

The second coming has been a greatly abused and perverted doctrine with many. False cults have greatly perverted the doctrine of Christ's coming. People set dates. They speculate on signs. Should the rest of us Bible Christians, then, ignore the clear Bible doctrine of Christ's imminent return because the doctrine has been abused? Certainly not.

Nor should we ignore the Bible doctrine of the fullness of the Spirit just because many associate it with talking in tongues and with sinless perfection.

Just so—we would be very foolish to turn Christmas over to Satan and worldlings. If the world has a Christmas of revelry, let us make it a day of love and a time of honoring Christ. Let us make much of the Christmas story, of Christmas carols, of Christian love and fellowship.

Do other people make giving of gifts a mere form? Well, it does not need to be so for Christians. We can give gifts that really express our love. We can make the gifts the response of an honest heart. We can send greetings with Scripture verses and with holy admonitions.

Is it wrong to have a day of rejoicing? Is it wrong to feast and to send portions to others? No indeed.

When, under Nehemiah, the remnant of Israel went back to the Land of Promise from the captivity in Babylon, when the Law was read and explained, the people wept. It was not a time for weeping, but a time for rejoicing. The wall of Jerusalem had been rebuilt, the gates hung, the city restored as the city of God, and the worship had begun.

Let us listen to the plain commands of the Lord in such a case, as given in Nehemiah 8:9,10:

"And Nehemiah, which is the Tirshatha, and Ezra the priest the scribe, and the Levites that taught the people, said unto all the people, This day is holy unto the Lord your God; mourn not, nor weep. For all the people wept, when they heard the words of the law. Then he said unto them, Go your way, eat the fat, and drink the sweet, and send portions unto them for whom nothing is prepared: for this day is holy unto our Lord: neither be ye sorry; for the joy of the Lord is your strength."

And we are glad to learn in verse 12:

"And all the people went their way to eat, and to drink, and to send portions, and to make great mirth, because they had understood the words that were declared unto them."

If Israelites would honor God by having a day of joy and feasting and of sending portions to others because the wall was rebuilt, the gates set up, the worship established, then we today do well to have a day of rejoicing over the birth of the Saviour and to send portions to one another and to make merry with spiritual joy.

I feel nearer to God at Christmas than at any other time. I seem to love the Word of God more at Christmas, when we read and quote it again and again. I like the time as a good excuse to get into people's hearts and win them to Christ. And many have been saved because I brought a Christmas message, or urged sinners to accept God's great Christmas gift.

Let us have, then, a happy Christmas, and make Christ supreme on this day which we remember in honor of His birth!

6. "Is It Proper to Give Gifts to Others on Christ's Birthday?"

Certainly Christ should be first. But then He wants and deserves first place on every other day also! Giving should honor Christ, and certainly we should give ourselves and all we have to Him. But giving gifts to others is also a proper way to honor the Lord, according to Bible example and teaching.

At the feast of Durim, a feast to the Lord celebrating the great deliverance God gave the Jews in answer to the prayers of Mordecai and Esther and other devout Jews when wicked Haman planned to exterminate them, Jews were taught "that they should make them days of feasting and joy, and of *sending portions one to another,* and *gifts to the poor"* (Esther 9:22).

When the Jewish remnant who returned from the captivity began to mourn on an holy day, as they met to hear the reading of the law, they were instructed, "Go your way, eat the fat, and drink the sweet, and *send portions unto them for whom nothing is prepared,* for this day is holy unto our Lord" (Neh. 8:10). So they returned home for feasting and sending gifts.

Then giving gifts, if it be done in the right spirit and motive, honors God on special days set apart for Him.

Remember that God does not need our material things, except as He wants them for people. So, under some circumstances giving to others may be as pleasing to Him as giving to pastors and missionaries. We should take care to give in Jesus' name, remembering specially the poor at Christmas. But the right kind of giving to others is certainly fitting on Christmas.

When the rich young ruler wanted to be perfect, he was instructed to give his property to the poor, not to Jesus (Matt. 19:21); when Zacchaeus was converted, he was led to say "the half of my goods I give to the poor" (Luke 19:8). That pleased Jesus very much.

Jesus said that He would reward every one who gave a cup of cold water in His name. He also said, "Inasmuch as ye have done it unto one of the least of these my brethren, ye have done it unto me" (Matt. 25:40).

So giving to others must please Christ very much, if it is done in loving thought toward Him and in His name. Certainly we should give to missions, to the poor and also to loved ones and relatives at Christmas. But be sure your motives are right.

7. "Should Christians Tell Their Children There Is a Santa Claus?"

Certainly not! Lying and deceit are wicked. Lying on Christmas is as great a sin as lying on any other day. It is shameful that Sunday schools often choose to teach a lying fable at Christmastime, instead of teaching the marvelous true Christmas stories about the Baby in the manger, the shepherds in the field, the angel's announcement of a Saviour born, the heavenly chorus, and the Wise Men from the East. The story of the virgin-born Saviour is sweeter than any lie or fable invented by heathen people and spread by non-Christians.

I remember the sad, sad day when I, five years old, found that my father and mother and kin people had deceived me about Santa Claus—or Saint Nicolas. I was ashamed. I had been victimized. Those I trusted more than anybody else on earth, devout Christians, had lied. Perhaps other things they said were not true, too. So Christmas was something of a mockery to me for years, until I began to learn the sweetness of a Christmas centered about the birth of Christ.

Lying is wicked, is plainly forbidden in the Bible, and is certain to have bad results. And the lie about Santa Claus is specially hurtful in that it crowds out interest in Christ Himself. The Lord Jesus, in many so-called Christian homes, is crowded out by the old fabled gentleman always seen on whiskey ads at this season of the year.

Parents should always tell the truth. My own children were happier about Christmas than those children who have known Christmas as the celebration of a lie.

8. "What About 'Xmas'?"

Many people distribute leaflets urging us to "keep Christ in Christmas." In these tracts they sometimes attack the use of "Xmas" as an abbreviation of Christmas. X, they say, is a symbol for an unknown quantity, and this is a devious device of the Devil to remove the name of Christ from Christmas.

While I personally feel it best not to use the abbreviated word, "Xmas," it was not a deliberate attempt—at least at first—to "take Christ out of Christmas." Actually, in Greek language a large letter similar to an X stood for the letters *CH,* and thus for *Christ.* Originally, then, *Xmas* was *Christ-mas.*

Be that as it may, I am strongly in favor of putting "Christ back in Christmas," and I never use the abbreviated "Xmas."

XVI.

Decide This Christmas to Serve God Without Regard for Consequences

JOHN R. RICE

Matthew 6:25: "Therefore I say unto you, Take no thought for your life...nor yet for your body."

Verse 34, "Take therefore no thought for the morrow...."

As I meditated on the Christmas story and on Christ's birth, I was amazed at the attitude of heart of those whom God saw fit to bless. So in connection with this Scripture, I speak on "Serving God Without Any Regard for Consequences."

Our need is to serve God on this basis: our minds are already made up, we already know that it pays to serve Him and to put Him first. We will not worry about bread and meat, about friends, about whether we live or die. We will serve God without regard to consequences.

COUNT THE COST AND SETTLE IT ONCE FOR ALL

The Saviour said we are to count the cost. The Bible commands us to sit down and count the cost of serving Christ.

That is like a man who builds a tower: he must first sit down and figure the cost.

It is like a man who starts war: he had better figure whether with his 10,000 he can meet the other king with 20,000. If so, go ahead; if not, then send an ambassage desiring peace.

Do you mean business? Is your mind made up to serve Christ without regard to consequences? Christians ought to do that, but that should happen just once. Get it settled once for all: *I am for God; I can risk Him, and I will serve Him.* After that, then a Christian should come to the place where he can say, *I will not take thought for my life, for my body, what I eat or drink or wear. I will take no thought of tomor-*

row but leave tomorrow with God. Already I have counted the cost and tried God. Already I have found it pays to serve Him. Already I have found God can be trusted in the dark, without my knowing the future. I can serve Him without a guarantee. I can serve Him without any visible evidence as to how He will bring me out.

Would you like a woman to say, "Yes," then before you even married, have to re-convince her forty times; then after marriage, hear her say, "But I want to live with Mother," and have to settle that matter again and again? Then when the question came up as to what kind of house you would live in, hear her say, "Well, if I can't live in such and such a house, I think I would be better off back home"? All the time you had to fight it out again and again that you could give her more than her mother and dad could.

Or how would you like to live with her when it was an open question whether she could be true to you, live with you, wear your name?

Then what does God think about it when a man, claiming to be a Christian, argues about everything God tells him to do? How does God feel when that Christian says, "Yes, Lord, I will follow where You lead, will go where You want me to go," then even if it is only the 10¢ out of $1.00 it has to be argued out and weighed all over again whether it pays to tithe?

Every time there is a chance to serve God, you put it under a microscope and check it very carefully to see whether it pays or not! When you decide to teach a Sunday school class, you have to weigh whether to give up some habit, some amusement; whether you can be at church every Sunday! If you were God, how would you deal with a bunch of Christians who were never settled, and every time He tells them to do something, it has to be fought out again?

What I am talking about is that every Christian should settle once and for all, *I will serve God without regard to consequences. I have already counted the cost and decided it is worthwhile.* Make up your mind that whatever may come tomorrow, you will be right in the will of God!

MARY SERVED GOD IN THIS MANNER

I call attention first to those connected with Christ's birth.

One day as a virgin sat alone, the angel of the Lord appeared to her. Imagine how startled she must have been! Her face must have turned white at the sight of an angel, who said to her, "Fear not, Mary, thou hast found favour with God." She must have prayed a lot.

"Behold, thou shalt conceive in thy womb, and bring forth a son, and shalt call his name JESUS. He shall be great, and shall be called the Son of the Highest; and the Lord God shall give unto him the throne of his father David: And he shall reign over the house of Jacob for ever: and of his kingdom there shall be no end."

But Mary questioned, "How can that be? I am not married, and I have never known a man."

The angel answered, "The Holy Ghost shall come upon thee, and the power of the Highest shall overshadow thee: therefore also that holy thing which shall be born of thee shall be called the Son of God."

Do you suppose Mary pondered: "If I become a mother when I am not married, I must face public shame. No one will understand. People won't believe what I tell them. Can I stand it?" Did Mary weigh the whole thing? No. Rather, with a glad heart she said to the angel, "Be it unto me according to thy word," or, "Oh, let it be just as you have said!"

God sent Elisabeth to talk with Mary. Elisabeth exclaimed, "Blessed art thou among women... because you believed what God said!"

Mary didn't have to fight it all out, weigh the thing, count the cost. She didn't say, "Well, now—wait! Let me see how it will turn out." She gave herself to open and public shame that she might bear in her body the Baby Jesus and become the mother of the Son of God without regard to the consequences, taking no thought how it would turn out.

JOSEPH DISREGARDED THE SHAME AND MISUNDERSTANDING TO TAKE MARY AND REAR JESUS

Joseph loved Mary; but he was troubled. Wouldn't you be, too, in such a case? If your bride-to-be was such a pure girl, of noble lineage—of the house and lineage of David? Though poor and poverty-stricken, yet she was a princess. God selected this girl, out of all the women in the world, to be the mother of His Son. Don't you think you would have loved her, too? Oh, how much Joseph loved Mary! When he was with her, she no doubt was timid and blushed, and she couldn't speak of it to him. But the outward evidence grew until finally Joseph could see that she was going to become a mother.

Has Mary done wrong? He wept over the matter alone, but dared not mention it to her. *If I report her to public authorities, she will be taken out and stoned. And I don't want that.*

But one night in his sleep, in his troubled slumber, the angel of the Lord came to him and said: ". . . fear not to take unto thee Mary thy wife: for that which is conceived in her is of the Holy Ghost. And she shall bring forth a son, and thou shalt call his name JESUS: for he shall save his people from their sins."

Not much is said about Joseph. He must have died before the Saviour had grown to manhood, for we never hear of him after Jesus was twelve years of age; but Joseph was a great man of God. That day when he woke out of his slumber, he knew within himself, *It is of God. I will not fear the future. I will take Mary as my wife. I will care for her. Never mind what men say. The restraint and patience necessary—I will not mind that.* ". . . and he knew her not until she had brought forth her firstborn son."

So Joseph had no regard for the consequences. He took no thought. He did what God said.

THE WISE MEN DID NOT HESITATE TO SPEND MONEY AND TIME FOR GOD

The Wise Men traveled from the East to see Baby Jesus. They had read in the book of Daniel about the coming Messiah. That was the only part of the Old Testament that they had in Babylon, and it was written by Daniel the prophet while there in captivity. After reading the 9th chapter of Daniel, the Wise Men knew that after the decree of Cyrus to rebuild Jerusalem, there would be sixty-nine weeks of years until the Messiah would come. Now those sixty-nine weeks of years, 483 years, had already come to pass; it was now time for the promised King of the Jews. They were watching and ready; so when the star appeared, they knew it was His star, the evidence they had waited for.

The Holy Spirit told them the Saviour, the King of the Jews, had been born.

I do not know of their good-byes to family and friends, who they put in charge of their businesses, nor what words were said to their wives and families about being gone so long and so far. But arrangements were made and then they mounted their camels and rode away yonder toward the west from Babylon, some five or six hundred miles, riding on around the northern part of the desert and across the Jordan River, until they came to Jerusalem, where they inquired, "Where is he that is born King of the Jews? for we have seen his star in the east, and are come to worship him."

After looking it up in the Bible, the scribes said, "It must be at Bethlehem, for Micah 5:2 says he will be born there." Following the star, they came straight to the Baby Jesus and opened their treasures—gold, frankincense and myrrh. After leaving their gifts, they returned home.

Can you imagine the expense of such a journey with no cars, no trains, no paved roads—only camels to ride? It was from one nation to another nation, a nation of a strange language. Can you imagine the time involved—months, perhaps? They brought treasures along—gold, frankincense and myrrh. They came far, without regard to the consequences, taking no thought for the morrow and serving God with no reservations.

SHEPHERDS TOO DISREGARDED THE CONSEQUENCES TO SEE THE BABY

Remember the shepherds, recorded in Luke 2, keeping watch over their flocks? Seeing an angel, they were afraid. But the angel said unto them,

"Fear not: for, behold, I bring you good tidings of great joy, which shall be to all people. For unto you is born this day in the city of David a Saviour, which is Christ the Lord. And this shall be a sign unto you; Ye shall find the babe wrapped in swaddling clothes, lying in a manger. And suddenly there was with the angel a multitude of the heavenly host praising God, and saying, Glory to God in the highest, and on earth peace, good will toward men."

These men, these shepherds, said, "Let us now go even unto Bethlehem, and see this thing which is come to pass, which the Lord hath made known unto us."

No one was left to watch the sheep. They could have mused, *Suppose a wolf gets our sheep,* but no one thought like that. A Saviour is much more important than sheep!

So these shepherds hurry down to Bethlehem to find the Saviour. They find the Baby Jesus in a manger wrapped in swaddling clothes by the side of His mother. They forgot the consequences.

Then what did they do when they had seen the Saviour? Their hearts rejoiced and they said, "It is true! It is true!" The Scripture says they went out praising and glorifying God, telling the good news. Then after telling everyone, they came back to their pastures and sheep.

Were all the sheep still there when they returned? The Bible doesn't say, for it does not matter. If a Saviour is born, what if a wolf did get a sheep or two! I imagine they were all accounted for, but if not, the shepherds didn't grieve over it. They did what they should have done, without wondering if the sheep would all be safe. They served God without any regard to the consequences. They took no thought. They believed, and God blessed them for it.

Won't you today start serving God without always taking thought, and always counting the cost?

THE THREE HEBREW CHILDREN STAYED TRUE, DISREGARDING THE CONSEQUENCES

Turn back to Daniel 2. We need some iron in our blood like these men had.

Nebuchadnezzar built a great image, 90 feet high and 9 feet wide, demanding that the people fall down and worship it. While the orchestra played and the drums rolled, all were to bow down before the image set up in the plain of Dura, in the province of Babylon.

While all were bowing down to the image, someone peeked and saw that Shadrach, Meshach and Abednego were standing up straight. A tattletale hotfooted it to the king and told him about the three Jews who would not bow to the image.

When Nebuchadnezzar was told this, he said unto them, "Is it true . . . that you do not yet serve my gods, nor worship the golden image which I have set up?" They said it was true. He told them he would give them one more chance and if they worshiped not, they would be cast into the midst of a burning fiery furnace, seven times hotter than before. Listen to what they said: "O Nebuchadnezzar, we are not careful to answer thee in this matter." They asked for no time to consider the matter but said,

"If it be so, our God, whom we serve is able to deliver us from the burning fiery furnace, and he will deliver us out of thine hand, O king. But if not, be it known unto thee, O king, that we will not serve thy gods, nor worship the golden image which thou hast set up."

Those three had already voted! How wonderful when we find Christians who have already made up their minds, wonderful to find men who already know what they are going to do for God. If there comes a time of testing, they have already foreseen it and they say, "God is able to deliver us, and God will deliver us. But if He doesn't, we will do what He says anyway."

So these three said, "We will not bow down to the image."

Nebuchadnezzar had the music play again. Still they didn't bow.

Now the king got mad. He ordered, "Poke up the fire, and grab these men."

They were tied with their hats on their heads and with their court garments on and pitched into the fire. The fire was so hot that it killed those strong soldiers who put them in. But all the fire did to Shadrach, Meshach and Abednego was to burn their bands off so they could walk around in the fire!

One came and walked with them, and His form was like the Son of man. I think Nebuchadnezzar was converted right there. The proclamation he gave showed he believed in the true God.

Shadrach, Meshach and Abednego didn't have to count the cost —they had already counted it and considered whether it pays to serve God.

BRAVE DANIEL SERVED GOD FAITHFULLY, EVEN THOUGH THREATENED WITH THE LIONS' DEN

A decree was issued that no one could pray to any god for thirty days; the king was to be above everybody.

"Now when Daniel knew that the writing was signed, he went into his house; and his windows being open in his chamber toward Jerusalem, he kneeled upon his knees three times a day, and prayed, and gave thanks before his God, as he did aforetime." —Dan. 6:10.

Daniel knew just what they did, but it caused not a tremor in his voice when he prayed. It didn't cause him to hesitate and say, "O God, give me courage." He had already made up his mind to any consequences; so he opened the windows. This time he didn't pray in the secret closet. (There are times to pray in secret, and times to pray in public.) Rather, he opened his windows and prayed toward the God of Jerusalem, as he had done before, three times a day.

I say, Daniel served God without regard to the consequences, without taking thought for what might happen! Daniel already knew his God was greater than a den of lions!

My friends, what happens isn't your business but God's. Yours is to serve Him day by day, risking yourself with Him and letting Him do the rest.

PETER AND JOHN OBEYED GOD, TOOK BEATING AND SHAME WITHOUT CARE

In Acts 4 there came a time of testing:

"But Peter and John answered and said unto them, Whether it be right in the sight of God to hearken unto you more than unto God, judge ye. For we cannot but speak the things which we have seen and heard. So when they had further threatened them, they let them go, finding nothing how they might punish them, because of the people: for all men glorified God for that which was done." —vss. 19-21.

And in chapter 5 they were arrested again:

"And when they had brought them, they set them before the council: and the high priest asked them, Saying, Did not we straitly command you that ye should not teach in this name? and, behold, ye have filled Jerusalem with your doctrine, and intend to bring this man's blood upon us. Then Peter and the other apostles answered and said, We ought to obey God rather than men." —vss. 27-29.

If God said so, that settled it.

Wouldn't you this Christmas want to say, "I will, one time, give God a gift and not renege on Him. I won't take it back"? Give yourself lock, stock and barrel, and don't take it back tomorrow.

MAKE YOUR DECISION PERMANENT: "I WON'T TAKE IT BACK!"

The Jews had a rule, commanded in the Old Testament, that if a man had a Jewish slave, after seven years he could be set free.

But suppose a slave said, "I would rather stay here and be your slave." Then he is brought to the doorpost, the servant puts his ear to the post and his master takes an awl and pushes it through, making a hole in his ear, then he becomes a slave forever (Read Exod. 21:1-6).

I hope you will say, "God, take me to the doorpost and put a hole through my ear—not just until I find a better job, not just until I find a firm that pays more, but make me FOREVER Yours."

When I was ten, we were living on a ranch in West Texas. Christmas to us was special. For example, we got one orange at Christmas—we rarely had any at any other time in the year. Then it didn't take very much to make a happy Christmas. We had no orange groves in Texas then; they were shipped in from California and were rather expensive, and we were poor. So at Christmas we each got an orange, along with a few nuts and twisted candy.

My stepmother said, "Children, I can make a fruitcake but I will have to make citron with your orange peelings. I will candy the peelings."

We all agreed. That may seem funny to you now. Why should children object to giving the orange peel? But if you got just one a year, you could eat the peeling with a little sugar and it was delicious. Remember, we hadn't had an orange since last Christmas. When we got bananas, we not only ate the bananas but also scraped the inside.

We each gave Mother the peelings from our oranges. She put them up on top of the kitchen safe so we couldn't see them and be tempted. No refrigerator, of course. It was a safe with tin doors and nail holes punched in the doors. They were to be left there several days, then Mother would candy them.

I got to thinking about the orange peels: *That orange was given to me for Christmas and I didn't have to give it, did I? Why did I give it all? I ought to have kept a little, one good section. I could have eaten it with some sugar. Besides, I don't think she needs that much.*

So I went back, reached high on the safe and got one piece and ate it with some sugar. Boy, was it good!

A day or two later as I thought about it, I decided I could have one more piece. *It was mine anyway, wasn't it?* So I took another section from the top of the safe. You know, I lost count of how many times I went back!

But one day when I reached up there for another piece of *my* orange peeling, nobody's was up there!

I have many times told God, "Lord, You can have me. Send me anywhere. I will give up anything for You. You deserve it, and You can have it." When I said that I meant it; but soon I felt myself reaching back on top of the safe to take myself back and have my own way instead of God's way.

At this Christmas season, I hope you will tell Him, "God, I will, from now on, commit myself to Thee as a bond slave. I will take no thought for the morrow, nor worry today about what the future holds."

Someone says, "Dr. Rice, I would like to tithe, but I have so many bills." Can you never think about God without thinking about bills at the same time?

Another says, "God has called me, but if I go, I will have to leave my loved ones." Can you never think about God without thinking about family at the same time?

The Wise Men would never have come from the East had they thought or worried about their families. The shepherds would never have left their sheep if they couldn't think about the Baby Jesus without thinking about their sheep.

Some never get their minds enough on God to forget sheep. Some never get their minds enough on God to forget what they eat. That is why Jesus said to His disciples in John 4, "Lift up your eyes, and look on the fields; for they are white already to harvest." In other words, "Get your eyes off food and look on poor lost souls." Oh, if we would get our minds on God and forget other things! *Take no thought!*

You think, *If I teach in the Sunday school, I must give up this, that and the other, and be there on time.* Can't you do that much for God! Can't you count the cost and come to this conclusion: When God said do a thing, I don't have to stop and consider it anew?

CAN YOU NOT TRUST GOD WITHOUT SEEING WHERE THE ROAD MAY LEAD?

A certain horse belonging to my father was a great lesson to me.

This horse was blind. One could ride him, but others couldn't tell he was blind. Ride him down the road and though this horse couldn't see where he put his foot, yet he trusted the man riding him, and went right ahead as if he could see.

My daddy got him by trading a horse with the heaves.

He rode beside a fellow one night and seeing this horse had such a wonderful gait, said, "What about trading horses?"

"All right, I will trade with you."

My dad said, "No questions asked, and we will trade for good?"

The fellow agreed.

Right there they changed saddles. My father got on this blind horse and rode him home that night. The next day Dad discovered he

...SERVE GOD WITHOUT REGARD FOR CONSEQUENCES 215

had traded for a blind horse but one that trusted his rider.

My friend, can't you tell God, "I can serve Thee blind"?

If God came to borrow $10.00 from you, would you ask Him to sign a promissory note?

If God wanted to buy something from you on credit, would you look up His name in Dunn and Bradstreet?

Many of you have to weigh things out and check up on God before you say "yes" or "no" to Him! Shame on you!

Oh, if we Christians could learn to act without any fear of the consequences, without considering the consequences! The Bible says, "Take no thought for the morrow." Take no thought for your body. Take no thought for your life. Take no thought for what you will eat and drink.

Wouldn't it be great if what you put in the collection on Sunday was put in without regard for what you will need next week?

If God says to me, "John, I want you to go to Africa," then I should say, "All right, Lord, I will go." I should not sit down and say, "There is my wife. She will not want to leave her children." I should not tell God, "Wait! Let me check on this business before I say 'yes.'" What should I do if God says go to Africa? Before saying "yes" to Him, do I always have to take the whole thing up every time and find out whether it pays to serve Him, find out whether it is worthwhile to do what He says?

Christians, here is something you ought to get settled: "I will count the cost once and for all and find out if it pays to serve God. When I have found that out, I will have it settled. I will say 'yes' to God. If God says to me, 'Do so and so,' I will not hesitate, I will not take thought when I find the will of God."

Steam automobiles were a good deal cheaper to run than gas automobiles. We used to see many steam cars. Some things about them were better. One was, you didn't have to have a gear shift. For years experimenters have spent thousands of dollars trying to make an automobile without a gear shift. A steam engine automatically adjusts to any load and never stalls. The more power, the less speed, and the less power, the more speed.

Why don't we use steam cars? And why don't they make them now? *Because it takes ten minutes to get the water hot!* And we can't always wait that long. So steam cars are now museum pieces.

God wants people to serve Him, but He sometimes has to wait for you to get the water hot when He wants you to do anything! Is He going to always, always wait for you to take thought for everything else, when He says, "Go"?

Each time God brings up a duty, there is a big tussle, a knock-down, drag-out fight before He can get you to do something, while you again decide whether to serve God, while you again count the cost! Must you always count the cost anew before deciding you will do what God said?

My brother Joe had a model-T Ford. He told me, "Any time you jack up both hind wheels and crank it until the water boils, it will start."

If you go at it that way, you may get some to teach a Sunday school class. You may get some to tithe. You may get some to prayer meeting. You may get some to testify. If you jack up both hind wheels and crank until the water boils, you can get some to do something for God. But God is not content with the kind of service that comes with a grudge, always with the brakes on.

I was in a revival in Hico, near Lampassas, Texas. Live oak trees and white limestone were everywhere. I was hurrying to get to the revival when I came upon a fellow with car trouble. I tried to help get it started but couldn't, so I said, "If you want me to, I will pull you in."

I hooked on with a tow chain and over those rough, rocky roads we went, driving about thirty miles per hour. The man in the car I was towing couldn't see, so he kept putting on the brakes. Finally I stopped to see what was wrong. He said, "I will just sit here if you don't mind. Just unhook the chain and I will send my boy after the car later."

Does God want to take you when He always has to drag you, when you always have the brakes on, when you won't go unless you can see the road? You are always thinking about the cost: "Will I have sufficient to eat? I will serve You, Lord, if my family doesn't go hungry." Or, "I would sing in the choir but I don't think it is worth the trouble." Or, "I would take a class but I don't have time to study, and I can't give up going to see Mother every second Sunday."

Why don't you make up your mind, like the shepherds, who didn't worry over their sheep when the Saviour was born? Or like the Wise Men from the East, who left home and families to bring their gifts to this far country, giving all they had? Why not say, as did Mary, "Be it unto me according to thy word"? And like Joseph who, when he arose out of his sleep, went and took Mary home with him.

Don't count the cost. Tell God He can have all of you. Lay all on the altar, and take nothing back.

Some may be here who are unsaved, but you would like to be a Christian. Can you say at this Christmas season, "I will trust Him to be my Saviour. I will take Him as mine. God loves me, offered me the best Gift in the world—His Son—and I will take Him today"? Will you come and take Christ as your Saviour?

JOE HENRY HANKINS
1889-1967

ABOUT THE MAN:

"He was a weeping prophet" is the way Dr. Hankins was characterized by those who knew him best—one of the 20th century's great soul-winning preachers.

BUT—Hankins preached sharply, strongly against sin. Would to God we had more men of his mettle in a ministry today that has largely been given over to namby-pamby, mealy-mouthed silence when it comes to strong preaching against sin.

Dr. John R. Rice wrote of him: *"His method and manifest spiritual power would remind one of D. L. Moody. He has the keen, scholarly, analytical mind of an R. A. Torrey, and the love and compassion of soul of a Wilbur Chapman."*

Hankins was born in Arkansas and saved as a youth. He graduated from high school in Pine Bluff, then from Quachita Baptist College. He held pastorates in Pine Bluff, Arkansas; in Whitewright, Greenville and Childress, Texas. His last and most productive pastorate was the First Baptist Church, Little Rock, Arkansas. There, in less than five years, 1,799 additions by letter, 1,144 by baptism—an average of 227 baptisms a year—made a total of 2,943 members added to the church. Sunday school spiralled to nearly 1,400; membership mushroomed to 3,200 despite a deletion of 882 to revise the rolls.

In 1942, Hankins gave up the pastorate for full-time evangelism.

In 1967, Dr. Hankins passed on to the Heaven he loved to preach about. Be sure that he was greeted by a thronging host of redeemed souls—saved under his Spirit-filled ministry.

XVII.

"Good Tidings"

JOE HENRY HANKINS

"And the angel said unto them, Fear not: for, behold, I bring you good tidings of great joy, which shall be to all people. For unto you is born this day in the city of David a Saviour, which is Christ the Lord." —Luke 2:10, 11.

I wish I could find words with which to express the meaning of that announcement made by the angel that night to the shepherds on the hills of Judaea. But no human language can express what Christ has meant to one single heart and life, much less to put in words what His coming has meant to the world for these nineteen hundred years; and to the multiplied millions who have found cleansing from sin as they have been washed in His blood; that have found that "peace of God, which passeth all understanding" as He has lifted the burden of sin from their souls, as He has opened the prison houses and set the captives free. "If the Son therefore shall make you free, ye shall be free indeed."

One could not begin to express in human speech what He has meant in the hour of sorrow for these nineteen hundred years as men have walked into the valley of shadows and felt the touch of His hand and the joy of His presence; as they have leaned upon His rod and staff and found support and comfort. He has never yet failed a single one. We could not express what He has meant to dying saints as their feet have touched the brim of the swollen Jordan of death.

No wonder the angel said, "I bring you good tidings of great joy."

The Greatest Day in History

Beloved, it was a great day when "in the beginning was the Word, and the Word was with God, and the Word was God." And the Word spoke, and out of nothing came this universe, with all its mystery and wonders.

It was a great day when the Triune God held the council of eternity and said, "Let us make man in our image... in the image of God created he him, male and female created he them."

After sin had come, it was a great day when the great God came down in compassion, mercy and grace and called that hiding pair out from among the trees and said, "Adam, where art thou?" And there in the garden He gave the promise of a Redeemer to that sorrowing, heartbroken pair whose sun had gone out in the sky, whose hearts were seized and overcome with fear as they scurried away from the presence of God and hid themselves among the trees in the garden and, with futile effort, tried to cover their nakedness from His presence.

It was a great day when God said the seed of the woman shall bruise the serpent's head.

It was a great day when God took three million slaves by the hand and led them out of the land of Egypt, opened the Red Sea and delivered them dry-shod on the other side.

But the greatest day this old world had ever known was when the angel said, 'This day a Saviour is born.'

Jesus had come at last. Oh, how sweet that name! The redeemed of God have sung it in their sweetest anthems, in carols and hymns of praise. For nineteen hundred years the theme of our song has been "Jesus, Blessed Jesus."

>**Sweetest note in seraph song,**
>**Sweetest name on mortal tongue,**
>**Sweetest carol every sung—**
>**Jesus, blessed Jesus!**

And the redeemed of God shall sing it throughout all eternity. For when God took His hand that day on the Isle of Patmos and pulled aside the curtain of Heaven and gave His old Apostle John a peep into the home of the soul, John said, "A great multitude, which no man could number, of all nations, and kindreds, and people, and tongues, stood before the throne, and before the Lamb, clothed with white robes, and with palms in their hands" (Rev. 7:9).

They were singing and playing on their harps and their music was like the "voice of many waters." As the chorus swelled, it was like the voice of great thunders. On and on it went until it was like the voice of a great earthquake—until the very walls of Heaven resounded and reverberated with the beat of its music. And what are they singing? "Unto him who loved us and loosed us from our sins in his own blood."

Jesus, blessed Jesus. Don't you love Him? Isn't it great to be a Christian?

Poets have written their sweetest odes to Him.

Singers have sung their greatest songs in an effort to express out of the human heart what this announcement meant.

Painters have spent a lifetime in producing their greatest masterpieces as an expression of what He has meant to human heart and life.

Prophets and the writers of both the Old and the New Testaments have exhausted human language in trying to tell of what they felt.

Isaiah, the greatest and most eloquent of all the prophets, after exhausting his entire vocabulary and finding no other speech in which to describe the coming Saviour, said, "His name shall be called Wonderful." Again: "He is the Balm of Gilead, the Rose of Sharon, the Lily of the Valley; He is the One altogether lovely."

When the great Apostle Paul had exhausted the Greek language trying to tell us what he felt in his heart about the Christ, he closed with this burst of praise upon his soul: "Thanks be unto God for his unspeakable gift!"

"Thou shalt call his name JESUS."

"Fear Not"

But listen to the angel's announcement. "Fear not: for, behold, I bring you good tidings of great joy."

Yesterday afternoon I got my concordance and began to run through it to find where God had used those two words, "Fear not." More than one hundred times I found them spoken from the heart of God to the heart of humanity that is so beset and torn with fear. For, after all, the greatest enemy of our lives is our fears. The most unsettled thing in human life is fear and anxiety—anxious about the morrow; afraid of the future; afraid of the present; afraid of another war; afraid of what may lie out yonder in the immediate future for our gallant sons; afraid of what may come to the shores of our fair land; afraid that we may hear the hum of the plane motors of the invader and the burst of its bombs; afraid of what may happen to our homes, our lives and our loved ones.

Oh, hear God this morning as He says more than one hundred times in His Word to His people, "Fear not."

Then I began to search for that expression, "Be not afraid," and over and over again, spread all through God's Word from Genesis to Revelation, I found God saying, "Be not afraid."

Jesus says, "Let not your heart be troubled: ye believe in God, believe also in me. In my Father's house are many mansions: if it were not so, I would have told you. I go to prepare a place for you. And if I go and prepare a place for you, I will come again, and receive you unto myself; that where I am, there ye may be also."

You can count on it; you can depend on what Jesus says.

Just before He enters the Garden of Gethsemane, I hear Him saying, "Peace I leave with you, my peace I give unto you: not as the world giveth, give I unto you. Let not your heart be troubled, neither let it be afraid" (John 14:27).

Fear not! Fear not!

Alone yonder after his long journey from Ur of the Chaldees, having made his way over a thousand miles on foot not knowing whither he went and finally arriving in the land of Canaan, God appears to Abraham, a stranger in a strange land, saying, "Fear not, Abram: I am thy shield, and thy exceeding great reward" (Gen. 15:1).

Isaac was beset with the enemy on every hand. Everywhere he tried to settle, the enemy would come and drive him away. Then when he would go and prepare for a peaceful place to settle down undisturbed and dig another well, they would drive him away again. Finally he dug one and God came and said, "I am the God of Abraham thy father: fear not, for I am with thee, and will bless thee, and multiply thy seed" (Gen. 26:24).

When Jacob, in his old age, was hesitating, not knowing what to do about going down into the land of Egypt, the angel of God said, "Fear not to go down into Egypt; for I will there make of thee a great nation: I will go down with thee into Egypt; and I will also surely bring thee up again..." (Gen. 46:3, 4).

When Moses stood at the Red Sea with the hosts of Pharaoh behind, with the mountain wall on either side and a sea of rolling waters in front, the children of Israel lifted their voices to God in a heart cry of hopelessness and desperation. Then God told Moses, "Fear ye not, stand still, and see the salvation of the Lord."

When Daniel, down in the land of Babylon for twenty-one days, had been praying day and night to feel again the hand of God and to hear again the voice of God that his people might be delivered out of bondage, Gabriel stood by him and said, "O man greatly beloved, fear not: peace be unto thee, be strong, yea, be strong." Daniel tells us, "When he had spoken unto me, I was greatly strengthened" (Dan. 10:19).

When at Corinth Paul was discouraged, the angel of God stood by and said, "Be not afraid, but speak, and hold not thy peace...for I have much people in this city" (Acts 18:9, 10).

When the ship on which Paul sailed on that voyage to Rome was so tossed and driven by the storm, until they cast all the lading of the ship overboard, undergirded the ship with ropes, then gave up all hope and sat down in despair waiting for it to go to the bottom, Paul said, "There stood by me this night the angel of God, whose I am, and whom I serve, Saying, Fear not, Paul; thou must be brought before Caesar; and, lo, God hath given thee all them that sail with thee" (Acts 27:23, 24).

On the Isle of Patmos, John, in the Spirit on the Lord's day, heard a great voice behind him. As he looked around he heard a voice saying, "I am Alpha and Omega, the first and the last." John fell at his feet as dead. Then he tells us, "...he laid his right hand upon me, saying unto me, Fear not; I am the first and the last: I am he that liveth, and was dead; and, behold, I am alive for evermore."

There is only One who can cast fear out of human life and that One is Jesus. He is my Saviour. He has said, "My sheep hear my voice, and I know them, and they follow me: And I give unto them eternal life; and they shall never perish." Listen! "Neither shall any man pluck them out of my hand."

Science says that the thing that holds this universe together is gravity. But when you tell me that gravity holds this universe together, then I ask you, What is gravity? and you can't tell me—you haven't given me any information.

Science says that this earth on which we live is a sphere eight thousand miles in diameter, twenty-five thousand miles in circumference, and is almost as heavy as if it were made of solid steel. Yet it floats through space like a soap bubble blown from a child's bubble blower. And around the sun it goes in its stately march through space, year after year, not deviating one iota from its path.

Science tells us there are millions, yea, multiplied millions of stars, planets, moons and suns, some of them multiplied thousands of times larger than the earth, traveling through space at the rate of more than a million miles an hour, and it is all held together and moves in an unerring path as the centuries come and go.

Science says the power that holds it all together and keeps each in its place is gravity. My Bible says it is Jesus. All things were created by Him, and for Him, and He is before all things and by Him all things hold together (Col. 1:16, 17).

Oh, think of it! If He who holds this planet out in space like a child's soap bubble as it floats along, is holding me in His hand, then I am perfectly safe.

> I've anchored my soul in the haven of rest:
> I'll sail the wide seas no more;
> The tempest may sweep o'er the wild, stormy deep,
> In Jesus I'm safe evermore.

"Neither shall any man pluck them out of my hand." Fear not.

Fear not your sins. The Devil would keep you paralyzed all your life with the fear of your sins. But, "Though your sins be as scarlet, they shall be as white as snow; though they be red like crimson, they shall be as wool." And, "The blood of Jesus Christ his Son cleanseth us from all sin."

After you have been saved, the Devil then would go back into the past, drag up your sins to discourage you, to make you tremble before them and be afraid. But remember, He who in the beginning was with God and by whom all things were made, has said, "I will put your sins behind my back...I will forgive your iniquity, and I will remember your sin no more.... As far as the east is from the west, so far hath he removed our transgressions from us."

Let the Devil bring them all up; let him bring any accusation he will, but we can stand with Paul at the cross of Jesus Christ and say to one and all, "Who shall lay anything to the charge of God's elect? It is God that justifieth. Who is he that condemneth? It is Christ that died, yea rather, that is risen again, who is even at the right hand of God, who also maketh intercession for us" (Rom. 8:33, 34).

Good News for Everyone

"I bring you good tidings of great joy, which shall be to all people" —

not just a select few. He opens the door of salvation, the door of grace, the door of divine worship to everyone who breathes the breath of human life. He says to the one deepest in sin, to the one nearest to Hell, to the one who has been crushed, broken, trampled down, defeated on every hand by the power of the enemy, "Come unto me, all ye that labour and are heavy laden, and I will give you rest." "I bring you good tidings of great joy, which shall be to all people."

Thank God for a gospel message that is given to the high, the low, the rich, the poor!

Said the prophet,

"... come ye to the waters, and he that hath no money; come ye, buy, and eat; yea, come, buy wine and milk without money and without price. Wherefore do ye spend money for that which is not bread? and your labour for that which satisfieth not? hearken diligently unto me, and eat ye that which is good, and let your soul delight itself in fatness." —Isa. 55:1, 2.

> **Grace, grace, God's grace,**
> **Grace that will pardon and cleanse within;**
> **Grace, grace, God's grace,**
> **Grace that is greater than all our sin.**

Good news to all the people of all the world. For, "he is able also to save... to the uttermost... He is able to keep that which I have committed unto him against that day..." and, "My God shall supply all your need according to his riches in glory by Christ Jesus."

"Fear not: for, behold, I bring you good tidings of great joy, which shall be to all people. For unto you is born this day in the city of David a Saviour, which is Christ the Lord."

Beloved, this Christmas let us not be thinking about an event; let us not be absorbed in a holiday season, but God help us to let the Holy Spirit turn our eyes of faith to Him and fix our hearts upon Him who came to be the Saviour of the world.

"Thou shalt call his name JESUS: for he shall save his people from their sins."

> **Fear not, I am with thee. O be not dismayed,**
> **For I am thy God, I will still give thee aid:**
> **I'll strengthen thee, help thee, and cause thee to stand,**
> **Upheld by My gracious, omnipotent hand.**

When thru fiery trials thy pathway shall lie,
My grace all-sufficient shall be thy supply,
The flames shall not hurt thee: I only design
Thy dross to consume, and thy gold to refine.

The soul that on Jesus hath leaned for repose,
I will not, I will not desert to its foes;
That soul, though all Hell should endeavor to shake,
I'll never, no never, no never forsake.

ROBERT G. LEE
1886-1978

ABOUT THE MAN:

R. G. Lee was born November 11, 1886, and died July 20, 1978.

The midwife attending his birth held baby Lee in her black arms while dancing a jig around the room, saying, "Praise Gawd! Glory be! The good Lawd done sont a preacher to dis here house. Yas, sah! Yes, ma'am. Dat's what He's done gone and done."

"God-sent preacher" well describes Dr. Lee. Few in number are the Baptists who have never heard his most famous sermon, "Payday Someday!" If you haven't heard it, or read it, surely you have heard some preacher make a favorable reference to it.

From his humble birth to sharecropper parents, Dr. Lee rose to pastor one of the largest churches in his denomination and head the mammoth Southern Baptist Convention as its president, serving three terms in that office. Dr. John R. Rice said:

"If you have not had the privilege of hearing Dr. Lee in person, I am sorry for you. The scholarly thoroughness, the wizardry of words, the lilt of poetic thought, the exalted idealism, the tender pathos, the practical application, the stern devotion to divine truth, the holy urgency in the preaching of a man called and anointed of God to preach and who must therefore preach, are never to be forgotten. The stately progression of his sermon to its logical end satisfies. The facile language, the alliterative statement, the powerful conviction mark Dr. Lee's sermons. The scholarly gleaning of incident and illustration from the treasures of scholarly memory and library make a rich feast for the hearer. The banquet table is spread with bread from many a grain field, honey distilled from the nectar of far-off exotic blossoms, sweetmeats from many a bake shop, strong meat from divers markets, and the whole board is garnished by posies from a thousand gardens.

"Often have I been blessed in hearing Dr. Lee preach, have delighted in his southern voice, and have been carried along with joy by his anointed eloquence."

XVIII.

Consider Christmas

ROBERT G. LEE

"And the angel said unto them, Fear not: for, behold, I bring you good tidings of great joy, which shall be to all people. For unto you is born this day in the city of David a Saviour, which is Christ the Lord."—Luke 2:10, 11.

God does everything in due time; no lapse of ages can subdue His power. No past successes of man in bringing wicked devices to pass can limit God's conquests. No geographical boundaries can circumscribe His activities. No conversive throes that shake the earth can thwart His purposes. No power of Satan or man can bring to naught God's promises of salvation through Jesus Christ. No powerful rebellion of angelic hosts can change the time when the claims of Deity are to be vindicated, when Omnipotence shall signalize itself by an outlay of Godlike power— and that in independence of human aid, and above and beyond all human knowledge.

Believing this, let us stand at midnight in Bethlehem of Judaea and listen to these words: "And thou Bethlehem, in the land of Juda, art not the least among the princes of Juda: for out of thee shall come a Governor, that shall rule my people Israel" (Matt. 2:6).

Let us look from the little village of Bethlehem, nestling in its quiet seclusion like some landlocked harbor away from the storms of the wild oceans, to Jerusalem yonder where thousands are wrapped in slumber. All is still in Jerusalem. All is still in Bethlehem that has nursed its busy population to rest.

But hark! There is heard the wail of an infant from a neighboring cattle barn. A queenly star, unseen before, does sentinel duty over the spot. Angelic legions are on the wing—and the skies resound with a new anthem from Heaven.

Then an announcement is made which takes us back to Eden's garden where there was a

1. Devil-Devised Downfall

There, in Eden, Adam, the first representative of our race—yea, the federal head of our race, was, after his creation in the image of God, the fit companion of angels—together with Eve, the first woman, the first wife, who in Eden became the first sinner, even as, cast out from Eden, she became the first mother. There, inhaling the pure atmosphere of his innocent home, Adam stood in the dignity of his Godlike manhood, with the earth around him blooming in the freshness of its green beauty—the heavens above him radiant with the Creator's smile, no ominous cloud to darken the background of his life. There he stood, in sweet fellowship and love, with Eve, in the undimmed luster of priceless purity.

But—alas!—what a wasting hurricane swept over the lovely Garden of Eden where Adam was the richest crown jewel in the kingdom of God, leaving a scene of desolation. Satan, the vindictive monarch of Hell, big with hate toward God, guided to his task by a deadly strategy, approached and praised and stirred ambition's fires, and then bartered on this jewel. Knowledge was lying tendered as the tempting equivalent of its worth. How deep and damning was this deception! The fiendish swindler triumphed—and a beggared and sin-blasted and expatriated race lived to date their crime and their curse from Paradise, where Despair pitched his black pavilions on man's sterile and blasted estate. That is why Paul spoke of how "through the offense of one many be dead" (Rom. 5:15), saying: "Wherefore, as by one man sin entered into the world, and death by sin; and so death passed upon all men, for that all have sinned" (Rom. 5:12).

If, at the Christmas season, we consider lightly this Devil-denied downfall of man, we shall miss much of the real meaning of Christmas. This sober truth we must think upon:

"For what the law could not do, in that it was weak through the flesh, God sending his own Son in the likeness of sinful flesh, and for sin, condemned sin in the flesh."—Rom. 8:3.

But we should find comfort in these words:

"But where sin abounded, grace did much more abound: That as

sin hath reigned unto death, even so might grace reign through righteousness unto eternal life by Jesus Christ our Lord."—Rom. 5:20, 21.

Those blessed words teach us that God's mercy lingered over the doom of the rebel, and taxed the resources of His unspeakable goodness and grace to avert His final fate, despoil the infernal monster of His prey, and make sure that immortality, once more restored to her ancient honors, could claim her perennial bliss in the smile of Heaven.

In Eden, where sin with foul invasion wrought havoc and brewed in Hell's caldron all our woe, God, in mysterious purport, preached the first gospel sermon wherein was this promise—gleaming like a bright star in the darkness and doom of that day:

"And I will put enmity between thee and the woman, and between thy seed and her seed; it shall bruise thy head, and thou shalt bruise his heel."—Gen. 3:15.

Then many prophets, while darkness brooded over mankind for one hundred and twenty generations, ascended, in deliberate succession, the mount of prophecy. From its mysterious height, they flung the light of hope far down the vista of future ages. Malachi was the last to catch the glowing theme—and following in the train of many great prophets, say, swan-like, his last and sweetest notes:

"Behold, I will send you Elijah the prophet before the coming of the great and dreadful day of the Lord: And he shall turn the heart of the fathers to the children, and the heart of the children to their fathers, lest I come and smite the earth with a curse."—Mal. 4:5, 6.

Then the harp of prophecy was unstrung and laid upon the altar—and silence reigned in the synagogues for four hundred years, called by historians "the four dumb centuries."

But at length the destined hour arrives—and the day of Christ arrived, the day which Abraham rejoicing saw: "Your father Abraham rejoiced to see my day: and he saw it, and was glad" (John 8:56).

Of the manger of that day Isaiah had spoken. Of the cross of that day David had sung. And then was vouchsafed to the world deliverance from the Devil-devised downfall of man—as testified to by the prophecy of Zacharias:

"Blessed be the Lord God of Israel; for he hath visited and redeemed

his people, And hath raised up an horn of salvation for us in the house of his servant David; As he spake by the mouth of his holy prophets, which have been since the world began."—Luke 1:68-70.

That brings us to think of the

2. Dutiful Diligence

Simeon had waited long for "the Consolation of Israel," the Holy Ghost being his guide.

"And it was revealed unto him by the Holy Ghost, that he should not see death, before he had seen the Lord's Christ. And he came by the Spirit into the temple: and when the parents brought in the child Jesus, to do for him after the custom of the law, Then took he him up in his arms, and blessed God, and said, Lord, now lettest thou thy servant depart in peace, according to thy word: For mine eyes have seen thy salvation, which thou hast prepared before the face of all people; A light to lighten the Gentiles, and the glory of thy people Israel."—Luke 2:26-32.

Simeon took up in his arms the Christ who in Eternity rested motherless upon the Father's bosom, and in Time rested fatherless upon a mother's bosom, clasping the Ancient of Days who had become the Infant of Days—the Christ who had glory with God before the world was, the Christ who was loved by the Father before the foundations of the world, the Christ who was co-equal and co-essential and co-existent and co-eternal with God.

And the shepherds had joy akin to old Simeon's joy. After Israel's glory had faded, after strength had decayed, after tribe after tribe had shrunk toward the enfeebled center, after the land of their fathers had become a despised and conquered promise, these shepherds saw a stable in the suburbs of the poorest town in Judaea. There God hung the morning star of hope—a herald of the highest day that ever dawned. Beneath that wretched roof, so small He was held in a woman's two hands, so weak He must of necessity feed at a woman's breast, was God's only-begotten and well-beloved Son.

**Cold on His cradle the dew-drops are shining,
Low lies His head with the beasts of the stall.**

But that Infant is destined to wear the diadem of the universe. That dimpled arm will sustain a sinking world. That Child, the sovereign

Saviour of the world, will lead captivity captive, will conquer death, will despoil Hell of its hopes, and re-open the gates of Paradise.

And in this subject nation—with the yoke of Roman authority upon its neck, with the heavy heel of Roman oppression upon its chest, with the grasping hand of Roman greed upon its purse—there were dutifully diligent shepherds.

"And there were in the same country shepherds abiding in the field, keeping watch over their flock by night. And, lo, the angel of the Lord came upon them, and the glory of the Lord shone round about them: and they were sore afraid."—Luke 2:8, 9.

These shepherds—poor, honest, industrious—were not leaders of armies, not expounders of philosophies, not advocates of political theories, not bankers counting piles of money—rather just throwers of stones to keep the wolves away. Watchers of their flocks, to these who were dutifully diligent in their common tasks, the good news was first announced—teaching us to be "diligent in business"—urging us to remember that our modest work and the hero's sacrifice are one in the unseen realm of duty, showing a woman's two mites and a rich man's great gifts are the same in the realm of love, showing that God seeks people in humble places for service and the honors of service.

Telling of how we, according to God's promise, look for a new heaven and a new earth, wherein dwelleth righteousness, the Apostle Peter writes: "Wherefore, beloved, seeing that ye look for such things, be diligent that ye may be found of him in peace, without spot, and blameless" (II Pet. 3:14).

Peter also urges diligence in these other words, "Wherefore the rather, brethren, give diligence to make your calling and election sure: for if ye do these things, ye shall never fall" (II Pet. 1:10).

The writer of the epistle to the Hebrews writes, "And we desire that every one of you do shew the same diligence to the full assurance of hope unto the end" (Heb. 6:11).

As we look upon Bethlehem, as we listen to the voices of all who speak in relation thereunto, let us see to it that Christian diligence in service to Christ possesses us with strength.

And now let us give ear, as did others in the days gone forever into the tomb of Time, to the

3. Divine Declarations

Isaiah, the great prophet, in whose preaching were always the thunders and lightnings of Sinai and the foregleams of crimson Calvary, declared:

"Therefore the Lord himself shall give you a sign: Behold, a virgin shall conceive, and bear a son, and shall call his name Immanuel. Butter and honey shall he eat, that he may know to refuse the evil, and choose the good. For before the child shall know to refuse the evil, and choose the good, the land that thou abhorrest shall be forsaken of both her kings."—Isa. 7:14-16.

To Joseph, the angel of the Lord appeared, when Mary, espoused to Joseph "before they came together, was found with child of the Holy Ghost." And in these words we find divine declaration:

"Then Joseph her husband, being a just man, and not willing to make her a publick example, was minded to put her away privily. But while he thought on these things, behold, the angel of the Lord appeared unto him in a dream, saying, Joseph, thou son of David, fear not to take unto thee Mary thy wife: for that which is conceived in her is of the Holy Ghost. And she shall bring forth a son, and thou shalt call his name JESUS: for he shall save his people from their sins. Now all this was done, that it might be fulfilled which was spoken of the Lord by the prophet, saying, Behold, a virgin shall be with child, and shall bring forth a son, and they shall call his name Emmanuel, which being interpreted is, God with us."—Matt. 1:19-23.

To Mary, a virgin espoused to a man whose name was Joseph, the Angel Gabriel, sent from God unto a city of Galilee, named Nazareth, made divine declaration:

"And the angel came in unto her, and said, Hail, thou that art highly favoured, the Lord is with thee: blessed art thou among women. And when she saw him, she was troubled at his saying, and cast in her mind what manner of salutation this should be. And the angel said unto her, Fear not, Mary: for thou hast found favour with God. And, behold, thou shalt conceive in thy womb, and bring forth a son, and shalt call his name JESUS. He shall be great, and shall be called the Son of the Highest: and the Lord God shall give unto him the throne of his father David: And he shall reign over the house of Jacob for ever; and of his kingdom there shall be no end. Then said Mary unto the angel, How shall this be, seeing I know not a man? And the angel answered and

said unto her, The Holy Ghost shall come upon thee, and the power of the Highest shall overshadow thee: therefore also that holy thing which shall be born of thee shall be called the Son of God."—Luke 1:28-35.

To the shepherds the angel of the Lord and angels of Heaven made declarations:

"And the angel said unto them, Fear not: for, behold, I bring you good tidings of great joy, which shall be to all people. For unto you is born this day in the city of David a Saviour, which is Christ the Lord. And this shall be a sign unto you; Ye shall find the babe wrapped in swaddling clothes, lying in a manger."—Luke 2:10-12.

To the same startled shepherds, a multitude from the heavenly choir made declaration—singing: "Glory to God in the highest, and on earth peace, good will toward men" (vs. 14).

Listen:

"And, behold, there was a man in Jerusalem, whose name was Simeon; and the same man was just and devout, waiting for the consolation of Israel: and the Holy Ghost was upon him. And it was revealed unto him by the Holy Ghost, that he should not see death, before he had seen the Lord's Christ."—Vss. 25, 26.

To Mary, old Simeon, in the glory of the righteous sunset of his life, made declaration, "When the parents brought in the child Jesus, to do for him after the custom of the law" (vs. 27). Simeon declared to Mary this, as he spoke to God while Mary listened:

"For mine eyes have seen thy salvation, Which thou hast prepared before the face of all people; A light to lighten the Gentiles, and the glory of thy people Israel."—Vss. 30-32.

Had they made a declaration that poverty would be no more among men, that war and plague and disease would be forever banished from the earth, that tears of sorrow would never be again, such an announcement would have been as discord to melody, as the chatterings of nonsense and idiocy to the speakings of wisdom, when put in the light of this divine declaration.

But we should think now upon the

4. Deep Descent

What is that deep descent? The coming down of Jesus from the heights of the Deity to the depths of errant and moneyless humanity.

He came down from the adorations of Heaven to the abominations of earth.

He came down from the blessedness of Heaven to the bruises of crucifixion tortures.

He came down from the coronations of Heaven to the condemnations of earth.

He came down from the delights of Heaven to the defamations of earth.

He came down from the excellencies of Heaven to the executions of earth.

He came down from the favor of the Father's face to the fury of men's faces.

He came down from the glory place to the gory place.

He came down from the hallelujahs of Heaven to the hisses of earth.

He came down from the intercessions of Heaven to the injustices of earth.

He came down from the joys of Heaven to the jeers of the mobs of earth.

He came down from the kindness of Heaven to the killing of earth.

He came down from the love of Heaven to the lying accusations of earth—yea, even to the iniquities of earth.

He came down from the majesties of Heaven to the miseries of earth.

He came down from the notableness of Heaven to the nothingness of earth.

He came down from the praise of Heaven to the persecutions of earth.

He came down from the quietness of Heaven to the quarrelsomeness of earth.

He came down from the riches of Heaven to the revilings and ridicules of earth.

He came down from the songs of Heaven to the sneers and scars of earth.

He came down from the throne of Heaven to the tree of Calvary.

He came down from the unison of Heaven to the unmitigated unjustness of earth.

He came down from the virtues of Heaven to the vices of earth.

He came down from the worship of angelic hosts to the homeless wanderings over earth and to the wrath and wrangling of unprincipled men.

CONSIDER CHRISTMAS

Isaiah spoke of this deep descent in these words:

"He is despised and rejected of men; a man of sorrows, and acquainted with grief: and we hid as it were our faces from him; he was despised, and we esteemed him not. Surely he hath borne our griefs, and carried our sorrows: yet we did esteem him stricken, smitten of God, and afflicted. But he was wounded for our transgressions, he was bruised for our iniquities: the chastisement of our peace was upon him; and with his stripes we are healed." —Isa. 53:3-5.

Paul spoke of the deep descent of Him for whom the innkeeper had no room—no place for Him who made all places—as He came down from heavenly honor to earthly humiliation, the Creator born of the creature, woman:

"Let this mind be in you, which was also in Christ Jesus: Who, being in the form of God, thought it not robbery to be equal with God: But made himself of no reputation, and took upon him the form of a servant, and was made in the likeness of men: And being found in fashion as a man, he humbled himself, and became obedient unto death, even the death of the cross. Wherefore God also hath highly exalted him, and given him a name which is above every name: That at the name of Jesus every knee should bow, of things in heaven, and things in earth, and things under the earth; And that every tongue should confess that Jesus Christ is Lord, to the glory of God the Father." —Phil. 2:5-11.

But His deep descent was the dawn of mercy; because we could not ascend to Him, Christ descends to us.

Now, let us think of the

5. Delayless Doing

The shepherds, startled by the revelations from Heaven, said: "Let us now go even unto Bethlehem, and see this thing which is come to pass, which the Lord hath made known unto us" (Luke 2:15).

"Let us now go...."

The information God gave, the shepherds wisely put into action, immediately. Not the delay of a week—nor a day, nor an hour, nor a minute. The Saviour of men born in the City of David? "Let us go and see him *now*." Not "when a more convenient time presents itself." Not "after we go home and talk it over with our families." But NOW. Not "after we visit again the sheep markets." But NOW! Not "when we make sure no wolves will attack our sheep." But NOW! Not "when we make sure no money will be lost." But NOW! And the Wise Men made the same improvement of their information. In a distant country they saw His star and followed its direction, defiant of all distances, discouraged by no vast expanse, downcast by no far reach of miles.

"Let us *now* go." What—at midnight? Cool and calculating reason would have argued that it was an unreasonable hour. Had covetousness spoken, it would have asked questions as to the welfare of the sheep. Had procrastination prevailed, it would have put off until "a better time." But these plain men, who had left their beds to attend their flocks, now left their flocks to inquire about the Saviour. "They came with haste."

To inquire after Jesus, to see Jesus, to serve Jesus, to follow Jesus is our first business—the one thing most importantly needed. And what we do for Him, let us do quickly. The sooner the better. Without a minute's delay.

Let us not be found guilty of letting "tomorrow and tomorrow and tomorrow creep in our petty pace from day to day."

Then, again, standing worshipfully at Bethlehem, we see

6. Deity Displayed

God's first promise to guilty man was that the seed of the woman should bruise the serpent's head (Gen. 3:15). As to the flesh, Jesus is the seed of the woman. But He is infinitely more. Paul says,

"But when the fulness of the time was come, God sent forth his Son, made of a woman, made under the law, To redeem them that were under the law, that we might receive the adoption of sons."—Gal. 4:4, 5.

Necessary it was to our redemption that the Saviour of men should be a *man*. But had Christ been produced in the ordinary way of human generations, He must have been a partaker of a sinful nature. This was prevented by the miraculous way of His conception—by the power of the Holy Spirit. Thus the virgin-born Christ was "holy, harmless, undefiled, separate from sinners"—fit to become sin for us because He knew no sin.

Jesus is God manifest in the flesh. Let us go to Bethlehem and see this great sight. Glorious mystery! We cannot fully comprehend it. Men may speak and write of it, but as they attempt to describe it, a woeful sense of inadequacy oppresses the mind. We may speak of it, but the most we can say is that it is unspeakable. And the most we know is that it passeth knowledge.

CONSIDER CHRISTMAS 241

God, in Christ, was made flesh. Thus was Deity displayed before the eyes of men.

"In the beginning was the Word, and the Word was with God, and the Word was God. The same was in the beginning with God. All things were made by him; and without him was not any thing made that was made." —John 1:1-3.

"And the Word was made flesh, and dwelt among us, (and we beheld his glory, the glory as of the only begotten of the Father,) full of grace and truth." —John 1:14.

"Concerning his Son Jesus Christ our Lord, which was made of the seed of David according to the flesh." —Rom. 1:3.

This pre-existent Christ Jesus was not flesh back yonder when the morning stars serenaded the advent of our infant earth as it lay, "wrapped in swaddling clothes of light," in the arms of the great Jehovah, for "all things were made by him, and without him was not any thing made that was made" (John 1:3).

He was not flesh back in creation days when there was the gathering together of the waters called the seas for "the world was made by him" (John 1:10).

He was not flesh when the first ray of light shone, when the first bird sang, when the first lion "panted in the jungles of roses," when the first flower bloomed, when the first fire burned, when the first river flowed, when the first rose opened wide its rubied heart, when the first wind blew, when the first lily bared its white bosom. "For by him were all things created that are in heaven, and that are in earth...and he is before all things, and by him all things consist" (Col. 1:16, 17).

But! But "he was made flesh"—and every nerve was divine handwriting, every bone was divinely sculptured, every muscle was a pulley divinely swung! It was in the flesh that He conquered the sins of the flesh, healed the diseases of the flesh, drove away the fever fires that burn up human bodies, conquered the loathsome leprosy that lays waste the flesh of the body, and straightened out the crippled bones of lame bodies. "It behooved him to be made like unto his brethren" (Heb. 2:17).

His supernatural birth is the Alpha of our Christian Faith. Let that be accepted and the whole alphabet follows as a matter of course. Deny it and, like a planet that leaves it orbit, there is no telling where unbelief will carry you. The virgin birth is the seal of the Father's approval affixed to the claims of Jesus as His only begotten Son!

His birth into our world by a virgin was a translation at the same time it was an incarnation. It was a transfer of His person from a previous condition of existence to this earthly one. It was His being clothed upon with our human nature. He saith, "A body hast thou prepared me" (Heb. 10:5). Before incarnation Jesus was God's instrument in creation. During incarnation, Jesus was God's instrument in redemption.

Then it is not just poetry and rhetoric and fiction when we say: "When the Lord of power determined to forsake His royal chariot and to alight on this earth, He undressed Himself first. He gave to the clouds His bow! He gave to the sky His azure mantle! He gave to the stars His jewels! He gave to the sun His brightness, AND, receiving instead of these the strange homespun clothes of one who had not where to lay His head," He was "made flesh," "made of a woman"! His incarnation meant, and means, that the pre-existent Christ was embodied in human flesh, demonstrated in human life, exemplified in human action, crystallized in human form.

We must, amid the bright lights of our Christmas festivities, think of the long-ago

7. Deplorable Darkness

When Jesus came, it was night in Egypt, night in Rome, night in Athens, night in Syria, night in Palestine—night everywhere. Darkness blacker than "a murder's mark of crepe." Darkness as Keats would say, like "the parentage of chaos." The world was dark "as if it were dipped in the death shadow." Poe spoke of the darkness "as the caves wherein earth's thunders groan"—and it was groaning "ever darker and darker like the shadow of advancing death." Thomas spoke of a condition "dark as the inside of a whale," and Whittier of a matter "dark as the brooding thundercloud."

The world was, as Milton described Samson, "dark, dark, dark, amid the blaze of noon."

Yes, deplorable darkness had long covered the earth—and the wisest of men bowed down "to an unknown God." But, glory to His name, "the only begotten Son, which is in the bosom of the Father, he hath declared him" (John 1:18). This is He who is "the brightness of [the Father's] glory, and the express image of his person" (Heb. 1:3)—"the image of the invisible God" (Col. 1:15). This, too, is unspeakable. But we believe and adore. Let but the light shine into our hearts to give us "the light of the knowledge of the glory of God in the face of Jesus Christ," and it is enough.

And there is a deplorable darkness in our world today—the wide world over, too.

Dr. S. H. Jones, editor of the *Baptist Courier* wrote that the darkness upon our world is great. There is the darkness of unbelief, coming from sin and intellectual pride; the darkness of ignorance, evidenced by the stupid railings of people devoid of understanding; the darkness of moral depravity, born of the unregenerate people who are incapable of high moral attainments; the darkness of prejudice, as people bar their souls against the light; the darkness of selfishness, which is insane blindness and the abnormality of life; the darkness of hate that lurks in human hearts as it leaves houses desolate and hearts forlorn and lives under blight; the darkness of fear, which, with its cold and soul-chilling grip, strangles the spiritual breathing of many; the darkness of pain and death, naturally associated with darkness rather than light.

But because Jesus came the prophecy of Isaiah is an experience greatly authenticated in the lives of many:

"The people that walked in darkness have seen a great light: they that dwell in the land of the shadow of death, upon them hath the light shined. . . . For unto us a child is born, unto us a son is given: and the government shall be upon his shoulder: and his name shall be called Wonderful, Counsellor, The mighty God, The everlasting Father, The Prince of Peace."—Isa. 9:2, 6.

Moreover, forget not what Luke writes about "the light to lighten the Gentiles" (Luke 2:32), nor what Matthew records in repetition of prophecy, "The people which sat in darkness saw a great light; and to them which sat in the region and shadow of death light is sprung up" (Matt. 4:16).

Let us recall and cherish with joy and gratitude the wonderful words which Jesus spoke during the days of His flesh: "I am the light of the world: he that followeth me shall not walk in darkness, but shall have the light of life" (John 8:12).

He said, "I am come a light into the world, that whosoever believeth on me should not abide in darkness" (John 12:46).

Again, "This then is the message which we have heard of him, and declare unto you, that God is light, and in him is no darkness at all" (I John 1:5).

Amid the deplorable darkness of our times, let us emphasize the design of the death of Him who was born of Mary in Bethlehem's barn to die at the place called Calvary.

What was the grand design of the Saviour's birth? The redemption, by His death, of fallen, guilty, helpless man. That was the grand design. "God sent forth his Son, made of a woman, made under the law, To redeem them that were under the law" (Gal. 4:4). He was named Jesus—because He came to "save his people from their sins."

There is something so sublime, so delightful, in the name *"Saviour."*

Cicero, the Roman orator, said that when traveling in Greece he saw a pillar inscribed with the word "saviour." He admired the fullness in the name, but he was as ignorant of its Christian meaning as an owl is of astronomy. How much more may every redeemed sinner admire the name—*"Saviour!"*

In conclusion, let us, having seen the things God made known to men in Bethlehem, have and hold holy hatred for our today's

8. Despicable Disgrace

What mean I by that? As, at Bethlehem, we see God in all His glorious perfections manifested in the person of Jesus, we should engage our souls to adore and love and praise Him—magnifying "the Lord God of Israel." "The Lord...hath visited and redeemed his people."

But we see the disgraceful way in which some celebrate the season called CHRISTMAS. Vain, frothy, carnal—these three words can be written over the celebrative ways of those who "make merry" at the Christmas season. Foolishly, even iniquitously, do they contradict as much as possible the design of His coming as the "Infant of Days" to Bethlehem. Jesus came to "destroy the works of the devil." What do the works of the flesh have to do with the birth of Jesus? Jesus came to save His people *from* their sins—not to urge them to participation *in* them. Why should more sin be committed at the Christmas season in a few days than in many weeks at other times? Why should sin be aggravated by letting it pass under the guise of religious joy? Such disgraceful observance of the birth of Christ is an affront to a holy God, a reproach to the Christian name, a ruinous matter to the souls of men.

At the Christmas festival, which is the commemoration of the incarnation of Him to whom God hath given a name which is above every name, many are found at any place or every place rather than at Bethlehem. More attracted are they to every trivial thing than to the glorious sight, for which the shepherds left their flocks and made haste to view. The sight which the Eastern sages came such a vast distance to behold, which drew all Heaven down to earth, is nothing to them. Some, while they observe the day of Christ's birth by doing no work, not only neglect but insult Him—and by riotous living and indulgence in the works of the flesh, revive the works of the Devil, which the Son of God was manifested to destroy. Instead of fixing their eyes on the Star of Bethlehem, they give attention to the little, debasing, vexing, defiling things of the world. The iniquitous incongruities of many Christmas celebrations are abominations to be avoided. Wickedness instead of worship oft prevails.

Let us not seek to be distinguished by worldly grandeur, but to be great in the sight of the Lord. Looking upon the Babe of Bethlehem, the Desire of all nations, let us give Him the glory which is due unto His holy name. Let us behold in Him God's provision for our recovery from sin and sin's ruinous damage. Let us look upon Him as the one most suitable to our wants—the most adequate to our relief. Since He is placed entirely within our reach, let us embrace Him and exclaim: "Lo, this is our God! We have waited for Him, and He will save us! This is the Lord! We have waited for Him! We will be glad and rejoice in His salvation."

And let us see to it that our zeal and our gratitude be equal to our joy. Let us follow the example of the shepherds not only in our going, but in our return. "And when they had seen it, they made known abroad the saying that was told them concerning this child."

And when we are always bearing about in the body the dying of the Lord Jesus that the life also of Jesus may be made manifest in our mortal bodies, we shall make known abroad many truths concerning Him who is the Truth.

Let us, as Peter counsels, show forth at the Christmastime and at all times and in all places "the praises of him who hath called you out of darkness into his marvelous light... but now have obtained mercy" (I Pet. 2:9, 10)—remembering that "We have also a more sure word of prophecy; whereunto ye do well that ye take heed, as unto a light that shineth in a dark place, until the day dawn, and the day star arise in your hearts" (II Pet. 1:19).

XIX.

A Thrilling Christmastime on the Frontier

By a Pastor's Wife

I remember a day one unusually cold winter that stands out like a boulder in my life. Our salary had not been regularly paid, and it did not meet our needs when it was.

My husband was away much of the time, traveling from one district to another. Our boys were well, but my little Ruth was ailing and, at best, none of us were decently clothed. I patched and repatched, with spirits sinking to the lowest ebb. The water gave out in the well, and the wind blew through the cracks in the floor.

The people in the parish were kind and generous but the settlement was new, and each family was struggling for itself. Little by little at the time I needed it most, my faith began to waver.

Early in life, I had been taught to take God at His Word, and I thought that my lesson was well learned. I had lived upon the promises in dark times until I knew, as David did, who was my Fortress and Deliverer. Now a daily prayer for forgiveness was all that I could offer.

My husband's overcoat was hardly thick enough for October, and he was often obliged to ride miles to attend some meeting or funeral. Many times our breakfast was Indian cake with a cup of tea without sugar.

Christmas was coming—the children always expected their presents. I remember that the ice was thick and smooth and that the boys were each craving a pair of skates. Ruth, in some unaccountable way, had taken a fancy that the dolls I made were no longer suitable—she wanted a nice large one and insisted on praying for it.

I knew it was impossible, but, oh, how I wanted to give each child his present! It seemed as if God had deserted us. But I did not tell my husband all this. He worked so earnestly and heartily that I supposed him to be as hopeful as ever. I kept the sitting room cheerful with an open fire, and tried to serve our scanty meals as invitingly as I could.

The morning before Christmas, James was called to see a sick man. I gave him a piece of bread for his lunch—the best I could do—wrapped my plaid shawl around his neck and then tried to whisper a promise as I often had, but the words died away upon my lips. I let him go without it.

That was a dark, hopeless day. I coaxed the children to bed early, for I could not bear their talk. When Ruth went, I listened to her prayer. She asked for the last time most explicitly for her doll and for skates for her brothers. Her bright face looked so lovely when she whispered to me, "You know, I think they'll be here early tomorrow morning, Mama," that I thought I could move Heaven and earth to save her from disappointment. I sat down alone and gave way to the most bitter tears.

Before long James returned, chilled and exhausted. He drew off his boots. The thin stockings slipped off with them, and his feet were red with cold. "I wouldn't treat a dog that way, let alone a faithful servant," I said. Then, as I glanced up and saw the hard lines in his face and the look of despair, it flashed across me that James had let go too.

I brought him a cup of tea, feeling sick and dizzy at the very thought. He took my hand, and we sat for an hour without a word. I wanted to die and meet God and tell Him that His promise wasn't true—my soul was so full of rebellious despair.

By and by there came a sound of bells, a quick step and a loud knock at the door. James sprang to open it. There stood Deacon White. "A box came by express just before dark. I brought it around as soon as I could get away. Reckoned it might be for Christmas. 'At any rate,' I said, 'they shall have it tonight.' Here is a turkey my wife asked me to fetch along, and these other things, I believe, belong to you."

There were a basket of potatoes and a bag of flour. Talking all the time, he hurried in the box, and then, with a hearty good night, he rode away.

Speechless, James found a chisel and opened the box. He drew out first a thick red blanket; and we saw beneath it, the box was full of clothing. It seemed at that moment as if Christ had fastened upon me a look of reproach. James sat down and covered his face with his hands. "I can't touch them," he explained. "I haven't been true, just when God was trying me to see if I could hold out. Do you think I could not see how you were suffering? And I had no word of comfort to offer. I know now how to preach the awfulness of turning away from God."

"James," I said, clinging to him, "don't take it to heart like this. I am to blame. I ought to have helped you. We will ask Him together to forgive us."

"Wait a moment, Dear. I cannot talk now." Then he went into another room. I knelt down—and my heart broke. In an instant all the darkness, all the stubbornness rolled away! Jesus came again and stood before me, with the loving word, "Daughter."

Sweet promises of tenderness and joy flooded my soul. I was so lost in praise and gratitude that I forgot everything else. I do not know how long it was before James came back, but I knew that he, too, had found peace.

"Now, my dear wife," he said, "let us thank God together." Then he poured out words of praise—Bible words, for nothing else could express our thanksgiving.

It was 11 o'clock—the fire was low, and there was the great box with nothing touched but the warm blanket we needed. We piled on some fresh logs, lighted two candles and began to examine our treasures.

We drew out an overcoat. I made James try it on—just the right size—and I danced around him, for all my lightheartedness had returned. Then there was a cloak, and he insisted on seeing me in it. My spirits always infected him, and we both laughed like foolish children.

There was a warm suit of clothes also, and three pairs of woolen hose. There was a dress for me and yards of flannel, a pair of arctic overshoes for each of us and in mine a slip of paper. I have it now and mean to hand it down to my children. It was Moses' blessing to Asher: "Thy shoes shall be iron and brass; and as thy days, so shall thy strength be" (Deut. 33:25). In the gloves, evidently for James, the same dear hand had written: "I the Lord thy God will hold thy right hand, saying unto thee, Fear not; I will help thee" (Isa. 41:13).

It was a wonderful box and packed with thoughtful care. There was a suit of clothes for each of the boys and a little red gown for Ruth. There were mittens, scarves and hoods, and down in the center—a box. We opened it, and there was a great wax doll! I burst into tears again, and James wept with me for joy. It was too much! And then we both exclaimed again, for close behind it, came two pairs of skates. There were books for us to read—some of them I had wished to see—stories for the children to read, aprons and underclothing, knots of ribbon, a gay little tidy, a lovely photograph, needles, buttons and thread, actually a muff, and an envelope containing a ten-dollar gold piece!

At last we cried over everything we took up. It was past midnight, and we were faint and exhausted even with happiness. I made a cup of tea, cut a fresh loaf of bread, and James boiled some eggs. We drew up the table before the fire. How we enjoyed our supper! And then we sat talking over our life and how sure a help God always proved.

You should have seen the children the next morning! The boys raised a shout at the sight of their skates. Ruth caught up her doll and hugged it tightly without a word. Then she went into her room and knelt by her bed.

When she came back she whispered to me, "I knew it would be here, Mama, but I wanted to thank God just the same, you know."

"Look here, Wife—see the difference!" We went to the window, and there were the boys out of the house already and skating on the crust with all their might.

My husband and I both tried to return thanks to the church in the East that sent us the box—and have tried to return thanks unto God every day since.

Hard times have come again and again, but we have trusted in Him—dreading nothing so much as a doubt of His protecting care. "They that seek the Lord shall not want any good thing" (Ps. 34:10).

For a complete list of books available from the Sword of the Lord, write to Sword of the Lord Publishers, P. O. Box 1099, Murfreesboro, Tennessee 37133.